MAKING PEACE
WITH THE
UNIVERSE

PERSONAL CRISIS AND
SPIRITUAL HEALING

MICHAEL SCOTT
ALEXANDER

Columbia University Press   *New York*

Columbia University Press
Publishers Since 1893
New York   Chichester, West Sussex
cup.columbia.edu

Copyright © 2020 Columbia University Press
All rights reserved

Library of Congress Cataloging-in-Publication Data
Names: Alexander, Michael Scott, author.
Title: Making peace with the universe : personal crisis
and spiritual healing / Michael Scott Alexander.
Description: New York : Columbia University Press, 2020. |
Includes bibliographical references and index.
Identifiers: LCCN 2020010175 (print) | LCCN 2020010176 (ebook) |
ISBN 9780231198585 (hardcover) | ISBN 9780231198592 (paperback) |
ISBN 9780231552707 (ebook)
Subjects: LCSH: Religious biography. | Psychology and
religion—Case studies. | Spiritual healing—Case studies.
Classification: LCC BL71.5 .A44 2020 (print) | LCC BL71.5 (ebook) |
DDC 203/.10922—dc23
LC record available at https://lccn.loc.gov/2020010175
LC ebook record available at https://lccn.loc.gov/2020010176

Columbia University Press books are printed on permanent
and durable acid-free paper.
Printed in the United States of America

Cover design: Julia Kurshnirsky
Cover image: NASA/JPL/Texas A&M/Cornell

For Cathy, Nick, and Thea—
Love builds up.

"I accept the universe" is reported to have been a favorite utterance of our New England transcendentalist, Margaret Fuller; and when someone repeated this phrase to Thomas Carlyle, his sardonic comment is said to have been: "Gad! she'd better!"

—William James, *The Varieties of Religious Experience*

CONTENTS

MAKING PEACE
WITH THE UNIVERSE

I

THE PROBLEM

1

THE PATH OF JOY

TOUCHING DOWN

In five minutes the plane would be landing on the exquisite Italian island of Sardinia, playground for Europe's richest people. I'd been asked in three languages to put away my electronics and to store any loose belongings. I stared down at the yellow pad sitting on my lap. Its open page contained the sum total of my notes regarding a speech for a wedding ceremony I needed to help officiate that afternoon for my friend Sanjay. The page was blank, reflecting my heartfelt thoughts on the subject.

Another page of the pad contained my practical thoughts about marriage. It held the telephone numbers of half a dozen Los Angeles divorce lawyers. I intended to call them from JFK while waiting between flights to return home. My own marriage was an insoluble disaster. Insoluble. Disaster. That's all I could think about it, and I thought about it constantly. On Sardinia, I hoped to muster enough courage to move forward with my life. Perhaps a lovely few days in the Italian sun among friends and intoxicants would hush the swirl of rationalizations that prevented me from declaring victory and just getting out. High hopes for a friend's wedding, I know.

I shoved the pad away and closed my eyes for landing. My two beautiful young children stared back at me from beneath my eyelids. So did my beautiful wife.

I'll think of something, I told myself. *I have to.*

WHAT SCHOOL CONFERRED

Who am I? Let me try to explain.

A rental agreement I filled out in my last year of graduate school asked how many years of education I had completed. I swallowed hard before writing down twenty-five. That was twenty years ago and I'm still in school. These days I teach college. My subject is religion.

My strange obsession started at age eighteen when I discovered a class in my college catalog about the book of Genesis and began studying Hebrew and Aramaic with a man whose academic specialty had been a single biblical word—a hapax legomenon, a word that occurs only once in world literature. The joke is, the word still can't be translated and probably never will be. An unknowable mystery compounded by the aura of the remote human past—I was hooked like a flounder. My more reasonable classmates turned away after a semester or so, but I couldn't. The more abstract, the more unknowable and, above all, the more impractical for real life, the more I poured my soul all in. I hadn't blinked when I graduated with a degree in the Ancient Near East and was off to graduate school to discover unimaginable mysteries and doctoral-level esoterica.

My parents were proud but concerned. They feared I might never leave campus, and as it turns out I never did. These many years later I typically prefer a carrel in some airless library and there settle in to work, although it never quite feels like work.

How can I describe it? It feels like *school*. Every time I crack open a musty book, I am returned in time to the feet of its master.

"Take a seat," the master seems to say.

"And stop chewing gum."

So there I sit and learn for a while. By some miracle, life has allowed me to pursue my own esoteric hunt through human civilization to follow my questions. I'm a geek, I've loved every minute of it. I've had a fun career among like-minded geeks. That's what my education conferred.

But even the strangest compulsions tend to have an understandable rationale, an interior logic that drives a behavior to absurdity. So I do ask myself why a reasonable person would travel so far on such an ethereal quest. For a couple of years in college, maybe as an undergraduate minor, sure, why not: learn a dead language or two; draw some nudes in art studio; ingest some psychedelics; take time to figure things out. Just make sure you outgrow it. But what if you don't outgrow it? What if you never end the adolescent experiment "to figure things out?" For me, it's still just as compelling to imagine, as I did when I first opened Genesis as a freshman, that on some utterly forgotten path, in the remnants of some eclipsed civilization, perhaps along some long dry riverbed that once sustained human life, there lying dormant I might discover a set of washed-out footprints. Whose are they? Has anyone else discovered this path? Once found, if I can only follow these steps, perhaps they'll lead the way to . . .

To where?

To a better place?

To a better way of doing things?

To knowledge?

To some *answers?*

Do the ages really contain secrets? Do they offer answers?
If they do, my education didn't confer any to me.

WHAT SCHOOL DIDN'T CONFER

This is the sentimental part of my story, because none of that
learning seemed to matter a whit when my dominoes fell. I
thought I'd built for myself some firm surroundings. I thought
I'd put together a solid family and a directed career. I hadn't.
Once pushed, everything tumbled. First my job foundered. I
ended up on airplanes trying to keep my career together (a hundred thousand miles earned me corporate chairman status and
many much needed drink vouchers). That schedule of course
kept me away from my family and, predictably, my marriage
turned to excrement. We didn't fight, but we never talked either.
Cathy cried while I froze. Or I cried while she panicked. We
never cried together. Then the crying stopped, and no better
mode of communicating came to replace it. We just weren't facing life's tumult as partners anymore. I looked back to consider
what had really changed. What had we seen during these wed-
ded years? Nothing extraordinary. Many wrenching miscarriages; finally two fighting and screaming kids; four states scat-
tered across four American time zones; cycles of sexlessness and
wanderlust; bouts of unemployment; and seven jobs between us.
And a lot of poorly made decisions to boot. Was this the reality
of marriage? Or was I simply in a bad one? Would a divorce
even solve my problems?

What is my problem? I thought.

Wasn't I supposed to know better? Shouldn't I have had some
understanding of spiritual well-being and the care of the soul? I
didn't. I only knew I needed to find something to motivate me

in a world that might not include anything I had once depended on as stable emotional facts. Yet despite all my supposed learning, I just couldn't figure out what that might be.

THE REALITY OF MARRIAGE

Then my old college friend Sanjay Sharma called. Since we'd left school, Sanjay had been on Wall Street becoming rich, which was no small feat for an Indian in the 1990s. Though in India his family was of the Kshatriya caste of kings and warriors, in America he was the outcaste son of immigrant parents, a man with dark skin navigating four centuries of Manhattan ethnicity and wealth. Sanjay's considerable bravado seemed to me always checked by his knowledge of the accidental distribution of advantages, which is I why I liked him.

The gift of a humble view did not, however, save Sanjay from getting himself into a good deal of trouble in New York. His perspective on the chance of advantages didn't stop him from enjoying his own advantages, including, of course, his newly found wealth but also his gift of good looks. He was Valentino handsome and still is. As a young man I'd heard tell of a modeling agent stopping him on a Greenwich Village street to present a card, while Sanjay's girlfriend, a gorgeous and successful actress, waited in his shadow. Each girlfriend seemed to me to be more beautiful and intelligent than the last, and the parade of them kept stepping forward. Sanjay did occasionally confide to me his concern about whether he could ever finally commit. Until then, he spent his wealth and good looks on this passion, and divided his resources between fancy dinner reservations, bottles of Veuve Clicquot, and a nightlife considerably more active than my own. As my marriage took its toll, I grew envious of his freedom. So

I was taken by surprise the day he called to say two unthinkable words:

"I'm engaged."

Oh god, was all I could think. After all my own troubles, I'd begun to consider that Sanjay might have had his romantic priorities right all these years. Perhaps mine had been all wrong.

"Congratulations," I think I managed to say.

He'd already begun the great domestic negotiation. He was calling about the wedding. His fiancée Emma insisted that her best friend read a love poem at the ceremony in lieu of a sermon. Sanjay had no problem forgoing religion. However, now close to forty years old, he was finally committing himself to marriage and he wanted some words of gravity to mark the change. I was his longest-married friend and, at least professionally speaking, his most knowledgeable friend regarding arcane rites like matrimony.

"I'd like you to say some something at the ceremony regarding the reality of marriage," he said.

The reality of marriage. I covered the phone before laughing. Me, the marriage virtuoso. I'd provide the words to launch these two good people into marital bliss. Then I'd go home and file for divorce, else have it handed to me.

What, me bitter?

MY SERMON

I squinted through Sardinia's orange evening sky toward the wedding dais. Sanjay was beckoning me to come up. It was time to speak my piece. As I stood to button my coat, I touched the yellow sheet of paper in my inside pocket with my sermon notes. Still blank. I'd tossed out every last-ditch imbecilic idea. I walked quickly down the aisle and took my place before the beaming array of Sanjay's closest family and friends. There sat his mother, Pat, absolutely gorgeous yet suffering from stage-four breast cancer, as she had been for most of that year. Beside her sat Sanjay's father, Samesh, a quiet and serious man, a scientist, who I reckoned worried as much about his wife as he did about his only son. What could I tell them about marriage and family? What could I say to any of them?

I touched my yellow sheet again. Still blank.

Sanjay smiled at me. I tried to smile back. He was making a good decision, right?

"Maybe you would like to face the audience," Sanjay said as he motioned for his bride to move out of my line of view.

And that's when the words finally came to me.

"No," I said. "I want to talk to you."

And I did. Like a streetlight flickering on at dusk, a single verse appeared in my mind. It arrived from among all the thousands of aphorisms, stories, and parables I'd come across in my work. I hadn't thought about this one in years. Where had I even learned of it? Why had it come back to me now? I had no idea. It didn't matter. I would tell Sanjay and Emma a curious story from the Upanishads of ancient India. I would tell them about the path of joy.

NICEKETAS'S QUESTION

The Upanishads tell the story of a man who is given a strange gift by the gods. He may ask Death any question and be guaranteed a true answer.

What if Death really could speak? What special knowledge could it reveal? Since Death is present at the conclusion of every life, presumably it would know what finally came of each dream, hope, and plan. In the end, did we ever really succeed? Did we ultimately fail? Did any of our successes, failures, or strivings make a bit of difference? That is to say, Death knows what a life finally amounts to. So if Death could speak, it might also reveal the answer to one of life's greatest questions, which Niceketas decides to ask: *In a world in which so many things we pursue seem futile, is there indeed anything that is not?*

Death responds with a concise verse that, for me on the dais, revealed a realistic possibility for fulfillment in marriage—and perhaps also in life. It's what I quoted to Sanjay and Emma:

> There is a path of joy and there is a path of pleasure.
> Both attract the soul.
> Those who seek joy come to find it.
> Those who seek pleasure never come to the end.[1]

Joy and pleasure. One path finds satisfaction and the other winds on endlessly. Was that even correct? It *felt* right. Comparing these two feelings raised up in my memory very different life experiences. *Joy* and *pleasure*. One set of experiences tended to leave me feeling edified and fulfilled, and the other set . . . well, these left me something less than fulfilled. Death's distinction between these two flavors of happiness seemed credible. Yet at the same moment the distinction also felt slippery. Maybe it was trite or merely semantic. Even the very word *joy* felt like an irrelevant antique from a bygone era, like *groovy* or *twenty-three skidoo*.

Still, recalling the verse as I did suddenly on the wedding dais, the ancient Indian wisdom cut straight through the confusing morass of my own troubles and seemed to clarify the means for fulfillment and happiness in marriage. I now knew what to say. I even had a faint understanding of what to do.

After the wedding ceremony in the excitement of the evening celebration, guests came up to me to learn more about the verse. Where did it come from? What did it mean? Some people had their own ideas. A young married couple caught me on my way to the champagne flutes. The husband tried to articulate his own understanding of the verse, perhaps too honestly.

"I always love my wife," he explained. "But I don't always *like* her."

Too much truth. I saw her fist careen into his bicep.

"What's wrong with pleasure?" another guest said accusingly.

"I'm not sure anything's *wrong* with it," I said.

"Can't pleasure be a joy?" asked another.

"Probably," I stuttered. "I think sometimes it can."

I didn't really know the answer to any of these questions. I had only just begun to wrestle with them myself. Every unanswered question made me think I'd said something pretentious and indecipherable at my friend's wedding. Still, I thought there was *something* to it.

When I had a moment to myself, my mind was thrown back in time to try and piece together the life of the ancient Brahmin priest and reciter who had first uttered it. Could joy and pleasure have meant the same things to him as they did now to me? How disparate the Brahmin's worldview must have been from my own. How unfamiliar all his daily routines of ritual memorization. How different was his river civilization along the Ganges from anywhere my ancestors had been. Surely the rhythms of his innermost feelings couldn't be related to my own. I mean, I had instant internet access to whatever sick pleasure I could imagine; he didn't even have the *Kama Sutra* (which was written later). So what could he possibly tell me about the path of pleasure? What could he say about twenty-first century joy? What could he know about the internal mess that *I* was feeling?

Maybe the best thing was to set aside these questions for a while and just ignore all the circumstances and centuries that separated me from the Brahmin priest. Whatever the distance between us, the Brahmin had been a feeling human being, and so was I. He had spoken to *me*, directly: my Brahmin therapist. His ancient psychological distinction seemed to make sense of *my* confusing knot of impulsive attractions, *my* enduring joys, and *my* ever-receding pleasures. I'd felt both joy and pleasure in my life. Were they different paths? To me, there was nothing to debate. I damn well knew they were.

THE ENDS OF PLEASURE

At dinner I was sitting next to my buddy from freshman year, Brian. He'd been thrown out of our dorm for smoking a six-foot bong. I had occasionally helped him manage that two-person operation, which is how we met. Now he was a professor of functional neurosurgery who cured debilitating diseases such as Parkinson's and obsessive compulsive disorder. He did this by soldering implants deep inside the brain. Recently he had been working on developing a surgery for clinical depression, actual psychosurgery. Brian Harris Kopell was an impressive guy. He wore five-thousand-dollar suits and five-hundred-dollar sunglasses, the constant sunglasses being a habit he picked up in his psychedelic days. He was also clueless when it came to relationships, just like me.

"Let's take a walk around the bay," he said. He had something on his mind. I knew what it was. Brian had brought his girlfriend with him to Sardinia.

"Is bringing her across the globe for a wedding something of a statement?" I wondered.

"That's what I seem to be asking you," he said.

The menacing tang of commitment hovered around us, my commitments and his potential ones. He wanted to know if it was going to be OK, whether getting hitched would be the best or worst decision of his life. What was I supposed to tell him? To look at the divorce rate?

I thought of the attorneys still listed on my yellow pad.

"Rabbi," Brian said, "tell me something."

"Everything I know about marriage I said today at the wedding," I replied.

"Not good enough," he said. "I'm a practical person. I need a yes or a no. Is the surgery feasible, or isn't it?"

"Thumbs up or thumbs down," I said.

"Exactly," he said. "Would you do it again?"

Would I?

We looked down over a cliff into the harbor of Costa Smeralda. In daylight its waters had been cobalt blue, with a kind of lucid clarity usually reserved for gems. At night the tide sparkled with colored lights coming off the decks of the yachts standing in the marina. Each boat was a more colorful peacock than the next. Brian pointed down to an enormous vessel at the very end of the line of them. The boat was easily the size of a cruise ship.

"Holy mother, what is that?" I said.

"A yacht," Brian replied cooly.

"For just one guy?"

By the morass of antennae and satellite receptors it had on its roof I guessed the boat was capable of launching its own satellite. Brian said its owner was probably a Russian oligarch, a multibillionaire created in the massive crime scene that was the aftermath of the Soviet Union. There he was, presumably, in his boat. An entire hotel at sea for one man. As I looked upon it, a set of emotions were stirred in me including awe and wonder. But I also wondered about the chain of emotions and drives by which the boat was acquired. What pushes someone to buy such a ridiculous boat for himself? A boat like that could serve no rational purpose for any individual—not even for his family and friends.

"That's your path of pleasure right there," Brian said. "'Those who seek pleasure never come to the end.'"

Brian was right. The yacht owner's motivation now seemed obvious. *This wasn't the man's first boat, nor would it be his biggest, nor would it be his last.* Each additional foot along the bow only pushed the owner to crave the next size up. Each new Star Trek contraption initiated the need for its own technological super-session. These were pleasures gotten completely out of hand. The grandest ship on earth would not satiate the oligarch's quest to find a ship that satisfied him. *There would always be a bigger boat.*

"It's Zeno's paradox come to life," Brian said.

"What's that?"

"What's in motion must arrive at a halfway point before it arrives at the goal. Each step forward creates a new halfway point. You can't reach the end."

"An infinite path of shortcoming?" I said.

"Exactly," he said. "Grasping and shortcoming. Almost being there. Always *almost.* But not quite."

What other explanation could account for this insane hotel anchored in the harbor? And what about my own ridiculous purchases, my own inane quests? They, too, felt like going forward by halves. Did I really need professional cameras for family snapshots and selfies? While in hot pursuit of products like these they seemed reasonable, but in the clarity of time their glorious stupidity shone through. And this wasn't only true for purchases. In theory, one could always find a better orgasm.

During my dating years, I'd felt that Sunday mornings consistently dissolved the achievements of Saturday night. Even later, during my family years, when my pursuit of pleasure was typically quite mundane, I found myself needing just one more click on an internet news aggregator while my kids waited for me to read them a book. With all that clicking, what was I looking for? Where was it taking me? Could I ever get there? *Then why hadn't I gotten there yet?*

While pursuing some pleasure, in that moment it did feel as though I might be accomplishing something. What I was doing *seemed* reasonable and important. I'd feel an initial pulse and rush. *Yes, this is it!* Then suddenly that feeling would slip away. I'd been down a path with no end.

"Is marriage like that yacht?" Brian asked. "Because that boat looks a lot more practical to me than some kids and a wife."

"Sometimes," I muttered.

THE ENDS OF JOY

When we got back to the party, I looked again toward the lovely, stylish, women thumping on the dance floor. They were in states of even further undress and abandon. My erotic charge rose as my confidence in my sermon fell. *Nice theory, egghead.* The actual impulses in the blitzkrieg of life were simply too overwhelming and impossible. Or maybe it was just me. I was just too far gone: falling out of love with my wife, frustrated with the bottomless needs of my kids, utterly spent in my vocation. Sure, I recognized when I felt premonitions of regret (seemingly all the time), but a drink took care of those. Or two drinks. Maybe a quick affair on an isolated Italian island, no big deal. Or maybe a protracted affair. Maybe a six-month stay in Margaritaville.

As I watched another bridesmaid kick off her shoes, I enhanced my bravado by finishing off the last dregs of a cocktail. *I'm going to hit the dance floor,* I thought. *Whatever happens happens.*

I took a first step out. Yet something intervened exactly when I felt the wooden slat beneath my foot. I heard the voice of my Brahmin therapist again. "Those who seek joy come to find it." Suddenly I understood the wisdom of the verse. Unlike pleasure, the experience of joy contained *an ongoing feeling of fulfillment,* even after the direct experience had passed. Wasn't that a great feeling to have? When I did achieve it, it came with neither guilt nor the sneaking suspicion that something else could be more important to do at that moment. I was making my best choice. I was taking my ideal way. Unlike pleasure, the feeling of joy transcended the immediate moment.

I could now understand the practical value of the Brahmin's ancient psychological distinction. Decisions I made throughout the day were ultimately choices between which flavor of happiness to pursue—pleasure or joy. I held in me a primordial tug of war of contesting therapeutic drives, with life itself forged in the competitive balance. The terse verse of the Upanishads had even articulated a kind of test for distinguishing these. It was an *endurance* test. With it, a simple set of questions might help direct me in every instance and moment, despite all intensity of temptation:

Would this impulse finally achieve the edification of joy, or the ephemeral moment of pleasure?

Would the happiness of this action endure, or would it slip away in the night?

When faced with a fork in the road or a choice along life's way I could always break out the Brahmin's endurance test. I could always ask: *How will I feel about my decision after the initial rush is gone?*

"What time is it in California?" I asked Brian.

"About 3:30 in the afternoon."

The kids would be having snack.

"Can I borrow your phone?"

My wife Cathy picked up. "Hey Mickey!" she said and called to the kids: "It's Dad!"

I found a quiet vista and settled in to chat with all my family about their day's little adventures and mine. Would my marriage last unto death? I had no clue. I still don't. Nobody knows the future—nobody will ever convince me otherwise. But *in that moment* I had taken my path of joy. I couldn't really ask for more. Decisions come in steps; in the passing of every moment there is a choice. And in that moment I felt really, really great—*and without any premonition of regret.* In that moment I'd done the right thing. In the next, would I do it again? What would the right thing even be? Would it be a marital reconciliation or a merciful divorce? Would it be reinserting myself back into my kids' lives or getting my sorry, sulking self out of their way? God only knew, but somehow I was going to figure it out, moment by moment, choice by choice. "Those who seek joy come to find it": that guy was going to be *me*. Joy or bust.

Groovy, baby. Twenty-three skidoo!

TAKING OFF

There, as my plane pushed off the runway in Sardinia, I still had the telephone numbers of attorneys scrawled out on my yellow pad. Though, since then, I had also jotted down many other notes as well. Even after the wedding ceremony and the glow of the party, my Brahmin's advice stayed with me, and I had stayed up to think. Did I have something here more than pretty words? Could I walk the talk in my own marriage and life? Could the Upanishads heal *me*? I began thinking about the relevance of the ancient Sanskrit lines to Sanjay's new life and to my own. And what other gems had I happened upon in my career whose personal value I had all but repressed? I had to find out. I now realized that for me going forward meant going back, back to my first classrooms, back to my first encounters with the big questions of life. I had to reconsider everything I thought I knew, everything I'd taught for decades as though a barker for a sideshow. Now I remembered what had brought me to the carnival in the first place: I was one of the freaks. It was time to admit that, like so many people who are drawn to spirituality, all along I had actually been seeking therapy. As so many do, I too was searching. I was looking for some answers.

Believe me, I was prepared to find a trail of quackery. Being made a fool is an unavoidable hazard in the pursuit of happiness. There on the tarmac in Sardinia, I realized that whatever came out of my earnest search might turn out to be nothing but a record of absurdity and embarrassment. Perhaps I'd find myself banging a djembe drum on the coast of Malibu; or sitting in silence for thirty days at a *sayadaw* retreat with my mind wandering most consistently to fantasies about lunch. (Alas, both puerile excitements came to be). But what the heck, the stakes were already high enough. Continuing to fake confidence in my purposes as husband, father, teacher, friend—I was done with that. It was time to ante up. It was time to say *I'm all in*. I was ready either to find real footing on the floor of this tempest or to drown in embarrassment while trying. So, as I clicked myself into my airplane seat and felt the engine vibrations grow, I could feel myself preparing for a new adventure. I decided there on the tarmac to put my other research interests on hold for a while and to take some time to reconsider classics I'd learned about over the course of my long career. I'd also consider things new to me, arenas of thought I'd always wanted to look into but so far hadn't. What was my purpose? For what was I searching? It was simplicity itself. I was looking to locate any wisdom at all that might help me make heads or tails of my life.

2

MAKING PEACE WITH
THE UNIVERSE

INFERNO

Being a scholar working in the history of religions, trained in
the country's great academies, and now teaching at a fine public
university, I decided to start my therapy with what I thought I
knew. Could anything from the long history of spiritual wisdom help direct me through the thicket of dark impulses, or
couldn't it? *Which beliefs and practices might actually heal?* I
decided to search across cultures, denominations, and human
history, to consider anything that struck me as potentially personally orienting. I'd also go into the annals of psychology,
including positive psychology ("the scientific study of positive
human functioning and flourishing," according to one well
received definition), cognitive science, and neuropsychiatry,
seeking what current science may have confirmed or rejected
of the older wisdom.[1]

I would read with utter skepticism, particularly of metaphysical assumptions. This could be no soft exercise in religious
toleration, carried on for the benefit of a liberal college education. I didn't need that again. I wasn't even sure I still *believed*
in that. So many spiritual platitudes pass for wisdom. So much

doctrine merely supports the bluntest overt political aims—
sexism, racism, sexual phobia, and, these days especially,
nationalism. In the classroom, I felt obliged to remind thinking
students of this impolite history of religions. Yet in private I still
found myself wondering, *But is there anything to it?* I knew I
finally needed to test any purported therapeutic affects for
myself, once and for all, in this life, now.

I mean I wouldn't abide any puerile drivel. I couldn't do that
anymore.

Soon I discovered something that shocked me. Many others
in the long history of the human record had also asked these very
questions during personal crises. I realized this while coming to
review the first sentence of Dante's *Inferno*, which in midlife now
halted me.

> Midway upon the journey of our life
> I found myself within a forest dark
> For the straightforward path had been lost.[2]

Suddenly Dante's famous journey through hell and redemp-
tion reflected a pattern I could see represented in so many spiritual masterpieces I knew. These in effect comprised notes of personal breakdowns, typically set off by dark reminders of the
human condition, whether illnesses and episodes of bodily
demise, addictions, or just the silent pangs of purposelessness
common to midlife. Right away, I recalled Augustine's *Confessions* (begun after a failed relationship), William James's famous
epiphanies with nitrous oxide that culminated in *The Varieties of
Religious Experience*, and countless examples before and since.
When had Socrates lost faith in sophistry, begun devotion to
Apollo, and started denouncing the inanity of Athenian leaders? In midlife, after an existential crisis. Why had Ghazali, the

sultan's legendary attorney, run away to Damascus to study mystical Sufi teachings? To reassess his life, after the likely murder of his sultan. Even Chinggis Khan (once more typically known as Genghis Khan) decided to begin spiritual study of the Dao while dreading a forced retirement from an arrow in the knee. Less renowned contemporary cases also came to mind, such as that of my own jazz hero, the pianist Mary Lou Williams, who walked off stage mid-career in an alcoholic despair, only to emerge writing the most gorgeous Catholic masses, insisting that these African American masterpieces be played at the Vatican. The current Pope Francis himself sought psychoanalytic therapy at age forty-two.

And so on. Like Dante, somewhere well along the path of life's journey these capable and successful people lost track of themselves. Once they had seemed perfectly normal, with important day jobs and social responsibilities; then something happened, and they collapsed, doubting everything they had achieved. Still, with the onset of crisis, they did not take leave of reason. None claimed mysterious prophetic contact with divinity; none announced the godlike founding of a new faith. In fact, in their darkest moments of confusion and indirection they all went and did something very normal, even reasonable: they sought spiritual grounding.

Fortunately each also came to find that grounding. Their confessions ultimately portray the achievement of a kind of spiritual mood, a peace with the universe and with one's place in it. This made some sense to me. Religion had certainly been the primary forum for therapy before scientific psychology existed. It was how one oriented oneself therapeutically amidst scarce resources and inhospitable environments. Yet I had never considered the classics of spiritual exploration and confession from this explicitly therapeutic point of view. I should have, because once I looked again, nearly all revealed these purposes explicitly: someone described a personal crisis and then recounted the steps taken to achieve personal reorientation. Nevertheless, after I began reconsidering these spiritual masterpieces, I never expected to find profound, radical, and even subversive therapeutic theories and practices. So my investigative purpose sharpened. I would now focus on the harrowing personal backstories to some classic works of spirituality in order to understand how therapeutics once operated and also to see if these might still contribute to personal well-being.

THE SPIRITUAL MOOD

Thinking about these things brought William James back to me, the founder of both American psychology and American religious studies, who only in his late forties finally succeeded in publishing his first book, *The Principles of Psychology* (1890). His would become the first American textbook in psychology, still cited frequently in the scientific literature. Cognitive behavioral therapy, for instance, is inconceivable without James. He also predicted neuroplasticity a century before it was demonstrated.

I had been reading William James for years. I knew his biography well, especially his own serious episodes of anxiety, insomnia, and depression. So I began to think about where James had been midway through his life's journey, around forty. He wasn't doing too well. He was married, with children, and in a difficult relationship; he was years late with his first book manuscript and not even close to finishing; he'd been sucking down nitrous oxide in his offices at Harvard and calling it "research" (he claimed it helped him to understand Hegel!); and ultimately he'd suffered a complete meltdown and fled to Europe to try and pull himself and his career together. Years later he wrote to a friend: "I take it no man is educated who has never dallied with the thought of suicide."[3]

So James too had suffered a personal crisis. Accordingly, he began to ask a very personal question of the academic concepts he had studied: *Is there any therapeutic potential to anything I've learned? Can any of this help* me?

James in fact came up with an answer to this question, and an interesting one. To what had the great psychologist turned when his own dominoes fell? He *re*turned, actually. He returned to the spiritual masters he first heard of as a child and had perused as a curious student. But in returning he realized that, whatever he'd once thought about those old masterpieces, he had not understood them as he now could with his own life experiences. So he started rereading those masters who had inspired him in youth: Marcus Aurelius and Ignatius Loyola, the radicals Spinoza and Swinburne, the American mystics Whitman and Emerson. He turned to Jonathan Edwards and John Henry Newman, Saints Paul, Augustine, Teresa, and also Madame Guyon. And he looked out as far off as he could as well, finding fresh points of view from regions that the English-speaking world of the nineteenth century had only begun to encounter with any seriousness: the Ramakrishna and the Upanishads, the revered Abu Hamid al-Ghazali and the obscure Lutfullah, and even little glimmers of translated Buddhist thought just barely understood at that time anywhere in the West.

These spiritual masters were the therapists James consulted when his own dominoes fell. They changed his life. After the crisis of his fortieth year, the long record of his mood difficulties dwindles and is replaced by writings describing an almost unbearably optimistic view. He thought, wrote, lectured, refined, and proselytized about this optimistic view for the rest of his life.

Twenty years after his crisis, an invitation came from Scotland to lecture about psychology and religion. For James, given what he himself had gone through and how he thought about the science of psychology, this could only mean he would discuss with his Scottish hosts the therapeutic affects of religious experiences—*affects* in the psychological sense of the word, indicating experiences of feeling and emotion. *Does spirituality contain a particular feeling or set of feelings? Can cultivation of these feelings cure ailments of the mind? Can they even make a person happier?* These lectures culminated in *The Varieties of Religious Experience* (1902), best-selling then and mandatory for students still.[4]

And what did James learn from his investigations? Could spiritual experiences translate into *therapeutic affects?* That is to say, could spiritual experiences induce feelings and emotions of mental well-being, and even sustained states of these? He thought sometimes they could.

He contended that across all denominations and traditions the most fundamental spiritual achievement is in discovering a more therapeutic mood for oneself, a better way of experiencing life's often impossible moments. The spiritual mood helped one embrace the hard circumstances of reality, not just tolerate them. "Dull submission is left far behind," he noticed, "and a mood of welcome, which may fill any place on the scale between cheerful serenity and enthusiastic gladness, has taken its place."[5]

To explain his point, James compared a spiritual person to a stoic one. He said the stoic merely submitted *to* the cosmic scheme; the spiritual person agreed *with* that scheme. A stoic might be "stunned into submission" by reality and typically invoked "resignation to necessity." The spiritual person, however, though working with the same set of facts and perhaps even agreeing to the same set of cosmic rules, also submitted to reality—but with "enthusiastic assent," "passionate happiness," and basic gratitude for the privilege of experience. "The difference of emotional atmosphere," James said, "is like that between an arctic climate and the tropics."[6]

When this discussion from the *Varieties* came back to me, I took in my lung's full capacity of air. To me, James on the spiritual mood still sounded like a compelling psychological understanding of personal religion. It also seemed to offer a peace treaty with the universe.[7]

MAKING PEACE WITH THE UNIVERSE

How did a person actually achieve this improved mood? Under which conditions did one come to find "enthusiastic assent" and "a mood of welcome," even with insurmountable situations? James himself made only preliminary suggestions about this. So that's what I set out to investigate. I wanted like James to return to spiritual masters who had turned their lives around. I had some twenty-first century questions for them.

How exactly did traditional therapies work before the advent of scientific psychology? Did these indeed turn personal crisis into something like an integrative and homeostatic psychological health? Did their basic therapeutic models and assumptions differ from those that finally took hold of modern psychology and counseling? Were their concepts and practices at all consistent with what we now understand from science about the human mind and brain? In short, did these spiritual therapies still have anything to offer?

This book became my attempt to locate the means of therapy in a diverse handful of the world's most articulate spiritual masterpieces, which I now understand as classic cases of spiritual therapy. By this I mean these are records of personal crisis and resolution through spiritual exploration. In them, readers may ultimately discover that the spiritual mood is not so mysterious after all. Many have experienced something of this natural human feeling before, perhaps while contemplating a rocky stream or while observing a child gaze in wonder or simply while swapping stories with old friends. For a moment, the world revolves on well-oiled hinges. Often that's really all there is to it.

Yet neuroscientists have just begun to study the physiological manifestation in our brains of this symphony of affects establishing inner peace and James's "mood of welcome." Health and spirituality is now an emerging subfield of medicine, offering help for those grappling with anxiety, stress, post-traumatic stress disorder, depression, and a host of other problems. Their initial scientific findings are fascinating and helpful, but medicine and pharmacology are still some way from invoking the benefits of spiritual experience precisely, consistently, and safely, let alone integratively. In the cases studied here, cultivating a spiritual mood seems to have achieved whole-person solutions. So although my study is certainly a work of medical humanities and not sciences, there may be something to learn by inspecting classic cases of therapy and spiritual genius. For millennia, the world's astounding array of spiritual traditions have *cultivated* the edifying spiritual mood and made of it daily practices. Seen this way, religion was indeed the forum for therapy before the modern scientific undertaking existed. Its annals may still hold insights and perspectives of value even today.[8]

JAMES VERSUS FREUD

At the time William James looked to the annals of religion for clues to therapeutic mood and affect, Sigmund Freud also turned to the same sources, but for clues to pathology. Unlike James, Freud was a medical doctor and clinician, a practicing neurologist, who took a medical view regarding the pains of his patients. This medical view, shared with many doctors of his time, worked with a therapeutic model based on specific pathology and its release. In his view, a specific debilitating problem existed at the root of pain, which Freud called a neurosis. A therapist's work was to find and alleviate this specific pathology. Unfortunately, also like most medical theorists of his time, Freud then offered no integrative or homeostatic state of stable affairs for the patient: a state of health, as it were. Far from it. In a particularly dark essay, in which he considered the question of when to terminate therapy, Freud admitted that the moment never came. The manufacture of neurosis and psychic pain was a continual function of normal mental processes, he said. The primal appetites of the id (which neuropsychologists now think of as the limbic system, still considered the seat of primary, innate, preorganized, indeed Jamesian emotions and drives) faced unrelenting conflict, frustration, and torment in any human habitat. The appetites of the id (i.e., the limbic system) would always face yet another frustration in the environment. Thus the very structure of human motivation created a permanent state of agitation, even war. Sickness itself was normal. Therefore psychotherapeutic efforts could only be specific, inconclusive, and interminable.[9]

James thought about relief very differently. Most obviously, he did not share with Freud the view of spiritual phenomena as debilitating symptoms. As we have already seen, James shared almost nothing of Freud's suspicion of religious expression. Indeed, James often understood these as signs of health. More important, I think, James differed in believing in the very *possibility* of an integrative psychological health. Through cognitive and behavioral efforts (beliefs and rituals), a person could come to feel many of life's inevitable torments and pains as occurring within a larger and more significant context, beyond oneself. So contextualized, the effect was to temper some of the immediacy of an individual's innate and preorganized (i.e., limbic) emotions. To James this recontextualization seemed especially successful for general types of pain, including generalized anxiety and major depression (to use modern diagnostic language). "Easily, permanently, and successfully, it often transforms the most intolerable misery into the profoundest and most enduring happiness."[10]

Here then, over a century ago at the very dawn of the cognitive and affective revolutions in psychology and cognitive science, and in stark contradistinction to models of permanent pathology being laid down by psychoanalysis, William James set forth an integrative model for achieving general and homeostatic psychological health. Amazingly, the great Harvard psychologist proposed that this health could be had through conversion to a saving *spiritual* point of view.

THE REALITY OF THE UNSEEN

James's claim seemed backward and unscientific even when he presented it in 1902. So why did he insist on the *spiritual* nature of the therapies he had explored in his study? Which elements of these therapies, for James, always sat *beyond* the capacities of human understanding and reason? His discussion of the definition of religion itself addressed these questions most directly. Religion, James offered, "consists of the belief that there is an unseen order, and that our supreme good lies in harmoniously adjusting ourselves thereto."[11] By an "unseen order," he meant beyond apodictic proof. Reason alone could never quite demonstrate the reality of such an order. Philosophy had no power to decide in this domain. Nevertheless, one's cognitive *belief* in such order constituted its own psychological reality. But was that all? If not reason, then did anything actually ground this reality or support this belief? What might be detected and *seen* of the unseen? James thought feelings themselves comprised a detectable reality. Though the beliefs were indemonstrable, the emotional states and feelings were real to those who felt them. Which is to say, *affects* constituted the reality of spiritual beliefs. Very often these appeared as *real therapeutic affects*. James called this "the reality of the unseen."

James's certitude in the "reality of the unseen" was intellectually difficult, even fraught, for thinking patients and psychologists alike. That was the case in James's time and even well before him. In fact, each master we will meet in these pages at first held dark doubts about the reality and worth of spiritual curiosity and feelings. Abu Hamid al-Ghazali in particular, we will learn, began his journey with a brutally skeptical Cartesian inquiry (five hundred years preceding Descartes), before finally locating for himself an integrative therapeutic orientation. And nearly a thousand years before James, Ghazali already understood that while spiritual suppositions lay beyond reasonable demonstration, their therapeutic affects could be altogether real. Ghazali gave his study of this phenomenon the intriguing title *The Alchemy of Happiness*, which readers will come to know shortly. Thankfully, Ghazali, along with the other masters we will consider, recorded for us both their doubts and their breakthroughs.

SPIRITUAL GRAVITY

Before finally starting off, I would like to offer my own formulation of the therapeutic work described and advocated by the spiritual masterpieces explored herein. My emphasis differs slightly (though I hope significantly) from the "belief in an unseen order" offered by James.

In my view, the oldest continuing human experiments regarding affect, or how things feel, have been recorded for us in the annals of religious confession. For that is what religions do: they cultivate feelings. Whether by the sudden uplift of one's attention and spirit achieved within a Gothic church or by the unity of cosmos and self experienced during the beating of a Sun Dance drum, religions exist to cultivate particular affects, which themselves are organized to bring the feelings of healing, orientation, and fulfillment.[12]

To be sure, there have existed a wide range of spiritual affects. Yet most have shared in their articulation of one feeling in particular: *gravitas.* By this I mean something like spiritual weight. The world often feels as though it has weight. People are born and die; things are created and destroyed; the world evolves and devolves; and typically these changes feel as though they matter. When one does slip into a mood of believing that nothing really matters, even *that* view can come with its own feeling of gravitas, an unbearable lightness of being.

Somewhere along the way, the geniuses described herein came to realize that recognizing and facing their personal feelings of spiritual gravity was an essential element in learning to live with themselves. They began taking such feelings seriously and exploring them. Like many others, these hurting people found themselves pulled toward spirituality, the forum in which so many had been considering the weight of the world for so long, and the place where people tried to align their own actions with this gravity. Why did they all bother? What was the point? They discovered that, for them, turning toward gravitas felt orienting, integrating, and grounding—as opposed to disorienting, scattering, "lite," and empty. That is to say, turning toward gravitas felt therapeutic. It felt healing. It felt edifying. It felt *good* in the weighty sense of the word. They report becoming suddenly clear minded and justified when finally abiding by this suprarational orientation, often when reason warned that they were just being naive. If I may suggest, the gravitas affect *is* the higher power articulated by these spiritual masterpieces, the mysterious inwardly felt tug to return to one's own right way, despite all sirens.[13]

Through these several cases, I will argue that noticing gravitas (spiritual weight), and orienting oneself to it, achieved for these masters the affect that James called "enthusiastic assent" and "a mood of welcome." The mechanism for coming to this state rested precisely in directing attention to some larger concern when one's private energies (whether conceived of psychoanalytically as id, cognitively as the Jamesian emotions, or neurologically as the limbic system) had become problematically self-obsessive, even self-destructively so. Put another way, the pains and frustrations of the private appetites became tempered by contextualization beyond themselves.[14]

The means of spiritual therapy then had two levers:

- *One felt the weight of the world.* One experienced gravitas, an unseen but discernible orientation towards some larger concern beyond the private appetites—a higher power, as it were.
- *One discovered a therapy of commitment.* One found that personal welfare could best be addressed by giving oneself to this gravity.[15]

Across diverse cultures and irrespective of historical moments—from ancient Athens, medieval Baghdad, and Beijing to modern day Paris and New York—each genius recounted in the coming pages did this. Each discovered his or her own common cause with a looming universe. This seems to me to be the very means of spiritual therapy as it has been practiced classically for millennia: noticing the weight of the world and *giving into gravity*. In so doing, each one managed to change the quality of emotion from that of grudging consent to worldly circumstances, and found a position of "enthusiastic assent" to those very same circumstances.[16]

Admittedly, my viewing the varieties of spiritual experience this way, as comprised fundamentally of a gravitas affect, differs in emphasis from James's major formulation that religion "consists of the belief that there is an unseen order." This subtle shift, from belief (cognition) to feeling (affect), I think is best addressed in the conclusion, after readers have traversed these several examples.

SPIRITUAL ADVENTURE

At the very least, I've set down the human backstories and crises to some of the world's great spiritual adventures. Of the dozens of documents I investigated, I choose to represent these few for their sustained human power and depth of insight, despite their religious, cultural, and historical diversity. First a brief case from the traditional sources, that of Socrates, initiates the discussion by presenting a classical model of integrative therapy, and with it a thoroughly radical understanding of happiness. It also provides a clear and almost commonsense example of divine orientation and commitment to gravitas. Then each of the following studies correlates with one of three basic arenas in the contemporary study of positive psychology: learning, labor, and love (interpersonal responsibility).[17] In all cases, we hear from an eyewitness to a crisis. The resultant masterpiece is either an autobiographical confession (Abu Hamid al-Ghazali), a biographical report of direct observation (of Socrates and Chinggis Khan), or an artist's personal rendition along with her own verbal explanations (Mary Lou Williams). Finally, after discussing these classics, I offer a recent case in which I was myself involved.

Although the cases are presented chronologically, each can be read independently, as a reader's interests may direct. Each also notes the primary documents and spiritual masterpieces on which the study was largely based. Inspired readers may turn to these as well.

What follows are the stories of a few hurting people and how they came to locate higher powers for themselves, by which I simply mean a personally orienting and therapeutic gravity. In all cases, this occurred after years of cynical beliefs and concomitant world-weary behaviors. Then, during a very personal crisis, each acquiesced to his or her total ignorance regarding personal well-being and so started over. In a sense, having reached the end of the reasoning tether, each finally let go, allowing the feeling of gravitas itself to make the therapeutic adjustments.

Now decades into the algorithm-driven information age, some readers may find quaint the value in keeping human company with specific figures of the past and in learning about the ideas and principles they came to embody. Here I must admit, while I admire the quantitative foundations and abstract prescriptions offered by scientific psychology, I myself find something rich in observing real people in the full dark wood of life experience. The private thicket of crises and gravities may not be exactly replicable by others who try the experiment, but there is still something gained in following through to the therapeutic epiphany of another, especially of a genius.[18]

I have presented these classic works by telling historical narratives of their compositions, at times using historical and literary evidence to consider possible motivations of the actors. All psychological biography must employ a degree of sympathetic introspection, our imagining the imaginations of others, and I have intentionally displayed this method explicitly. Yet I have taken no liberties with facts. We need to understand what we can of those times and places supporting the therapeutic claims. Consequently, each case here must display considerable historical and cultural depth. For similar reasons, while I have tried to locate recognizable human voices behind these revered works, I also hope to have retained the subtlety of their insights. A spiritual genius once cast a message out upon the waves, and we have picked up the bottle. We are together indeed delving deeply into James's unseen order of the universe. Not so many travelers have been out to these parts.[19]

Once found, the spiritual mood may finally seem simple, but maintaining it never becomes easy. None of these reports advocates some painless Pollyanna perspective that just barely hides anxiety and fear. For how long could that have held together anything as complicated as a relationship or marriage, a family, a career—a life? Rather, each of our adventurers explored with utter emotional and intellectual honesty the nasty mess that living can be. Many people feel opposing tugs—toward gravity and toward emptiness. All the world's scriptures and confessions are filled with this struggle. In the fog of living one can sometimes forget which of these ultimately feels therapeutic and which pathetic. Overcome by daily assaults, sometimes it seems easiest just to scurry after quick reliefs and releases, despite knowing all too well that, when pursued for themselves, these can come to feel more emptying than edifying. Yet, at the same time, a simple hope persists that there must be some better choice than the endless course of turning away. These geniuses also articulated this same hope and then went on to heal themselves. They did this by submitting their dark impulses to higher gravities and purposes. All of us do this, in fact we do it all the time—in our families, with our friendships, in our schools and communities, in our vocations, and sometimes even in our places of worship. So perhaps in these masterpieces we will simply find a prompt or two to recall how those myriad and miraculous experiences of tranquil orientation are sometimes achieved. I mean the peace with the universe once felt by poet Wallace Stevens as he walked through the streets of New Haven one ordinary evening, breathed down deep, and, despite all the chaos, terror, and strife of life, could think to himself: "God is good. It is a beautiful night."

II

THE CLASSICS

3

SOCRATES

An Old Man and His Daemon

A man's character is his daemon.

—Heraclitus Fragment 54

HAPPINESS

The spiritual masterpiece informing this case is among the earliest recording a personal crisis regarding life's purpose. Some suppose The Apology *to be the first thing Plato wrote about his teacher, probably put to papyrus while still fresh from having attended the trial himself.*

Herein one learns how Socrates upon reaching maturity discovered an unfathomable truth about himself, thus drawing him into a genuine existential crisis: he no longer knew what he was supposed to be doing with his life. He then also began his career of humiliating the Athenian elite when he could no longer tolerate hearing their platitudes pass for wisdom.

Socrates's anxiety over losing his life's purpose, and his obsessive quest to find it again, will feel contemporary and even familiar to some. From the moment of Socrates's crisis to the very final minutes of his life, he dedicated himself totally to discovering what constituted

his best life and how to reorient his actions accordingly. He called this
eudaemonia, or happiness, and said he achieved it by heeding what
he called his divine voice.

COURTROOMS

Opening the pages of *The Apology*, we are returned to an ancient
courtroom of some kind, where fragrant oils infused with flower
and spice once filled the air. Everyone dressed formally for this
particular occasion in brightly colored gowns and jewelry. That
is, everyone except the defendant, since he appeared clothed like
a vagabond. The poor old man looked a mess. He had a puffy
face, almost like a drunk, and what was left of his hair tufted up
into a greasy crown, matching an equally scraggly gray beard.
His tattered gabardine tunic couldn't conceal his overflowing
belly or the fact that he was about to address the court without
the dignity of underwear. What a sight. He walked around the
courtroom in shreds. Yet something charismatic remained about
him. He stood upright, chest level, with eyes incongruously clear
against his bulbous nose and face. Maybe it was a certain weight
in his step. But what was this? He had no shoes. He'd come *bare-*
foot to his day in court.

As he walked out before the jury, five hundred citizens of
means and import perked up to listen.

To a derelict?

Who was this person?

His defense began. The disheveled man talked with surprising forthrightness and articulation. He apologized, he said, for
speaking in a style foreign to legal proceedings. He asked jurors
to please excuse the idiosyncrasies of his phrasing; he realized
his language was more suited to the malls and parks where he

spent most of his time. At age seventy, this was his first appearance in court, and he had no intention suddenly of learning a
new way to speak. The defendant stated all of this simply and
respectfully, without any hostility in his tone. Yet there was *bite*
in his meaning. The jury must have felt it. The aged defendant
wouldn't concede an iota of deference to the expectations of the
court. He wouldn't temper a single word on account of the circumstances. Those circumstances were considerable. He was on
trial for his life. This was but the prologue of his final defense,
what he called in Greek his *apologia*.

Who *was* this?

Could this have been the father of Western inquiry?

Was this really Socrates?

THE MOST DANGEROUS IDEA
IN THE WORLD

So it happened that in 399 BCE the people of Athens put a
seventy-year-old teacher on trial for his life. The crime had something to do with what Socrates had been saying to the city's
teenagers. Chatter in the city indicated that the notables who
had made the charges were themselves having trouble with their
sons, especially General Anytus, scion of wealth, former com-
mander in the Peloponnesian War, and finally an important politician in Athens. Perhaps that was really the cause of this spec-
tacle, because otherwise it didn't make much sense.

Most of the city knew Socrates as a harmless pest. As in other
villages and cities, the idle teenagers of Athens roamed its streets,
or hung out in the park (*lyceum*) or at the mall (*agora*), and those
kids sometimes gathered around Socrates as they might have
for any street entertainer. Most moved on at the first flicker of

boredom, but the brighter ones stayed to listen. Plato had been one of those bright kids.

Socrates wasn't even a teacher really, at least he never considered himself one. He didn't grant degrees or distribute technical knowledge. He never accepted payment for what he said, and he was amazed that others thought they knew something of value. Socrates didn't even have a classroom. Even though he enjoyed a home, a wife, and a few children, he really did spend his days like a vagrant, taking loans from his friends, accepting their charitable meals, and, most often, simply walking the streets in search of any passing conversation he could find regarding his favorite subject: What is *arete*?

Arete to Socrates roughly meant something like "excellence" or "virtuosity." It meant doing one's best. If anyone would talk to Socrates about his question—*What is arete? What is excellence? What is one's best?*—he'd talk to them, and when he got started asking he didn't stop. Most conversations with the inquisitive elder ended with an exhausted participant feigning some excuse for needing to leave. Nothing ever got settled either. One famed orator on the subject of personal excellence (apparently the ancients had motivational speakers too) said that after having been questioned by Socrates about the subject of his supposed expertise, he felt as though he'd been touched by an electrical torpedo fish, "for it too makes anyone who comes close and touches it feel numb, and you [Socrates] now seem to have had that kind of effect on me, for both my mind and my tongue are numb, and I have no answer to give you."[1]

Stupefied, that's how Socrates left the city's sages and experts, stupefied and numb. That must have embarrassed a lot of people around town. Still, how much of an actual threat could he have been? Since he didn't *do* anything, any danger must have come from what he knew, or at least what he'd been saying he knew.

So what was this dangerous idea, this knowledge worthy of execution? What did he claim to know?

"Not anything worthwhile." According to Plato, that's what Socrates told the jury.[2]

Let's consider what Socrates explained to the jury about how he came to his unusual way of life and his embarrassing and dangerous conclusions.

Socrates said he once had a best friend from childhood who had since passed away, Chairephon, an outgoing person whom most of Athens still remembered. The two once went around as quite a pair. Like Socrates himself, Chairephon would also corner people and grill them with questions and conversation. Even in adulthood the men wandered the streets or arrived at parties late together for having been waylaid by some discussion along the way.

Twenty years before, the playwright Aristophanes had produced a comedic send-up of the two friends called *The Clouds*, referring to the airy location where they typically pursued their lofty thoughts. The premise of the satire had been that these two clowns ran a technical school for so-called philosophers, where students could learn how to convince people that a bad argument was actually a good one, the worse argument the stronger. What a send-up of a play! Athens loved it, and when the friends Socrates and Chairephon themselves saw the piece they may have chuckled a few times themselves. But what the playwright satirized by exaggeration and inaccuracy had, twenty years later, become the central criminal claim held against Socrates by the court. That is, "he busies himself studying things in the sky and below the earth; he makes the worse into the stronger argument; and he teaches these same things to others."[3]

It was Chairephon who had gotten Socrates started in his strange career as gadfly of the city. Years ago, when the men were in middle age, Chairephon had decided he wanted to know just how smart his best friend was. Perhaps it was a lark when Chairephon saddled up and traveled out a few days to Apollo's temple at Delphi, a temple known for its inscriptions of sayings of the god such as "Know yourself," "Nothing in excess," "Fulfill the limit," "Bow to the divine," and "Curtail hubris."[4] There among these maxims lived the priestess of the temple, the oracle who spoke truth in the name of Apollo. Hidden in the inner chamber of the temple, she met pilgrims to answer all queries great and small, from the questions of politicians and aristocrats regarding the future outcomes of war and diplomacy to lowly matters of one's personal potential and fate.

Chairephon's question for the oracle was of the personal kind. He asked if anyone was wiser than his friend, Socrates, the humble stonemason. The priestess simply said no, nobody was wiser.

The oracle stunned Socrates. In fact, he lapsed into a personal crisis. He had always thought of himself as not wise at all, a simpleton really, quite content as a stonemason. But with this pronouncement of the god, could stonemasonry comprise Socrates's arete, his best? The god had proclaimed his to be the top mind, maybe in the world. But Socrates wouldn't believe it. What could the oracle have meant? Perhaps Apollo's priestess had spoken some sort of riddle. Socrates tried to unravel its meaning, but could not.

So Socrates conceived a plan to refute the oracle. He would wander about, seeking this sage and that elder statesman, anyone reputed to be wise, and Socrates would then examine the person. If Socrates learned something of any worth whatsoever (for he believed he knew nothing of the kind himself), the oracle would be proven wrong: case closed.

This quest led only to frustration and disappointment. Instead of refuting the oracle, Socrates ended up disproving everyone he met. He'd visit a sage and ask some questions. "Then, when I examined this man," Socrates reported at his trial, "my experience was something like this: I thought that he appeared wise to many people, and especially to himself, but he was not."

Listening to Socrates's position, some jurors must have recalled similar experiences. How often had they left some city council meeting, only to think: *And why is that idiot making policy?* or *What's this windbag doing giving advice?*

"So I withdrew," Socrates said to the jury, "and thought to myself: 'I am wiser than this man; it is likely that neither of us knows anything worthwhile, but he thinks he knows something when he does not, whereas when I do not know, neither do I think I know; so I am likely to be wiser than he to this small extent, that *I do not think I know what I do not know.*'"[5]

This then was the purported origin of the famous Socratic method, the style of questioning that whittled down a claim by scrupulous refutation until there was one less windbag in the world. But was this really the whole of the famous Socratic wisdom? Could it have been simply that nobody knows anything? That couldn't have been it, because Socrates seemed to have thought he was at least wiser than the supposed experts, so he must have known *something* more than them, no?

What again did he think he knew better than anyone else?

"I do not think I know what I do not know."

Seems a little thin for the father of rational inquiry.

Some on the jury considered Socrates's position carefully. He wasn't claiming total ignorance for everyone. He said people could know things, all sorts of things. During this very defense before the court he'd spoken of his admiration for the knowledge of politicians, poets, and craftsmen. When the oracle said nobody was wiser than Socrates, Socrates had gone out systematically to interview those professionals, since quite obviously they all knew *something* about their jobs. Of course there were those who claimed expertise and didn't have it, but there were also people who claimed to know things and *did* know them. Doctors, metalsmiths, farmers—people knew how to do all kinds of important things, and it would have been silly of Socrates to say otherwise. And Socrates didn't say otherwise. People, he said, indeed knew things, "many fine things."[6] Then what exactly was his concern? What was it that nobody knew, but only Socrates *realized* he didn't know?

"Anything worthwhile," is what he said.

What could he have meant by that?

Given what all of Athens knew about Socrates from talking with him over the years, it was no great jump for most on the jury to recognize what Socrates considered worthwhile knowledge: What is arete? What constitutes one's excellence and potential? What does it mean *to do one's best*? And how could anybody really *know?* For all those years Socrates had been asking any sage who passed through Athens for a rational, logical way to recognize what it is that anyone *should* be doing to achieve arete and excellence in one's life. And all he'd found were technical experts who admittedly knew how to do "many fine things"—though none could say which of these fine things constituted excellence. Everybody knew *how*, but nobody could say *what*. And then there had been the supposed arete experts who made grandiose claims about becoming one's best self but whose words crumbled the moment anyone bothered to ask: And how would anyone know *what that is?*

To be fair, Socrates wasn't being contrarian just for the sake of boosting his own ego. He often said he was as clueless and useless as the rest of humanity. How he had responded to the stupefied and numbed arete expert is interesting: "Now if the torpedo fish is itself numb and so makes others numb, then I resemble it," Socrates had said, "but not otherwise, for I myself do not have the answer when I stupefy others, but *I am more stu-pefied than anyone* when I cause stupor in others."[7]

What a strange career of bringing himself and humanity to stupefaction. The word is actually *aporia*, or "impasse." Along with *arete*, *aporia* was one of Socrates's favorite words, and it remains among the most enduring legacies of Socratic thought.

Aporia originally meant an impassable ford across a river. One might have a sense of where one needed to go, and possibly could even see the opposite shore, but then there would be no way to get across.[8] *You can't get there from here.* Plato's dialogues recounting the conversations of his teacher have come to be called apo-retic since Socrates talked so much about his own perplexity in them, his own personal impasses before the question of how to know excellence. These dialogues all end inconclusively and hav-ing demonstrated nothing, except perhaps reason itself as an inadequate means to find arete.

Maybe that was the Socratic point. Rational analysis worked well in some matters. Step-by-step, it led sometimes to the knowledge and mastery of many fine things—except what any-one should be doing with their lives. There reason left Socrates in aporia, numb and stupefied, high and dry.

Some on the jury must certainly have reacted badly to Socrates's position. As these jurors fathomed his assessment of all the sages of Athens, and the worthlessness even of his own knowledge, it must have stung some of them personally. How could it have not? All adults, most of them in the middle of prosperous and seem-ingly important careers, they too must have realized that Socrates had accused them along with the rest of the Athenian sophists and so-called experts. *Nobody knows anything worthwhile.* Not all the jury could have enjoyed realizing this about themselves. Behind the clarity of the old man's eyes, some surely recognized danger.

THE SOCRATIC PARADOX

Perhaps some among the jury considered whether they had mis-understood Socrates. After all, despite all aporia and inability to move forward with knowledge, there had never been any resulting anarchy in Socrates's actions. No nihilism or void emp-tied his character. The great paradox of Socrates's life, noted now by readers for quite a while, is that despite the Socratic claim not to know "anything worthwhile" about human excellence, Socrates always seemed to have ended up doing *exactly the right thing*. He became the hero of the Platonic dialogues not just for his relentless refutation of falsity and hubris; nothing he did was ever anything but heroic. Among his many good qualities had been his courageousness, justness, virtuousness, temperance, piety, and loyalty as a friend; yet when he used reason to try to explain any of these, time and again he only came to stupefying aporia. His very life seems to have been a living paradox.[9]

But was it really?

Maybe one shouldn't assume that Socrates needed to *know* about these arenas of arete in order to have made good life decisions. Did arete need to be discovered *rationally* in order for a person to achieve it?

Despite his life of investigation, Socrates never said as much. The father of inquiry seems to have gotten on perfectly well in life without having figured out a thing about what constituted excellence. This didn't stop him from investigating rigorously in order to try and reach the noble end of rational discovery (which is what he did all day in the park), but neither did his ultimate lack of knowledge prevent him from living an excellent life.

Was it possible, then, that for Socrates the aporia of reason did not also mean moral stupor?

Could this have been Socrates's *greatest lesson*?

But how was this possible? If it wasn't knowledge achieved through reason, what then motivated heroism, excellence, and good choices? If one didn't *know* the right thing, how could someone always end up *doing* the right thing?

In fact, Socrates said how. He told the people of Athens how he did this explicitly and often. His strange explanation was precisely why Socrates sat on trial for his life.

THERAPEUTIC REALITY

Just a few days before the trial, a friend had spotted Socrates wandering near the courthouse looking dazed. He wondered why Socrates wasn't making his typical rounds through the park accosting people with philosophy. Socrates said he had been indicted. He'd come here to familiarize himself with the court grounds, he said, but probably he was also trying to wrap his head around the gravity of the charges. In his seventy years, he'd never once been to court, even as a juror, and suddenly General Anytus indicted him. A young man named Meletus, a complete stranger from the far side of the city, had accused him of the capital crime of corrupting the young.

"Tell me, what does he say you do to corrupt the young?" asked the friend.

"He says that I am a maker of gods," Socrates said, "and that I create new gods while not believing in the old gods."

The accusation bewildered Socrates. He didn't understand it at all. He'd always thought of himself as being respectful of the traditional gods of Athens, ever conscientious to do his duty for them. Socrates had behaved practically as a monk for Apollo, wandering the streets penniless as he did. His obedience to the oracle left his whole family in poverty, his young children were

often in want. What more could this Meletus need to demonstrate Socrates's piety to the old gods? And beyond this, what
evidence could Meletus have to accuse Socrates of *inventing*
gods? Hadn't his whole career been dedicated to *refuting* speculation? Wasn't the Socratic method the enemy of ungrounded
human invention?

But the friend thought he knew: "This is because you say that
a daemonic sign keeps coming to you."[10]

The daemonic sign of Socrates is among the most mysterious
parts of the Platonic canon. Plato consistently reported that
Socrates, throughout his life, talked about having some kind of a
spiritual or divine sign—literally a daemonic sign (*to daemonion
sēmeion*).[11] Socrates talked about this sign so often that typically
he simply abbreviated it, calling it by a pet name: *daemonion*,
"a daemonic something." Thinking of daemonic as "divine" or
"spiritual" may help readers, and these are perfectly accurate
translations. Before the middle ages, daemons weren't consistently understood to be malevolent. A daemon in ancient Greece
wasn't yet an evil competitor to the authority of a monotheistic
god. A daemon was simply a nonphysical presence that could
influence people. A spirit. Eros for instance was considered a
daemon, the spirit of desire.[12]

Of course, today anyone who has taken some biology understands how to view erotic desire in a material sense, as hormones
interacting with organs, and neurotransmitters connecting neurons, thus animating a material creature. Biology constitutes
the material stratum of desire, locatable under a microscope or
fMRI. But then there are also the powerful *experiences* of desire:
the all-consuming ideas one hears ricocheting as words in one's
head, the obsessive pictures that flash up on the mental screen,
the uncontrollable drive to activate the body. *I want that. I won't
stop until I get that.* Those experiences of erotic desire, cognitive

and emotional, although certainly somehow working in consort with neural activity, can't themselves be put under fMRI. So perhaps it is still understandable today why the Greeks understood something as experiential as erotic desire to be a daemon or spirit, an intangible reality that at times feels so powerful it seems beyond one's personal control. Sometimes these intangible elements of uncontrollable sights, sounds, and feelings commingle to give the impression of a coherent whole, an animate though immaterial presence almost in possession of a person. This is the classical Greek conception of daemon or spirit. Writing a century before Socrates, Heraclitus had probably meant something like this when he said: "A man's character is his daemon (*ethos anthropoi daemon*)."[13]

Socrates often spoke of his daemon, his spirit. Actually, that's not quite accurate. He *never* spoke of his daemon itself. But he often spoke of his daemonion, his "daemonic something," his spiritual sign. And here at his trial for impiety and the invention of gods, he knew he had some explaining to do.

"I have a daemonic sign from the god which Meletus has ridiculed in his deposition," he said. "This began when I was a child. It is a voice, and whenever it speaks it turns me away from something I am about to do, but it never encourages me to do anything."[14]

So Socrates claimed to have a spirit whispering to him.

Really?

Let's take a moment to understand this. Maybe this divine voice even somehow addresses the Socratic paradox. Perhaps this voice was how Socrates achieved excellence without ever having been able to *know* excellence, without ever having been able to demonstrate it logically or even to show its positive effects empirically. Perhaps he'd employed for himself no reasoning here, no rational refutation. Yet he still could consistently achieve a refutation of a sort—a *spiritual* one. A spirit told Socrates what *not* to do.

Socrates never explained logically how he arrived at his own path of arete and excellence, because he *couldn't*. Reason itself could never say, because reason consistently led to aporia and stupefaction. So Socrates could then only describe his own experiences of how he personally came to know what to do, without the benefit of reason. Typically it went something like this:

- Arete disclosed itself with a kind of voice;
- it came seemingly from nowhere;
- it told Socrates with absolute reliability what he shouldn't do.

Hearing this, at least some on the jury must have wondered: *Wait a minute. Don't I have that voice?*

Many jurors had probably also been hearing some version of this since childhood, just like Socrates. *Don't do that. Don't sneak those sweets. Don't whack your sibling. Don't do it!* And when had the voice ever been wrong? No, it didn't provide logical arguments for its prohibitions. Sometimes what it banned might have seemed less than reasonable. *But why shouldn't I?* That was always a perfectly good question. But the voice wouldn't engage in Socratic discourse, it wouldn't be pinned down by reason, although it did provide a reason of a kind—a *therapeutic* reason: *Because your daemons will scream if you do.*

And when had the voice ever been wrong about *that*?

No, it couldn't quite be called objective. Not everyone heard the same prohibitions. Socrates's daemon had told him not to go into politics, though he had had sufficient ethical reasons for thinking he ought to.[15] Others probably turned away from teaching, medicine, metallurgy, and other perfectly good vocations, despite having personal aptitude and moral justification for pursuing any of these. There may have been rationales for these life decisions, but these couldn't quite ever be determined by objective reason. These jobs simply could never become a life of arete for some people, their spirits would have been crushed. A kind of voice told them so, perhaps a gut feeling.

Don't do this.

Don't. Do. This.

But Socrates's voice was never quite subjective either, and that remained true no matter how much he might have wished it were. Socrates didn't get to choose what the divine voice would prohibit. Perhaps sometimes during dark nights of the soul, when the voice coursed through his anxious muscles and tossing body as it does occasionally for everyone, he might have wished he could control it. But it simply didn't come to him like that. To Socrates, it was neither exactly objective nor righty called subjective. It was just personally *there.*

Perhaps some of the jurors didn't take Socrates's idea of a divine voice seriously. Many had probably grown to consider anxious feelings and browbeating voices as unpleasant but largely irrelevant parts of one's life. The daemonion could sometimes be so common that perhaps some had even stopped noticing its consistent presence. Socrates himself wondered whether he alone or perhaps just a select few even received such signs. Maybe that was because so few people behaved as though they did. Perhaps some had even learned to shove away their own signs, thinking: *Oh, that's silly, that's naive; you live in the real world, not Mount Olympus; just push that voice down and get real.* Yet for Socrates, and likely for some of his fellow citizens, the voice always came back. So the divine voice constituted its own reality—and ignoring it had its own consequences. To Socrates, there was no use in denying his daemonion as a reality that persisted despite all rationalizations to the contrary. What would happen if I were to take this voice more seriously when noticing it? Would I then look in the mirror a little more easily, or spend nights more peacefully? Would I have fewer interior screaming matches? Maybe I'd just be happier with myself.

HAPPINESS

In case anyone were to misunderstand the divine voice as imparting magical knowledge about how to fill one's world with polka dots and moonbeams, the jury in fact convicted Socrates. Apparently his daemonion did not have paranormal sway over earthly events. Obey it or not, the world kept turning as it would. Judging by Socrates's calm reaction to his conviction, he does not seem to have expected otherwise.

Not all jurors voted to convict, and surely even some of those who had were still inclined to temper justice with mercy. After all, the offender had been a senior citizen convicted only of speaking his mind. What would Socrates say now, as he was asked to suggest a fair sentence? What penalty would be appropriate for a vagrant who refused to hold a regular job because he needed time to humiliate the city's elite?

Here was Socrates's recommendation:

"Nothing is more suitable, gentlemen, than for such a man to be fed in the Prytaneum."[16]

What did he say?

The Prytaneum was the Athenian capital dining room and club, the central hearth of the city where power brokers took their plentiful lunches and potations. Olympic victors of the most popular sports took free meals there because politicians liked to have them around, which Socrates thought a questionable use of public money. "The Olympian victor makes you think yourself happy," he told the jury. "I make you *be* happy."

Did he actually just belittle the Olympics?

"So if I must make a just assessment of what I deserve," he said, "I assess it as this: free meals in the Prytaneum."[17]

It had to be the most fearless allocution in the history of the judiciary. Not only did he embarrass members of the sentencing jury, but he also smacked down their sports heroes. He might as well have told an American jury that following basketball is a waste of time and that national athletic heroes don't deserve their paychecks. Whether or not Socrates believed this to be true, should he have said it before a court of five hundred peers? What kind of compromise would it have been for Socrates to have offered just a smidgen of deference when speaking at his own capital trial?

The jury then handed down the death penalty. Talk about having a fool for a lawyer, although Socrates didn't seem to think so. While the court took some moments to come to order, he turned confidentially to those jurors who had voted to acquit. They'd tried their best to help Socrates, they'd put reputations on the line and cashed in political chips; so why hadn't Socrates tried to help himself? He wanted to explain.

"A surprising thing has happened to me, jurymen," Socrates said. "At all previous times my familiar prophetic power, my spiritual manifestation, frequently opposed me, even in small matters, when I was about to do something wrong . . ."

(Could he really still be going on about his "special friend"?)

"but now that, as you can see for yourselves, I was faced with what one might think, and what is generally thought to be, the worst of evils . . ."

(Meaning *dying . . .*)

"my divine sign has not opposed me, either when I left home at dawn, or when I came into court, or at any time that I was about to say something during my speech. Yet in other talks it often held me back in the middle of my speaking, but now it has opposed no word or deed of mine."

Again with the divine voice or, in this case, *without* it. When Socrates woke up in the morning and readied himself to come to court, his sign did not stop him. When he arrived at the court-room door, no righteous voice instructed him not to enter but rather to flee. During the entirety of his testimony, including his outrageous allocution, no halting thought crossed his mind, nothing told him to temper his speech because maybe he was out of line.

Therefore he had done nothing wrong. He'd done his best. The *voice* was the sole arbiter of his arete: not the jury; not Socrates himself; not even reason; but the daemonion alone.

That noble strategy had led Socrates directly to a potion of poisonous hemlock. What did his little voice have to say about *that*?

"I will tell you," Socrates said. "What has happened to me may well be a good thing, and those of us who believe death to be an evil are certainly mistaken. I have convincing proof of this, for it is impossible that my familiar sign did not oppose me if I was not about to do what was right."[18]

I think we're all within our rights to protest Socrates's certainty about the goodness of death. However what I'm not sure we can protest is his certainty about having done "what was right." Even at his own capital trial, he continued to do his job exactly as Apollo's Delphic oracle mandated. He'd spoken wisdom and refuted hubris. To the very end he remained the moral gadfly of the city, always speaking truth to power. If speaking truth meant death, then bring it on. Socrates explained calmly to his friends that he accepted this fate. They wished to understand how this was possible. How could he face certain death and still be OK?

Because he heard no voice telling him otherwise.

His daemons were still.

Could Socrates have chosen a better way to leave this life? Ready, calm in mind, without screaming daemons, having no regret over his actions: Could he have proposed any better definition of ethics? Is there a better understanding of *happiness?*

Etymology doesn't always prove a great deal. For instance the word *terrific* doesn't imply terror as it once did, and it hasn't for while. If somebody learning English wants to know what it means to say "That's terrific!," she shouldn't turn to the philology of the word.

That said, *happiness* has an interesting origin. It's fascinating that the Greeks had no word for it.

Some learned readers may protest. Of course they did. *Eudaemonia.* Socrates just talked about it! He said that unlike the Olympic victors who only make people believe they're happy, Socrates actually made people be happy. So Socrates talked about it, and Plato did too, as did Aristotle also. Eudaemonia, in fact, was the final subject of all their explorations, as well it should have been, human happiness—only it didn't mean "happiness."

Happiness is random, deriving from the old English *hap*, meaning chance or fortune, as in happenstance. The classical Greeks believed in chance and fortune, but they didn't believe it led to well-being. At least Socrates didn't. Arete led to it. Excellence led to it. Doing one's best led to it.[19]

So here's the philology lesson:

Eudaemonia parsed out is *eu-* (to be well with) *daemonia* (the daemon).

To be well with the daemon. To be right with one's spirit. To hear none of its browbeating. To live in the still and silent clarity of one's own best actions. *That's* happiness.

It seems obvious to me now that eudaemonia is the key to everything Socrates talked about. I can't figure out why I've heard so little about the "divine something," why most interpreters harp on Socratic reason and Socratic refutation, when these are only the setup for the real story. Daemonic interdiction is the payoff: the divine *No.*

Don't do that.

Don't. Do. That.

Belief in this daemon doesn't have the favor of step-by-step logic, but in its *therapeutic reality* it's just as real, just as solid, just as unquestionable as any reality comprehended by reason. When the daemon screams, there is torment. That's reality. It's also interesting that this divine refutation doesn't take the positive form of the more famous Socratic question: What *is* excellence? What *is* one's best? Maybe we can't know what our best is, but perhaps we can know what it's *not*. I know when I'm not doing my best, its torments are obvious. I know what *not* to do—it's as clear as the divine voice.

Closing the pages of *The Apology*, we drop out of the ethereal fog of thought to assess our lesson in classical therapy. We now know Socrates's own method for locating personal excellence; we recognize his understanding of happiness, perhaps a happiness worth dying for; and finally we see how the father of Western inquiry acknowledged a higher power beyond reason—an orienting spiritual gravity—and why he chose to commit himself to it.

4

ABU HAMID AL-GHAZALI

The Greatest Midlife Crisis in the

History of Islam

By the remembrance of God do hearts find rest.

—Quran 13:28

LEARNING

Over the past several decades the field of positive psychology has noted that the feature of continuous learning is important to satisfaction and fulfillment, on the job, in one's domestic life, and even with hobbies. Yet sometimes learning in these limited areas isn't enough. Sometimes the whole enterprise of life simultaneously feels both inscrutable and unimportant. This happened to Abu Hamid al-Ghazali, perhaps the greatest intellectual living during the golden age of Islam. His writings relay descriptions of a dark period, what we would now understand to be a severe episode of anxiety and depression. He needed a reboot, a fundamentally new way of looking at an old world. And so, five hundred years before Descartes, he wiped the slate clean and asked himself the Cartesian questions: What do I really know? What is there really to learn?

Upon discovering a deeper learning and finding a better way, Ghazali dedicated the rest of his life to writing a compendium of the insights that had gotten him through the terror called The Alchemy of Happiness. *He also composed his spiritual autobiography,* The Deliverance from Error. *For despite all prestige and accoutrement he had gathered as the most important lawyer in the sultanate, in the end the hubris of his former intellectual life was only a barrier to his awareness of God.*

THE BLOODBATH

One could tell almost everything about him from his academic robe and mount. He'd paid five hundred pieces of gold for these, or rather the benefactors supporting his deanship at the university had. Abu Hamid al-Ghazali wore exceedingly nice robes and kept an exceedingly nice mount. He'd also achieved everything an intellectual in his civilization could, which was no small feat for someone living in the Golden Age of Islam. This was a time of the greatest convergence of thought, art, literature, architecture, and science since Athens itself, and the good professor sat atop its intellectual hierarchy. Still, he was also human, and at thirty-nine he'd been having a walloping midlife crisis. His existential test had upended every value he'd ever held for himself, which was problematic enough, but he'd also begun to doubt everything he'd ever pronounced as lawful and right in the name of his sultan. So Ghazali did what so many reasonable adults think to do when suffering through a personal collapse. He decided to run away.

Most academics think big thoughts and those ideas are about as connected to reality as a genie bottled up in a lamp. When Ghazali had a thought, it actually mattered. As the dean of the Nizamiyya Madrasa of Baghdad, the top law school in the sultanate, he altered the lives of millions with short movements of his pen. In his career, those strokes had to this time mostly worked to temper tensions between two great houses, the Seljuq sultanate and the Abbasid caliphate. But then recently Ghazali's job had become all but impossible.

Over a century before, the sultan's ancestor, Seljuq, while dozing in a felt yurt somewhere in the wild northern Eurasian steppe, dreamed himself pissing fire over east and west, like a dog marking a tree.[1] His progeny achieved that end, first taking the fertile Persian plain, then coming to control vast lands and trade routes between the Mediterranean Sea and the Indus River, including Anatolia, the Levant, Mesopotamia, Persia, and the Hindu Kush. With the help of a savvy Persian vizier, the Seljuq sultans built a school system, Nizamiyya Madrasa (Nizam University named after vizier Nizam al-Mulk), to train administrators in rational tax collection, land grant procedures and subsidies, postal services, secret intelligence and reconnaissance networks—all the markings of a modern empire even by much later standards. The first such university went up in Nishapur in Persia, where Ghazali himself trained as a boy. Schools also rose in Balkh, Herat, Basra, Marv, Amul, Masil, Tabaristan, and, finally, the jewel of the system in Baghdad itself, all precursors to later European universities. Ghazali quickly proved himself to be the preeminent student among a new generation of Islamic scholar-jurists coming up in these Seljuq schools under the eye of the sultan and his cultured Persian vizier Nizam al-Mulk—quite pointedly *not* under the auspices of the Abbasid caliphate.

Yet Caliph al-Muqtadi remained the recognized authority on all matters of Islamic law. The Abbasid caliphate, an old household hailing from Mesopotamia, in these latter days functioned something like the papacy, and the Round City in Baghdad worked something like Vatican City in Rome. Once upon a time,

Abbasid caliphs ruled with armies and territories, but that hadn't been the case since the Seljuq domination. The Seljuqs had in fact placed Ghazali in the Baghdad law school to make sure that the rival Abbasid caliph and his theologians in the Round City continued to interpret Islamic law in a manner beneficial to the Seljuq empire. So, at age thirty-five, Ghazali became the sultan's attorney in Baghdad and thus the most important lawyer in the Islamic world.[2]

From time to time the sultan and his vizier traveled out from the Seljuq capital city of Isfahan on the Persian plain to make imperial visits to the Round City in Baghdad. Shockingly, during the last such excursion, on the tenth day of Ramadan in 485 AH (October 14, 1092 ACE), the unthinkable occurred. It happened on the road just outside Baghdad. What appeared to be a harmless panhandler and Sufi mendicant was not. A sparkle of polished metal in the sunlight, the briefest flash of silver and steel, and the mighty vizier Nizam al-Mulk slumped over like meat peeled off the shoulder of a slaughtered calf. Some said a radical Shiite enclave from near Teheran was responsible for the assassination. Others suspected the sultan himself. ("My inkbottle and the crown are linked together," the vizier had to remind his sultan in the midst of a recent unfortunate spat.)[3] Of course many noticed that the Abbasid caliph may also have benefited from the clever vizier's demise.

Then only weeks after the vizier's death, the sultan himself took ill during a hunting expedition in the lush Mesopotamian wilderness north of Baghdad. These sorts of imperial vacations were characterized by excessive eating and drinking, so it was not entirely unexpected that the sultan wasn't well after a few evenings of indulgence. But his fever persisted and finally forced him to return to Baghdad. The fever never broke. Sultan Malikshah died just a month after the murder of his vizier. Everyone in Baghdad noted the coincidence, including Ghazali.

Soon after the deaths of vizier and sultan, Caliph al-Muqtadi summoned Ghazali to the Round City. An interesting legal question had come up. The caliph trusted he could count on Ghazali's support in the matter.

As Ghazali dressed himself for the visit, he must have felt the weight of the gold threads holding together his academic robes. The Seljuq sultans had paid for these. As chief muderris and dean of the Baghdad Nizamiyya—top legal intellectual at the most prestigious university in the sultanate—Ghazali indeed had been the Seljuqs' attorney in Baghdad. He explained the sultan's legal positions to the caliph, often forcefully so. Though the caliphate technically made rulings, it could hardly do so without intellectual support from the dean of the law school. "The ink of a scholar is more holy than the blood of a martyr." That hadith uttered by the Prophet was the very motto of the Abbasid house. The caliph simply could not ignore Ghazali's opinions. Yet with sultan and vizier now deceased, political circumstances had changed.

Predictably the caliph wished to discuss sultanic succession. He claimed for himself sole authority to choose the next sultan, even over the dying instructions of the last sultan. On his deathbed, Sultan Malikshah had declared that his oldest son Berk Yaruq, then thirteen years old, would succeed him. Yet the caliph planned to ignore that directive and, rather, wished to appoint an even younger son of the sultan, Muhammad, just five years old. Given the boy's age, of course the caliph would also need to appoint the boy's cabinet. That would include both a new vizier and an amir of the army. The caliph wanted Ghazali's confirmation and support on the succession issue.

Ghazali considered the caliph's wily move. Through this swift exchange of chess pieces the caliph would dominate the new sultan's entire administration. With such influence in the sultan's court, the Abbasid caliphate could rally and perhaps even regain its lost empire. But was the plan legal? According to sharia, could the caliph cross and upend all division of powers, even against the dying wish of the sultan?

The caliph said he could. If anyone should believe otherwise, the law dean of the Nizamiyya school in Baghdad—our good scholar Ghazali—would confirm that the caliph's appointments were consistent with Islamic law.

Ghazali considered some more. The caliph's plan did sound a little unusual. There had never been a sultan so weak as to have his cabinet appointed *for* him. Ghazali ran through all the possible ways this political game could play out. Who were Ghazali's own friends and benefactors? Vizier Nizam al-Mulk: dead. Sultan Malikshah: dead. All of his protectors were dead. Ghazali could possibly support the dead sultan's own choice, the older son Berk Yaruq, but the boy was only thirteen. Did the adolescent really have any chance going up against a savvy politician like Caliph al-Muqtadi? Besides, the only politician left from the old days with whom Ghazali had any relationship was the caliph.

So that was it. Politically speaking there had been no real decision to make. Whatever the caliph said had to be. Ghazali pronounced exactly this: "Allowed is only that which the caliph says." Nicely done. A lawyer couldn't get in too much trouble with a statement like that.[4]

In less than a year, by the end of 1093, the child sultan Muhammad and his mother were both dead of the same strange and unnamed disease. How mysterious! The caliph had no choice but to summon the adolescent Berk Yaruq to Baghdad. He would finally pronounce Malikshah's first choice and eldest son to be sultan, which he did on February 3, 1094. The following day it was announced that Caliph al-Muqtadi himself had keeled over at the dinner table and died of natural causes. What grief! The good caliph was only thirty-seven years old![5]

What had happened here? It appears that every serious politician in the Seljuq sultanate and Abbasid caliphate had gotten themselves killed. A later chronicler would write of these strange days: "The affairs of the realm were thrown into disorder and confusion; there was chaos in the provinces . . . and turmoil and uproar in the kingdom."[6] Of course disorder, confusion, chaos, turmoil, and uproar are all euphemisms for violence and death. That would be the new state of the Seljuq empire until the teenage sultan Berk Yaruq could gain some control over his sultanate. The crown itself really meant nothing without sufficient displays of violence. Berk Yaruq would have to demonstrate ad nauseam that his threats really did imply disproportionate actions. Generations of Seljuq sultans had taught him that political edicts meant nothing until inscribed on the bodies of corpses. Berk Yaruq needed to frighten people viscerally, in their bones. He needed to be the bloodiest maniac in the empire. That's how rulers were forged; law would come later. So the next few years would not be a time of talk or lawyerly maneuvers. Until Berk Yaruq could prove himself in violent fashion, he would have what is antiseptically called a power vacuum, though people from Anatolia to India would know it as a bloody mess.

THE ERROR

According to Ghazali, nothing but "treachery and discord" characterized the following years.[7] In the aftermath of the deluge of assassinations, the politics of Ghazali's workplace became a knot of intrigue and nastiness with no apparent point or direction. People in the Nizamiyya law school spent all moments trying to figure out what the new adolescent sultan might suddenly demand of the judiciary. Ghazali himself likely thought about this question obsessively, spending his days attempting to forecast and then argue cases for any potential political scenarios that might arise. Yet Ghazali also knew full well that the young sultan couldn't care less about law while he battled in blood to regain control of the Seljuq empire.[8]

Then again, what good had been the rule of law anyway? Look what had happened to Ghazali's own rulings once the protectors of his integrity could no longer protect him. Ghazali had allowed holy sharia law itself to become a mouthpiece for the vain earthly pursuits of the caliph. What business could it have been of the caliph to appoint army generals and viziers? And yet in weakness Ghazali had supported it! Worse, he'd given blanket affirmation to the caliph: *You're in power now, so you command and I'll justify.* Had Ghazali's sacred office really devolved into nothing but the blanket legitimation of earthly interest? And with the caliph dead, would Ghazali simply tack in the direction of the next gust?[9]

The privilege of the academy is in having the time to follow a thought to the end of the mind. Learn all the necessary techniques and languages, read all the extant formulae and literatures, and then track an idea to the final point humanity has taken it. Who in the real world gets to do this? Done rightly, the privilege entails peeling back the scabs of accepted knowledge or, perhaps to use a better metaphor, pointing out cracks in society's foundation. Having followed a thought to the end of the mind, one becomes familiar with a surreal world where human knowledge simply stops. Here what William James called "the unseen order of the universe" unfurls out beyond the grasp of sensation or reason and ripples into infinity. It's only at the soft border of knowing that one recognizes the normative truths and scientific axioms for what they are: the educated hunches of others who have been to this limit before us.

Surreal exploration just beyond the border of knowledge is the purpose, privilege, and responsibility of scholarship. People in the real world are too busy solving real and immediate problems to spend time pondering the ways in which the normative approximations stop making sense. Yet it's only from these surreal outskirts where the best guesses of past generations can even be seen, let alone improved upon, and the cracks in the foundation of our collective edifice can perhaps be better set to carry the human load.

Sometimes the load crumbles, and sometimes it's the scholars who are most to blame for the failure. Despite the appearance of ivy surrounding the towers, universities do find themselves competing with worldly pressures to build up yet another floor on the accepted edifice of knowledge, money, and power and not worry too much about how the foundation is handling the weight. Ghazali knew the temptation, though he hadn't recognized it at the time. As a professional in the academy, he'd come to master every aspect of normative Islam, the way the world was *supposed* to work. Normative law pronounced society's ideal rules; normative scripture declared its ideal canon; normative hermeneutics proclaimed the proper interpretation of that canon; normative devotion set down the official rituals; normative epistemology set forth what human beings could investigate; finally normative theology announced the official description of the unseen universe. Normative! The way things were *sup-posed* to happen! *But what if they didn't?*

What happens when the world falls apart?

Ghazali had spent his professional life mastering the rules and defending them, always proceeding as though the foundation were sound, so don't look down, build up! For twenty years in the vizier's service it had seemed as though he'd really been building something. Then a single dagger stroke along the road to Baghdad brought the civilized world crumbling to the sand, and Ghazali saw his life of pronouncements and legal decisions at the Nizamiyya for what they were: rationalizations of an untenable system. What had happened? Had something gone wrong in the building up of the edifice? Or were the normative foundations themselves to blame?

Amidst this bloody devolution of civilization, Ghazali began to notice the weight of the gold threads holding together his academic robes. These apparent privileges of wealth and stature again began feeling contemptible to him, as they once had seemed when as a boy he'd been driven to investigate the essential questions out of the childhood purity of simple human curiosity. How long it had been since then. The professional expertise he'd since built up now felt far less essential than those initial childhood questions about God and the order of the universe. Certainly the world of power and violence Ghazali had come to serve couldn't be the best way to know God. Ghazali had realized this for quite a while. Of course jihad remained holy, and the world did need to submit to Allah. Such was the very meaning of Islam, submission. But Islam also meant peace; it meant safety; it meant security and wholeness; and Ghazali now wondered whether he would ever know Islam in these senses of the word. *What is real peace? What is true submission? How can I come to know God's will?* These simple questions no longer seemed so childish.[10]

TASTE

For years Ghazali had known about the existence of an intriguing manuscript, although he'd never found time to look at it carefully. It was by a doctor by the name of Ibn Sina who had lived up in Teheran about fifty years before. The Latin Christians in Europe came to know him as Avicenna. The writings of Ibn Sina had become the basis of a promising new way of thinking in Islam, one that Ghazali had trifled with since his own student days but had never made any systematic effort to understand: *falsafa*, philosophy.

Perhaps Ghazali hadn't yet addressed philosophy because it was not much of a path to worldly success. For instance, there was no chair of philosophy at the Nizamiyya. There were no emergency summons by viziers and caliphs for crucial philosophic rulings: *Professor, we really need to know the truth about our position.* That never happened.

The philosophers had, however, made some interesting advances, especially in the physical sciences. Medicine, biology, chemistry, physics, astronomy, architecture—for all of these physical questions the philosophers of Islam had turned to the Greek writings preserved mostly at the library in Alexandria, and these had proven to be helpful starting points for the Islamic renaissance in science. Young people were attracted to philosophy as well, as they saw philosophy as something radical, an intellectual movement bypassing the declarations of the authoritarian theologians and assuming egalitarian access to truth by mere thinking. Anybody could do it. Ghazali had no problem with this radicalism; he was as disgusted with authoritarian theology as he was with politics.[11]

The best of these Greek writings attempted to think about thinking itself. These included discussions of reason, logic, and mathematics and also more abstract discussions of what it even means to know something. Epistemology. Now *that* was an interesting subject to Ghazali. "I must inquire into just what the true meaning of knowledge is," he recalled in his autobiography. If one were truly interested in securing foundations, then this had to be the very first stone one would inspect. *How do I know anything?*

So first he tried to achieve an acceptable definition for what it means *to know*:

"Sure and certain knowledge is that in which the thing known is made so manifest that no doubt clings to it, nor is it accompanied by the possibility of error and deception, nor the mind even suppose such a possibility."[12]

Sure and certain knowledge. No possibility of error. Ghazali would accept nothing but manifest clarity as the litmus test for what it could mean to *know* anything.

His next question: Did the philosophers really *know* anything? They may have been achieving very fine things in medicine and the physical sciences. They may seem to have been building up fascinating and apparently solid edifices. But so had Ghazali in his own disciplines of law and theology, until an assassination fractured his foundations. So Ghazali wouldn't tolerate shifting sand no matter how wondrous its castles. He'd seen too much go wrong.

For about a year Ghazali pondered epistemology and the possibility of attaining "sure and certain knowledge . . . so manifest that no doubt clings to it." He studied whatever philosophical proofs he could find to determine if any actually proved that philosophical reason could ever meet such a high epistemological standard. He decided that none actually could. He then published twenty refutations of philosophical epistemology in a book he called *The Incoherence of the Philosophers*, which he published in January of 1095. His most brutal rebuttal, of causal necessity, preceded Scottish philosopher David Hume's identical argument by seven hundred years.[13]

At first, the collapse of philosophy and human reason actually threw Ghazali into a funk he couldn't shake. For two months he became "a skeptic in fact, but not in utterance and doctrine."[14] It was not an era that took agnosticism lightly. Few had been to this shadowy border before. His skepticism seems to have brought with it a dark mood. Though Ghazali still went about teaching and making legal pronouncements that affected every level of Seljuq society, inwardly he doubted the very possibility of knowing either divine truth or simple fact.

I'm a fraud. Everybody is a fraud. Nobody knows anything.

Despite this pessimism, the sermons of an old Sufi teacher came returning to Ghazali's mind from the storehouse of memory. As a much younger man, back in his hometown of Tus in Persia, Ghazali knew Abu ʿAli al-Faramadhi as the local Sufi master, an aged ascetic who like those in his sect wore the blue tunic of rough wool. He'd talk to students on street corners and in his tiny convent, but to Ghazali the master's sermons all seemed to repeat the same nonsensical point. There existed a state beyond the intellect, a suprarational "knowledge" that couldn't quite be called knowledge (*ʿilm*), but rather was awareness (*maʿrifah*). Awareness differed from knowledge in that it skipped clear over the intermediary step of thinking and allowed a direct experience of reality. The Sufi master used to call this taste (*dhawq*).[15]

At the time, Ghazali didn't know what to make of the sermons. He couldn't understand back then what the Sufi master meant when he distinguished between knowledge and awareness. It sounded like semantic games. *Awareness. Taste.* What did the words even mean? What would it be like to experience something directly without the intermediary of thinking? Didn't people think about *everything?*

Besides this conceptual objection, Ghazali still believed in the power of thought. He had believed then that, with sufficient raw intelligence and cultivated patience, the human mind could untangle even the greatest mysteries and come to stand more or less before the truth. Perhaps a person of thought wouldn't have the clarity of a prophet such as Abraham, Jesus, or Muhammad, but his reason could put him rather far along the same path. Yet after his world of legal learning totally devolved, and since he'd dismantled all proofs from philosophy as well, he was no longer sure where any of his education had gotten him. So those inscrutable Sufi teachings of his youth came bubbling back up.[16]

Specifically, the voice of Faramadhi returned as Ghazali composed the twentieth and ultimate refutation of philosophic certainty in his *The Incoherence of the Philosophers.* In the final chapter of the book, Ghazali considered the question of analogy, the comparison of a strange phenomenon with a familiar one, which is the method of all reasoning. Only by comparison can one transfer information about a known scenario to a strange scenario that one is trying to understand.

To demonstrate the limit of analogy, Ghazali asked a rather bawdy question. How could anyone explain the pleasure of sex to a prepubescent boy or to an impotent man? Sex is pleasurable, certainly. So by analogy we might tell the boy that sex is something like the pleasure he experiences during playtime. Likewise for the impotent man we might compare sex to the pleasure of eating. But then, of course, after we've made these helpful comparisons, we would also have to inform the boy and the impotent man "that what he understood by the example does not convey the reality of the pleasure of sexual intercourse and that this is only apprehended through taste."[17]

That word *taste* is what had repeated in Ghazali's inner ear as he finished the final refutation of *The Incoherence.* Direct *experience*—that's what the Sufis meant by taste. One can't tell an impotent man what sex is *like.* Nothing compares to the direct experience of sex. Just as nothing compares to the taste of sugar. If we want to experience sugar, we don't memorize its chemical formula. We don't explain the process by which it is reduced from cane plants. We don't compare its texture and color to salt. We *taste* the sugar. We direct our senses toward the sugar and then we have experiences of it. That's how people actually come to know sugar, sex, and all things.

Actually Faramadhi would have said that's how we become *aware* of things. There's no *knowing* involved, no thinking, no rational processing, no intellectual chain linking P and Q. Taste is unmediated by cognition. Rather it is experienced and felt. That's what his Sufi master had meant by distinguishing knowledge and awareness. As Abu Talib al-Makki had defined these things over two centuries before in his classic handbook of Sufi epistemology, awareness is the "knowledge (*'ilm*) of inward realities."[18] These Sufi masters had thus articulated the distinction between *cognition* and *affect* that cognitive scientists and neuroanatomists would only name and locate a millennium later.[19]

By denying the technique of comparison by analogy, Ghazali's final critique of philosophy had closed the door on the rational path of knowledge. So he completed *The Incoherence of the Philosophers* and ended his explorations of rational and philosophical epistemology. Yet the same stroke also suggested a way out of the bog of total skepticism, by considering the Sufi concept of taste. *Experience itself is a kind of reality.* Maybe it's the only reality we can ever really come to know.

One might object that experiences may be filtered through complicated and sometimes even faulty sense data. That's of course true; any reader of Descartes (or fan of *The Matrix,* for that matter) understands as much. Nevertheless, in the end the experience *itself* stands on its own as a phenomenon. *I feel what I feel, and nobody can tell me otherwise.* My experience is *mine.* I know what sex feels like *to me.* I know what sugar tastes like *to me.* The reality of these direct experiences have a certainty that I simply can't doubt. I may not know what they mean or signify. I may never know how my experience correlates with "external reality" or the perspectives of other people. I may never be able to construct useful comparisons or analogies with these experiences. As in *The Matrix,* I may be a brain floating haplessly in a jar. But my experience *itself* can't honestly be doubted. It's my experience; I can *taste* it. It's real to me. Thus it passes Ghazali's test of *sure and certain knowledge.* Awareness, in the end, constitutes what I know. Maybe Faramadhi and the Sufis really did have something coherent to say. Perhaps taste could be a kind of foundation.

Certainty now came to mean something different to Ghazali. He now realized that it "was not achieved by constructing a proof or putting together an argument." In his autobiography he put down a remarkable new formulation for what constituted for him certain knowledge. The new certainty that had allowed him to go on living was "the effect of a light which God Most High cast into my breast. *And that light is the key to most knowledge.*"[20]

When I first read that sentence from Ghazali's autobiography, a light turned on in my own mind. How many matters in my own life have really felt certain by means of rational proof alone? I don't think very many. Of course I've studied and thought and applied a good deal of logic and reason during my studies. I spend a lot of time thinking, pondering, and reasoning. Sometimes I've even come up with logical "proofs" during these intellectual processes. But the moments culminating in certainty for me seem to be more aesthetic, a *feeling*—a taste. I think, ponder, and reason, and then from out of nowhere a light comes on. Suddenly I *know*. I just know.

I think of Yale's motto: *lux et veritas*, light and truth. An idea is often described as a light having been turned on. Why is this? It isn't quite random. It's not an arbitrary pairing of one sensation (light) with another experience (knowing). Rather, something like light flooding in seems like *part* of the experience of knowing. How does it feel when I add together a string of numbers and the answer checks out? It *feels* right. What is the *experience* when the path to completing a complicated project suddenly dawns on me, seemingly out of nowhere? A *light* goes on. Even in the mathematical example, which seems so determined by logic and reason, in the end it's often an affective experience, passive and received, a *feeling*—something akin to light—which convinces me that I have been made privy to something true.

Why is that? Nobody really knows. It's still a question hotly contested by neurologists.[21] Nevertheless, I do know that *to me* the experience of knowing feels like a light having been suddenly turned on. The light indicates *personal* certainty. The light brings certainty *enough*. Perhaps most important, I realize that I concur with Ghazali regarding the therapeutic affect accompanying this light; it signals a profoundly personal orientation. I know that coming to this minor certainty and having my chest flooded by light, this all *feels* right. It feels significant. It also feels edifying, as though I've achieved something. And I realize that I may well be addicted to this edifying feeling. That's what I've been doing all of this time in the academy, trying to foster moments of sudden illumination, the *ah ha!* experience. Although that experience is there for me to pursue and to try to cultivate, in the end it's never quite under my control to make happen. Finally, after a good deal of preparatory thought and rumination, it just comes. I look and I search and I think, and then flashes suddenly occur amid a cloud of unknowing. The cloud brightens for just a little while, making my general state of darkness more tolerable, maybe even meaningful.

Thus Ghazali had discovered for himself the taste of learning.

LAKE OF FIRE

Ghazali then found himself alone with his direct experiences and the light which God Most High sometimes cast into his breast. That light as well as its accompanying *ah-ha!* he now understood to be the taste of learning, comprising his only certain epistemological test. Having the experience of the light, he'd learned something sure and certain.

This was not radical subjectivism, since Ghazali claimed no control of when the light would shine in. Would that he were in control. Unfortunately the inherited knowledge of theology, which had been the foundation of his worldly position and spiritual security, no longer lit his heart. That demotion hadn't been his choice. His former hubris simply fell away from him. And he'd learned that philosophic reasoning could only end up disproving its own certainty.

On the other hand, the taste of skepticism had also left his life, replaced by the possibility of *awareness*. Feelings and experiences themselves constituted their own reality and justified their own certainty. Ghazali now realized that Abu Talib al-Makki had been right: "Certitude is found uniquely in the hearts of those endowed with experiential knowledge."[22] For Ghazali, the world was no longer a vacuum of doubt, but had become full again with the reality of taste. Discovery of the light of awareness had proven to be knowledge enough. But having found the bedrock of phenomenal experience, it did tease

Ghazali's intelligence with a lingering question which came to take up increasing amounts of his interior dialogue and energy.

Can you taste God?

Of course that was a Sufi question. Over the past several centuries Sufi masters had put forth a great number of answers to this question. Some had built monasteries in which they tried to cultivate experiences of God. Some wrote down their experiences as best they could, invoking whatever analogy most closely reflected what were likely incomparable and even ineffable tastes. They used any language available to suit this purpose—theological, philosophical, technical, poetic, erotic, sometimes all in the same verse. Ghazali now poured over these writings as he had once taken to theology and philosophy. Only this time his studies did not convince him to abandon the avenue. What he read pushed him to probe even more deeply.

"I brought my mind to bear on the way of the Sufis," he recounted in his autobiography. "Theory was easier for me than practice. Therefore I began to learn their lore from the perusal of their books."[23]

What he read, however, consistently told him that reading about Sufi taste was derivative and insufficient. The theory of Sufism, spelled out with language, only brought one to the same epistemological limit Ghazali had already found in his refutation of philosophy. Going past those limits could not be achieved in theory but only by practice. *He needed to have direct experiences themselves.* There could be no other way.

Words were not the problem per se. Indeed, Sufis surrounded themselves with words in their poetry, manuals, prayers, lectures, and especially in their ecstatic practices of sacred remembrance and invocation of God's name and attributes. But it was how they experienced these words—the manner in which they directed their attention and senses toward them—that made all the difference between mere intellectual knowing, which always came up short of certainty, and the *feeling* of awareness that, according to the legendary Sufi master al-Nuri, finally entailed "the annihilation of the invoker in the invoked."[24]

What could *that* mean?

The ecstatic experience of words was *exactly* what Ghazali could not cultivate by mere reading and thinking, or even through his regular ritual of praying, despite the fact that he'd dedicated his life to words of this kind. Although he was certainly one of the most literate men in the world, as he read the masterpieces of Abu Talib al-Makki and al-Harith al-Muhasibi, he realized that his way of approaching words intellectually had simply failed him. "I knew with certainty that the Sufis were masters of states, not purveyors of words," he remembered, "and that I had learned all I could by way of theory. There remained, then, only what was attainable, not by hearing and study, but by taste and by actually engaging in the way."[25]

Then one day Ghazali got up to lecture at the Nizamiyya before his three hundred law students. It was June of 1095, three years after the murder of Nizam al-Mulk. A new sultan presided over the Seljuq empire, along with a new vizier, while a new caliph inhabited the Round City in Baghdad. At age thirty-nine, Ghazali looked about and saw he was the last standing of the old guard. He'd weathered the storm of intrigue and assassination and had become the most revered authority in Islam. Sultan and caliph alike sought his opinion to bolster their own frail authorities. As Ghazali ascended his lectern that day to deliver a lecture on jurisprudence, the sort of lecture he had now given a thousand times before, stray thoughts penetrated his mind regarding what he'd been doing with his life. He said:

> I saw that I was immersed in attachments which had encompassed
> me from all sides. I also considered my activities . . . and saw that

in them I was applying myself to sciences unimportant and use-less in this pilgrimage to the hereafter. Then I reflected on my intention in my public teaching, and I saw that it was not directed purely to God, but rather was instigated by and motivated by the quest for fame and widespread prestige.

As he looked out over the assemblage of his students, he couldn't quite bring their faces into focus. His inner landscape became dominated by a nightmare image—the Lake of Fire. "I became certain that I was on the brink of a crumbling bank and already on the verge of falling into the Fire, unless I set about mending my ways."[26]

He opened his mouth, but nothing came out. The man of words had been struck mute.

"God put a lock on my tongue," he remembered. "I struggled with myself to teach for a single day, to gratify the hearts of the students who were frequenting my lectures, but my tongue would not utter a single word: I was completely unable to say anything."

He stepped down from the lectern with uncontrollable fear and trembling. When he arrived home, he discovered that he could no longer put down any food; his throat wouldn't even accept broth. The finest doctors of Baghdad ran their tests and soon realized that the ailment was psychological. "This is some-thing which has settled in his heart and crept from it into his humors," they say. "There is no way to treat it unless his heart be eased of the anxiety which has visited it."[27] The doctors couldn't determine a source for the generalized anxiety. But Ghazali knew. When he saw the Lake of Fire pulsing before him, he understood the problem with the clarity of divine light.

I've been wasting my life.

I'm on the wrong path.

Closing time approaches.

My last chance to change is now.

Outwardly he remained mute, but his interior voice wouldn't be still. "Away! Up and away!" it scolded. "Only a little is left of your life, and a long journey lies before you! All the theory and practice in which you are engrossed is eye service and fakery!"[28] Lots of voices come and go from a person's interior dialogue, nobody can heed them all, nor should they. But the accompanying light in Ghazali's breast indicated that this one was sure and certain.

"AWAY! UP AND AWAY!"

After six months of second guesses and ingenious rationalizations about why he should stay the course in his current career, Ghazali finally told associates and family in December of 1095 that he had decided to fulfill a lifelong dream to make pilgrimage to Mecca. But he wasn't actually headed there. Rather, he'd resolved to flee secretly to Damascus. He'd heard that the greatest living Sufi master was affiliated with the main mosque there. Damascus had been beckoning Ghazali since the moment he'd lost his voice. So many masters of insight had come from that sacred city, including the authors of nearly all manuscripts on the subject. With the week of Hajj quickly approaching, which could serve as cover for his escape, Ghazali decided that he'd had enough of lying awake tormented at night. The Lake of Fire. Whatever rationalizations prevented him from leaving already, the period for internal debate was now concluded. A light had been cast into his breast. If the taste of God Most High were possible in this life, then it could be learning's only purpose. Every other knowledge constituted vanity.

Ghazali kept just two confidants in his escapade. One was his younger brother Ahmad, whom Ghazali installed as dean of the

Nizamiyya in his absence. Ghazali handed over his academic robe to Ahmad, and as the weight of its gold threads shifted between the men so must have its burden. In secret and by elaborate legal stratagem, Ghazali put a sliver of his considerable academic estate into a trust for the sustenance of his wife and daughters. He set aside an even smaller portion for his own welfare. The rest he returned to alms for the poor of Baghdad. He told his family, colleagues, and the caliph that he planned to be back shortly after the Hajj. They shouldn't worry if he also decided to tag on some minor touring afterward. Perhaps he would also visit Hebron and the tomb of Abraham. That trip, too, had been a life's dream.

Ghazali took with him his second confidant in this escapade, his best friend from college, Abu Tahir al-Shabbak. Perhaps boyish excitement built up as they mapped out their adventure. After so many jaded years working in government together they now had a purpose and quest. They had a mystery to explore, something new and significant to learn about. Although they could have but an inkling of the coming adventure, already they could likely feel between them a revival of mood. The pursuit of learning itself feels *good* in the edifying and weighty sense of the word. It's therapeutic. It lifts the spirit. Then, taking only light travel chests filled with simple robes and some of their beloved manuscripts, the friends fled Baghdad in search of God Most High.

REMEMBRANCE

It would take two weeks to get to Damascus. We can try to imagine how each mile ratcheted up the anticipation of the traveling friends. As they had no recourse to Sufi techniques just yet, they would have continued to resort to analogies of reason as they tried to piece together some mental portrait of what their Sufi retreat experiences would be like. Perhaps they passed evenings by lamplight pondering the meanings of their worn Sufi manuscripts. Though Ghazali would have known better than to dissect these writings by reason, how could he have helped himself? These last days and nights of pondering and speculation would constitute the final blooming of his intellectual ego as he tried to understand a divine taste he knew full well to be ineffable. He'd have realized that by the means of mere thought he was about as able to experience God as the impotent man is able to experience sex. He might even have chided himself with his own favorite analogy: "I thought you were just impotent! Now I know that you are impotent *and* stupid!"[29] Ghazali, the most authoritative mind in Islam, was left with only a schoolboy's virgin wonder when it came to the experience of God. That's where all of his thinking had gotten him. Ghazali understood this. Yet as he anticipated Damascus he still couldn't help but *think*.

When Ghazali finally arrived in Damascus, current headquarters of the venerable Junayd school of Sufism, he stopped thinking. Awe took over, awe such as he hadn't felt since he first walked into a schoolroom when he was eleven years old.

In Ghazali's writings, he never mentions the name of his Damascus instructor, but it could have been none other than Nasr al-Maqdisi, for here in Damascus Shaikh Nasr presided over Sufism. The elderly shaikh then had a small convent affiliated with the main Umayyad Mosque where he taught Sufi techniques by day and gave sermons most evenings. His stature as the most prominent Sufi master of his day displayed itself in subtle ways, though certainly not by the golden threads of an opulent robe. Shaikh Nasr would take no money for his lessons to the spiritually curious travelers who passed through his lodge and lived only by income from what he'd published.

In coaching students in the awareness of God, Shaikh Nasr continued a great Damascus tradition, as most of the Sufi masters that Ghazali read came from this ancient place, among the most continuously inhabited cities in the world. Syriac Christian mystics lived here before the advent of Islam, and in Ghazali's time one continued to feel their presence through local devotees of the Eastern Church. Even Paul first realized the reality of God while traveling on the road here, struck clear off his mule and into the Kingdom of Heaven. The shaikh himself was Palestinian, raised in Jerusalem and Gaza. At age eighty, he still maintained a close connection to the Sufi community at the Dome of the Rock, although in old age he had made Damascus his home. He would come to spend his last days here, of course teaching to the very end.

We can only imagine the first meeting between the two men: one middle aged, still embodying hubris despite all efforts to release the habits of worldly stature; one old, forthright with a confidence that comes from having given himself up long ago to annihilation in God.

Did Ghazali announce himself to the shaikh? Did he allow his companion Abu Tahir the customary role of announcing the presence of the great jurist? I try to envision the scene. I see Ghazali entering the lodge with his head properly bowed, even nervous with anticipation. I see him taking his place silently among the riffraff of students and devotees. They are all seekers, young and old alike, unmarried people and householders, retirees—all of them on quests to find their right places in the world. They are similar to one another only in the shared hope that maybe, just *maybe* the unseen mysteries of the universe will be unveiled here. Most are old hands in this hope, having been disappointed many times before. There may be doubters among them, there may even be skeptics, but there are no cynics in this crowd. These are people who, despite all former disappointments, continue to live in hope. Ghazali also lives in hope. He sits down among them and waits for the master to speak.

After the set of obligatory morning prayers, Shaikh Nasr would have given his instructions to the students. They were to engage in *dhikr*, the "mention" of God. Sometimes the term is translated as "remembrance" since Arabic holds both meanings. The Quran itself refers to the concept 270 times, but never explains how to do it. That was why all of these students were here, including Ghazali. They were to learn a simple technique they had heard about for their entire lives but had not been taught to do, at least not as the Sufis practiced it. It was a technique available to the humblest of supplicants, requiring almost no intelligence and the lightest physical stamina. It began by sitting with one's mind in open attention, empty of any intentional content. One should then not recite the Quran or think about its meaning. One shouldn't pray or supplicate oneself or consider any aspect of the hadith tradition. Those things have their place, but not in the remembrance of God. Not now. Ghazali reports:

> Then, as one sits in solitude, let him keep on saying continuously with his tongue, "God (Allah), God," and keep his heart attentive until he comes to a state in which his effort to move his tongue drops off and it looks as if the word flows on his tongue all by itself. Then, let him persevere in this until any trace of motion is removed from his tongue and he finds his heart persevering in the *dhikr*. Then, let him still persevere in this until the image of the word, its letters and its shape are effaced from his heart and

there remains the idea of the word alone in the heart, clinging to it, as if it is glued to the heart, without separating from it.[30]

And that's it. One mentioned the name of God first physically; then mentally by sound and image; then wordlessly by idea alone. The instructions were simple, especially the first two parts. One was to speak a word and concentrate upon it until the physical act of speaking actually became irrelevant to one's mental concentration upon the word, at which point one could let the speaking fall away. Then one continued the mental repetition until that interior vocalization and imagining also became irrelevant and even distracting to one's concentration on "the idea of the word." But what could it mean to mention "the idea of the word" without actually using the word? Ghazali didn't yet know. The instruction seemed inscrutable, but Ghazali knew there existed certain experiences, certain tastes, that must be *had* and could not be described. So he trusted that these steps would bring him to this inscrutable experience. If he persevered in the first two steps of physical and mental remembrance, maybe the third form of mention of God—"as if glued to the heart, without separating from it"—perhaps this ineffable type of remembrance would come.

To Ghazali's way of thinking, it made a kind of sense. The Quran described God's perfect unity (*tawhid*) as His ultimate essence. This unity in Ghazali's time was generally accepted as the foundational precept of Islam. Perhaps this wordless cleaving to the idea of God would be the taste of God's unity that had eluded Ghazali since he'd first learned of the concept as a child. Then he had pondered the possibility of God's pure unity with wonder and longing, only to find from the vantage point of adulthood that God, insofar as He was around at all, seemed estranged and differentiated from this world. Ghazali of course didn't know for sure whether the remembrance of cleaving to the idea of God would be an experience of His unity. But the Quran and its commentaries all seemed to point in this direction, and the world sometimes seemed to point this way as well. Ghazali himself, in his memoir and later mystical writings, relayed scores of accounts describing a feeling of fusion with one's surroundings—and simultaneously with something more. He described fleeting experiences of *at onement* that illuminated the breast like lightning and then quickly passed. Could dhikr then have been the remembrance of that unity? Was that sense of fusion a human glimpse of God's own tawhid? Had Ghazali he been tasting God *spontaneously* all this time and simply not understood it?[31]

When Shaikh Nasr concluded his instructions, his senior disciples directed each new student to a room. Ghazali went to a minaret in the southwest corner of the mosque, and there he began his practice. He practiced in that minaret for six months, probably for eight or ten hours a day, interrupted only by the requirements of Muslim rituals and prayers. He took down some notes regarding his experiences as well. Along with the typical student cycle of prayer, ritual observances, and sermon attendance, remembrance took up the bulk of Ghazali's time. He practiced the method of remembrance day and night, sometimes with great concentration and clarity, sometimes less so. Sometimes he needed to mention God's name physically throughout the session because mental mention too quickly receded into distraction. But as the weeks went by he sometimes became able to reach a place of wordless mention and remembrance. With practice, and over time, this state came more quickly and easily. There was progress and regress, and every day always seemed to contain something of a battle with distraction, but most days also brought with them a tiny taste of the unity that had so long escaped him.

He now had an inkling of the Quran's meaning when it said: "By the remembrance of God do hearts find rest," (13:28).

Nevertheless, despite this monumental success, Ghazali soon enough realized that the wordless mention of God was but the gateway to remembering God, and not the totality of that taste. The technique of remembrance might have been a door available to anyone who would persevere, but further states of unity could not be attained by perseverance alone. These came sporadically, like lightning, when one had opened oneself up to the possibility of such an experience.

> Indeed, after having done what one can, he lies bare to the breathings of the mercy of God. Nothing remains but to await the mercy which God reveals as He did to the prophets and the saints in this manner. Thereupon, if his aspiration is sincere, his wish is unmixed and his exercises are sound—and furthermore, his lusts do not disturb him and idle thought does not occupy him with worldly ties—then the light of Truth shines out in his heart.[32]

So it happened that six months after having arrived in Damascus, in the spring of 1096, Ghazali likely received the light of truth that he had so long coveted. Although Ghazali in his writings typically did not display his own mystical experiences, and preferred rather to describe these matters impersonally, he does claim to have enjoyed some personal taste of the unity he describes. Writing in his autobiography, for instance, he remembered this of his mystical study: "In the course of those periods of solitude things impossible to enumerate or detail in depth were disclosed to me. This much I shall mention, that profit may be derived from it: I knew with certainty that the Sufis are those who uniquely follow the way to God Most High." And so he left the lodge of Shaikh Nasr, never to see this Sufi teacher again. Ghazali would never come to mention the shaikh or say a great deal about his own experiences in the minaret, preferring the deflection of the Sufi poet Ibn al-Muʿtazz:

> There was what was, of what I do not mention:
> So think well of it, and ask for no account![33]

Ghazali did, however, offer one tantalizing sentence regarding the final state of remembrance. "Its end," he said, "is being completely annihilated in God."[34]

THE HEART'S MEDICINE

Wanderlust finally took Ghazali to Al-Aqsa Mosque in Jerusalem, shutting himself in for another six months next to the mystical Dome of the Rock, where Muhammad was said to have ascended directly to heaven to receive revelation from God and where, a thousand years earlier, ancient Israelite priests entered the Holy of Holies, the nexus of God and earth—whatever these claims may mean. To Ghazali they now meant something more specific than what he'd once imagined, as something like ascension to heaven now seemed possible even for mortals still here on earth when touched by "the breathings of God's mercy."

Ghazali now began to interpret all the prophets and saints as masters of awareness. He now spent his time continuing his own practice and writing about the world as it is experienced through Sufi taste. The world itself was of course the same and looked much the same as well. People still were born and then died; they bickered and wept and sometimes smiled. But, through awareness, it all also somehow could feel very different. Ghazali now would portray the world as though it were *new* again. He described the mystical state as though one were watching creation occur. It's as if awareness allowed one to observe the world being created, moment by moment, while one walked through life. So preferring not to try and describe what he couldn't (meaning annihilation in God), rather Ghazali jotted down as many insights about the created world as he was able to. After years of writing, this became his magnum opus and gift to Islam, his *Revival of the Religious Sciences* (*Ihya' 'Ulum al-Din*). In effect, it interpreted orthodox Islamic practices and claims from the perspective of Sufi taste. For Ghazali, the appeal to direct awareness was quite enough to revive the truth and reality of Islam. Just *live* Islam and be revived. Walk through life with it. *Experience* it. *Taste* it. That's the whole finding of his great *Revival*. So simple.

By sciences (*'ulum*), of course, Ghazali did not mean knowing (*'ilm*) based strictly on philosophy, reason, or cognition, as had been Ibn Sina's goal. Ghazali's revival of science and knowledge was founded on direct affective experiences of taste, and he now defined 'ilm as such. In this he followed the master Abu Talib al-Makki, who centuries before had defined awareness as "the knowing (*'ilm*) of inward realities."[35] It had been only just a few years ago, when the Seljuq empire fell apart and Ghazali retreated into the study of philosophy and, ostensibly, 'ilm, that Ghazali had had no idea what Abu Talib had meant by "the 'ilm of inward realities." But now it was the only thing Ghazali knew with perfect certainty. He would finally encapsulate his new epistemology like this: "Knowledge is above faith, and tasting is above knowledge; because tasting is finding, but knowing is a drawing of analogies, and having faith is a mere acceptance through imitation."[36]

His story from this point forward contained many wanderings on the earth to such places as Mecca, which he finally did visit, and to Hebron, where he swore before the tomb of Abraham never again to subject his heart and teaching to vain interests or

to the aegis of the state. After two years in the Levant, and at
the request of his young daughters, who missed their father, he
finally returned to Baghdad, taking up residence in a small Sufi
convent just across the way from the Nizamiyya. A contemporary witness noted: "When Abu Hamid originally entered
Baghdad we estimated the value of his clothing and mount
to be 500 gold pieces. After he turned ascetic, traveled, and
returned to Baghdad, we valued his clothing to be worth fifteen
pieces of copper."[37] A short while later, Ghazali returned home
to Persia, taking up with the modest faculty of the Nizamiyya
at Nishapur where Ghazali himself had earned his legal degree
as a boy. Ghazali remained in that humble position for the rest
of his life.

The more significant of his wanderings, however, took place
in innerspace. "For nearly ten years," he wrote in his autobiography, "I assiduously cultivated seclusion and solitude. During
that time several points became clear to me."

What points?

"That man is formed of a body and a heart—and by 'heart' I
mean the essence of man's spirit which is the seat of knowledge
of God, not the flesh which man has in common with corpse
and beast."

"That his body may have a health which will result in its happiness, and malady in which lies its ruin; and that his heart, likewise, may have a health and soundness . . . and it may have a
malady which will lead to his everlasting perdition in the next
life."[38]

And so Ghazali became Islam's first therapist, its first advo-
cate of an integrative positive psychology, its first happiness
expert, its first doctor of hearts. He dedicated pages upon pages
of his *Revival of the Religious Sciences* to this very subject, especially in a volume he named *The Marvels of the Heart*. It remains

salient and well worth investigation by those interested in traditional therapeutics. Its essential prescription for the heart's revival is taste of God's own unity; this is available to those who empty out the hubris of ego and self and submit themselves to the taste and experience of His comprehensive dominion.[39]

Let me be clear about one important point that some modern readers may find difficult. Ghazali argued lucidly and vociferously for the logical possibility of an afterlife. He did not claim proof, but rather argued for lack of disproof. Lacking demonstrable disproof, he held that Muslims were obliged to hold faith in the literal accuracy of the Quranic position regarding afterlife. More than this, Ghazali justified much of the work of remembrance as preparation for that afterlife and concluded his great *Revival of the Religious Sciences* with thorough arguments for its possibility.[40]

Nevertheless, he also acknowledged that other reputable mystics held Paradise to be the experience *of our own known world*. Ghazali himself often used language of God's unity to describe terrestrial experiences of remembrance, even indicating these to be a taste of Paradise in the here and now. Through the practice of remembrance, the sensory (*al-mulk*) and ideational (*al-malakut*) tastes of our world—the stuff of normal human experience and imagination—could reveal themselves as God's very presence in *this* world, thus turning this world into Paradise.

> The material world (*al-mulk*) and the world of spirits (*al-malakut*) taken together under one classification are called the Lordly Presence, for the Lordly Presence encompasses all existing things. For there exists nothing except God, the Exalted, His works, and His Kingdom; and His servants are a part of His works. What appears of this to the heart is, according to some, Paradise itself.[41]

Ghazali appears to have been arguing that something of God's Paradise could become available in the here and now by becoming *aware* of our normal sensations and thoughts. Still, to emphasize Ghazali's important position, I must repeat that he understood Quranic orthodoxy and orthopraxy as the very best means to taste God, and he believed this work should be done as preparation for a more important Paradise occurring after death. He took this as a matter of faith. Yet he also held that some portion of a future Paradise is available to us now, as a taste of divine unity. I want then to wrap up discussion of Ghazali's own spiritual adventure with some remarks from his *Alchemy of Happiness* (*Kimiya-yi Sa'adat*) that apply to happiness in *this* world, our world. The book itself is a précis of his *Revival of the Religious Sciences*, redacted and translated into colloquial Persian so that his common countrymen could reap the full benefits of his experiences. In it, Ghazali suggests one can grasp something of the joy of God's unity simply by recognizing the common, daily, perhaps even mundane miracles of creation, which become especially accessible during remembrance, but are also available with plain curiosity about one's experience of everyday surroundings.[42]

If you go to the abode of a prince that is painted and plastered, you would describe it for a long time and you are amazed; while you always see all these wonders in the House of God Most High and you are not amazed! This physical universe is the House of God Most High. Its carpet is the earth, its roof is the sky, but it is a roof without pillars, and that is more marvelous. Its treasury is the mountains and its storehouse is the seas. Its household goods and utensils are the animals and the plants. Its lamp is the moon and its torch is the sun. Its candles are the stars, and its torchbearers are the angels; yet, you are heedless of the marvels of this House. The House is very immense and your eye is minuscule and cannot contain it.

You are like the ant that has a hole in the corner of the castle of a king and is unaware of anything save its own nest, its nourishment, and its comrades. It has no knowledge of the beauty of the architecture of the palace, the multitudes of slaves, the king's throne, and his kingship. If you desire to be satisfied with the degree of an ant, do so! But if not, you have been given entrance to wander admiringly in the garden of the spiritual knowledge of God Most High. Come out and open your eyes so as to see its wonders and become astonished and amazed! Peace![43]

Thus the jaded jurist and lawyer saw his world revived. When one recognizes the severe limit of human knowledge through cognition, as Ghazali first demonstrated to humanity, and which every good scientist since his time has also realized, we are left with the inescapable fact that each and every experience is both a moment of creation and a miracle. Even a thousand years after Ghazali, *experience* remains a mystery utterly beyond the ken of contemporary neuroscience, which still today has no grasp of the mechanisms by which physical data are translated into the qualitative experiences Ghazali knew as taste. None. This mystery of qualia continues to be what neuroscience calls the "hard problem."[44] *We don't know how taste happens.* And those experiences comprise the *totality* of our world.[45] Or at least our "sure and certain" knowledge of it. These mysterious acts of phenomenal translation are the only kinds of creation to which human beings are privy. Which in effect means, despite all advances of mathematics, reason, and science, of which there is no doubt, creation entire is still an utter mystery. That mystery includes the external world, our experiences and interpretations of that world (rational and otherwise), and *especially* the ethereal mechanism by which we are permitted any experience or interpretation at all.

Ghazali saw this epistemological limit a thousand years ago. Yet by the miracle of our sentience—to use Ghazali's word, our *taste*—he claimed we are permitted phenomenally to witness existence as it comes into being, moment by moment. From this point of view, Ghazali believed all creation must be allowed the status of revelation.

> The masters of insight never see a thing without seeing God along with it.[46]

And in recognizing the miracle of taste and the gift of learning, was our hero finally healed? Had he located for himself an alchemy of happiness? Had he made peace with the universe? A contemporary by the name of ʿAbd al-Ghafir had this to say about Ghazali's changed, calmed, manner in his later life: "What we initially thought was pretension and an acquired mode was, in fact, his true nature and the realization of what he truly was. This was the sign of the happiness that had been ordained on him by God."[47]

So it would seem that the good Professor Abu Hamid al-Ghazali finally learned how to submit and assent to the mysteries of cosmos and self.

5

QIU CHUJI

Chinggis Khan Learns to Cherish Life

To know one has enough is to be rich.
—Daodejing, chapter 33

LABOR

The following is a strange travelogue, both geographical and spiritual. Although Li Zhichang's Travels to the West of Qiu Chuji *is not widely known outside of China, there it is still a classic. I turned to it initially for no other reason than its eyewitness depiction of Chinggis Khan's anxieties as he approached retirement. If a person of his accomplishments and powers could undergo a crisis regarding his labor—if he could lament the limitation of his achievements—then aren't we all entitled?*

This case addresses the alarm that can occur when one feels that a life's work is not enough. When Chinggis Khan faced this moment, he did not feel himself ready. So the khan located a Daoist monk whom he believed to know a secret alchemy for prolonging life. The monk, however, had another therapy in mind for the khan. Master Qiu Chuji preferred to help the khan reconsider what really constitutes a life's work. This work is not the pursuit of treasure, as the khan believed, but the cherishing of a treasure already held within. In fact, the monk explained that cherishing what one already possesses can prove to be the hardest human labor of all. We now explore this revaluation of wealth and labor by taking some first few steps along the Way.

THE HUNT

In early autumn, Chinggis Khan routinely commenced the Mongol sacred hunt by sending a whistling arrow skyward from his bow. Within seconds, hundreds more signal arrows followed, launched from a line of cavalry troops at least one hundred thousand strong. The horsemen stretched out for seventy or eighty miles, composing an enormous and menacing U-shaped front. One whistling arrow signaled the next, one flick of a banner set off a vibrant pattern of hundreds more, *thousands* more, and soon each horseman knew his function. Step by step, the *nerge* (Mongolian for "line") pushed forward a net of hunters sweeping across the Eurasian plain.

The nerge went along a set course for weeks, operating in closely coordinated shifts, signaled by flags in the day and by fire at night. Day or night, the line never stopped, and it never broke. Every creature with enough awareness to sense danger attempted to outrun the line or was forced to turn its feet inward toward the middle point, which accumulated thousands of wild steppe animals all moving forward as though a domesticated flock of sheep. No animals were killed initially. Without an order from the khan himself, no soldier dared to set off a hunting arrow. But neither would he allow any creature to make it past his point in the line. Those who were lax knew the range of penalties for failure, including death. Each of his commanding supervisors would then be beaten: his sergeant of his squad of ten, his captain of a hundred, and his colonel of a thousand. If the offense were egregious, the Khan himself might have a word with the commanding general of ten thousand, the need for such a conversation being a humiliation more painful than any beating. The regimen of punishments in the nerge were as well regulated as its every other aspect. This killing machine would operate by a single trigger—the word of Chinggis Khan.[1]

In the distance a flag marked the final killing plain. The khan and his honor guard rode ahead to a spot just above. Chinggis Khan surveyed as his troops tied the ends of their line into a circle. At first the circumference was eighty miles around, but the circle then contracted.

"Here," an observer noted, "there becomes massed together an extraordinary multitude of wild beasts, such as lions, wild oxen, bears, stags, and a great variety of others, and all in a state of the greatest alarm. For there is such a prodigious noise and uproar . . . that a person cannot hear what his neighbor says; and all the unfortunate beasts quiver with terror at the disturbance."[2]

Standing shoulder to shoulder, troops tied ropes together and covered these with felts, draping the cloth prison down to the ground. "Lions are becoming familiar with wild asses," said another observer, "hyenas friendly with foxes, wolves intimate with hares." Finally "the circle has been so much contracted that the wild beasts are unable to stir."[3]

The khan and his immediate retinue broke the line and entered the circle, pushing back against the animal pack. Once again Chinggis Khan raised up his composite bow, this time not with the signal arrow that began this ritual, but with an arrowhead scraped down to pierce through animal hide. The bow itself didn't appear to be anything special. By world standards the weapon was small and unadorned, seeming like the toy bow of a diminutive people. With it the emperor would personally take down the first few animals, after which the macabre portion of the hunt would begin. Chinggis Khan raised his bow; he took his thumb ring to the bowstring; his compact latissimus dorsi muscles pulled back the bowstring as though it were indeed a child's toy and . . .

His heart pounded in anticipation of the kill.

Did he hesitate?

Did he squint?

Did he *savor* something?

Whoooosh! THUMP!

The khan's arrowhead pierced through the neck of some poor creature, maybe a Eurasian elk or sable. Maybe it was a lion or bear. Blood spurted against the fur of neighboring animals which now bucked in terror, but the pack was dense with no space to move. Creatures twisted about, shuddering, panicking, sweating.

The khan's own life energy pulsed through his body with each release of an arrow. Adrenaline flooded his system and the focus of his sight narrowed. He knocked down a few more animals, and then the corral of wild creatures grew rowdy with fear. The animals brayed with every pulse of their own life energy.

After perhaps an hour of this sport, the khan had had enough. The strange force that fed the rush and thump of the kill then seemed depleted. The thrill was gone. Chinggis Khan retreated behind the line, allowing the next group of princes into the circle to continue the hunt. This sacred slaughter would now go on for days, one group of princes following the next, one cavalry unit following the next, all in orderly ranked procession "until nothing is left of the game but a few wounded and emaciated stragglers." Chinggis Khan ceremoniously remitted these inedible creatures from annihilation.[4]

After a day or so of bagging and counting, nine days of drunken feasting commenced, celebrating the successful accomplishment of the nerge hunt. It was the central ritual of Mongol civilization, occurring early each autumn when the land was full and the hard winter months lay ahead. It was also a simulacrum of the Mongol art of war, as the people of Khwarazm and their shah, Sultan Muhammad II, would learn all too soon.

A ROYAL ENVOY

The imperial envoy that approached the quiet Daoist monastery on Shandong Bay in the spring of 1219 had not been the first to do so. Actually this was the third such official invitation in three years. In 1217 the Jin emperor ruling north of the Huai River had summoned the master, and the master declined. Then, early in the year 1219, the Song emperor ruling south China made a similar summons and sent generals to punctuate the request. Master Qiu Chuji again declined. He used to travel more, proselytizing and teaching, but these days the master was much older; he could feel the pulse of his energies waning considerably. So when generals came with carriages to escort Master Qiu Chuji, the vehicles returned to their emperors empty.

The master's disciples worried about declining so many imperial requests. Didn't the master fear reprisals, if not against himself then against his church and beloved laity? But the master shooed away his disciples, reminding them that he hardly had any choice in the matter. The Way was constant and indomitable, dictating all happenings. "When the time comes for me to go, I shall go," he said, "and there is no more to be said."[5]

Then a new envoy strode through the monastery gates. The gold pendant dangling from the neck of ambassador Liu Wen was neither the charm of the Jin emperor nor the emblem of the court of the southern Song. The gold was molded in the form of a tiger's head, magnificent really, with some touch of the style of the wild steppe tribes. On it was inscribed: "This man is empowered with the same freedom as I myself should exercise had I come in person. Chinggis Khan."[6]

Why should students of spirituality be interested in one of the greatest killers in history, Chinggis Khan, emperor of Qamuq Mongol Ulus, the Great Mongol Nation?[7] Because the great khan at this moment had begun to think seriously about his final enemy, the decrepitude of his own body.

The khan had been at war for nearly all his fifty-seven years. The effects of a life of horseback and blood were wearing on him physically, and maybe they had also taken some toll on his mind as well. That arrow he took in the knee during this most recent war with the Jin hadn't helped his outlook any. Of course, the khan still retained the kind of bravery and inner strength it took to face the chance of death in battle or by capture. He'd ordered enough kings and princes wrapped in blankets and kicked to death to know that his own life might very well end by similar means, perhaps at the hand of the Tanguts in central China or maybe by a resuscitated Jin empire in the north. Or it could come from the dreaded Khwarazm shah of the Islamic world who had been sending out some rather inhospitable signals recently. So the khan knew death could come from every point of the compass. He'd made his peace with the chance of death.

The inevitable course of bodily demise felt different. This made itself known through unwelcome cricks in the joints and pains along the lower back. Sometimes his mortality took the khan by surprise, as when he flubbed a simple hunting maneuver he'd otherwise performed flawlessly since puberty. Or perhaps gloom crept in when he wondered whether his knee injury hadn't really come at the hand of the Jin enemy, but rather by the slowing of his own wit. So his personal decay had been on the khan's mind of late. As he looked out once again on a strange new horizon hosting a strange new enemy, likely this time in the Khwarazm shah of the Turko-Islamic empire, the khan had another morbid actor to consider as well. His own personal horseman of decrepitude also rode steadily forward from the horizon.

During his last campaign to take Beijing from the Jin, the khan learned of a strange Chinese monk rumored to be three hundred years old. His sect supposedly knew a secret alchemy by which one could prolong life and perhaps even become immortal. Nobody in the khan's court quite understood the medical details (the famed monk was the leader of a fairly new offshoot of the ancient Dao called Quanzhen, or Complete Perfection), but the idea was that, by carefully disciplining one's instinctual interior drives and forces, one could preserve the life essence itself.[8]

A secret inner alchemy of immortality—now that seemed interesting.

Could one master the treasure of life?

So the khan had decided to issue an invitation for Master Qiu Chuji.

The khan's note to Master Qiu Chuji had actually been endearing, even humble.[9] "Heaven has abandoned China owing to its haughtiness and extravagant luxury," the khan had said. "But I, living in the northern wilderness, have not inordinate passions. I hate luxury and exercise moderation. I have only one coat and one kind of food. I eat the same food and am dressed in the same tatters as my humble herdsmen."

This was all true. Naturally, the khan did enjoy a personal armed guard of ten thousand troops surrounding him at all times. But as for his more universal needs, of food, shelter, and dress, these he met in the manner of any of his minor officers and even his common soldiers. Chinggis Khan wore the same basic tunic and coat as his herdsmen. He ate the same basic goat stew as them, drank the same fermented milk from their mares, and like his men he consumed barely anything else.

The emperor's asceticism must have appealed to Master Qiu Chuji. The master, too, had had quite enough with the royal extravagances of the Jin and the Song, both dynasties having grown fat off taxation of populations ravaged by nearly a century of constant war. Like Chinggis Khan, Master Qiu Chuji also believed that, once one's basic human needs were met, any additional elevation of these staples only contributed to decay and not to nourishment. A body needed clothes, not costume. A person needed food, not delicacy. Both khan and master believed that luxuries were literally decadent: their pursuit misappropriated the precious storehouse of life.

"Do not be afraid of the thousand li," the khan had said, meaning three hundred miles or so. "I implore you to move your sainted steps."

> Have pity upon me, and communicate to me the means of preserving life. I shall serve you myself. I hope that at least you will leave me a trifle of your wisdom. Say only one word to me and I shall be happy.

GIVEN ON IST DAY OF THE 5TH MONTH (MAY 15, 1219).[10]

Master Qiu Chuji knew he had to accept this invitation. The Mongol nation of wild northern horsemen now constituted political reality in China and among all its neighbors. Over a million people had either been killed, dispossessed, or committed to slavery during the khan's Beijing campaign. So Master Qiu Chuji decided to take the thousand-li journey to Mongolia to meet the khan in his *ordo*, his city of yurt tents, along whichever river that camp might in summer reside. Hopefully it wouldn't be too far north of the Great Wall. In any event, the master was to travel from his tranquil bayside monastery up north to noisy Beijing, where he would stay in the Jade Emptiness Temple until the Mongol envoy would meet him for further transmission to the khan's tent city.

Once Qiu Chuji actually reached Beijing, however, new revelations regarding the rest of his itinerary surprised the old monk, to say the least. Upon his arrival in Beijing, Qiu Chuji learned that the khan's Chinese envoy Liu Wen had received further instructions from his excellency. For one, according to Qiu Chuji's chief disciple and eyewitness chronicler of the journey: "Master was distressed to discover that Liu Wen proposed taking with them on the journey all the girls whom he had collected for the khan's harem." Yes, that would be something of a shock to a celibate monk.

"I am a mere mountain-savage," the master had told envoy Liu Wen upon learning of the development, "but I do not think you ought to expect me to travel with harem girls."[11]

Liu Wen's next rude disclosure announced that the khan's ordo was no longer camped in Mongolia a thousand li away. Where on earth had his majesty disappeared to? He now resided *ten thousand* li away (three thousand miles) somewhere near Samarkand, great city of the Hui-Ho peoples (Muslims). "I am old and infirm," Qiu Chuji protested, "and fear that I shall be unable to endure the pains of such a long journey."[12] Yet the royal envoy had no authority to modify the khan's order. Although the khan promised to return Qiu Chuji to China within three years, that could not have been much consolation to an aging monk.

The expedition's chronicler says that as Master Qiu Chuji made his last preparations to go, a disciple brought in an antique painting. He hoped Master Qiu Chuji might inscribe something on it. The picture depicted the last trek of ancient Master Lao, over fifteen hundred years before, also crossing over the western frontier to teach. Master Lao had died in the barbarian west while spreading the Dao. Perhaps that would be Qiu Chuji's fate as well. Though we don't know what Qiu Chuji finally wrote on the picture, the feelings inscribed in his heart must have been profound. Qiu Chuji had seen a great deal since the time he first stumbled into a Daoist monastery when he was nineteen years old. Since then, he'd served kings and immortals. But he'd never been through something like this. Before the wagons rolled out, the master retreated to his cloister in the Jade Emptiness Temple for some final moments of practice in solitude.[13]

"I do my utmost to attain emptiness," Master Lao had written in the Daodejing: "I hold firmly to stillness."[14]

BENEATH THE SKY GOD

One should not underestimate the trepidation with which Chinggis Khan ascended Mongolia's sacred mountain Burkhan Khaldun to supplicate himself before the sky god. His birthplace lay in the shadow of this mountain, along the Onon River. Despite having come into contact with all sorts of religions and beliefs during his long lifetime (the Buddhism of the Qara Khitai, Tangut, Uighur, and Chinese; the Islam and Judaism of the merchant caravans; the Nestorian Christianity even among his own Mongol tribes), he had never considered any of these over his servitude to Tengri, the Mongol sky god who overlooked the vast steppe and treated the earth as his consort. After consulting with a shamanic interpreter about the burnt shoulder blades of a sheep, as he had always done for major decisions, Chinggis Khan ascended the holy mountain itself, unaccompanied, for three days of prayer and thought. Just as a supplicant did before addressing a khan, Chinggis Khan removed his own belt and placed it over his shoulder as he hiked up the mountain. Then, in some secret spot, he took a posture of deference and opened his heart to Tengri.

His hesitations to attack Samarkand were many. Sultan Ala ad-Din Muhammad II, shah of Khwarazm (our contemporary Uzbekistan, Afghanistan, and much of Iran) was said to have an army of two hundred thousand cavalry, while Chinggis Khan had perhaps half of that under his control.[15] Moreover, the sultan's domain was not a familiar steppe but mountains and valleys; these would be extraordinarily difficult terrain in which to utilize the usual open-field caracole and nerge tactics of the Mongol cavalry. And finally, Chinggis Khan realized Khwarazm to be far from his new holdings in China, requiring that he split his resources.

Yet not retaliating for the Khwarazm shah's insult to the khan's embassies would be worse. The Khwarazm shah had tested a trade agreement with Chinggis Khan by executing the khan's merchant envoy. When the khan sent an ambassador to demand restitution, the Khwarazm shah then executed the ambassador. Not responding to this abuse would amount to forfeiting the vast distribution riches of the western steppe. Taxing this region bought the very loyalty of the khan's Mongol nation. So the aging khan had a lot on his mind.

When the khan descended the sacred mountain, he sent out communiques to his sons and generals: gather the armies to meet along the banks of the Irtysh River in Kazakhstan, a thousand miles west, where they would conduct the sacred autumn nerge and replenish supplies. Then they would head south to take Khwarazm from its shah.

As the khan assessed his muscles and joints after three days of intense supplication on his knees, he may also have realized the field of his body to be in need of its own wartime preparations. Chinggis Khan's initial invitation to Master Qiu Chuji was likely among these wartime communiques, urging the monk to kindly travel west to meet the ordo. Please come teach an aging khan the secret of immortality.

The sources say it took Chinggis Khan five months to capture the northern gateway to the Khwarazm shah's empire, Otrar, culminating in his command to pour molten silver into the eye and ear orifices of its governor. If indeed it took as long as five months, this was because Chinggis Khan had been exceedingly careful in the face of his enormous enemy. He methodically cleared Otrar's environs of every fortress and enslaved the unprotected agrarian population. He then encircled the city. Slaves did the suicidal work of traversing the moats and walls of the citadels while under enemy fire. Slowly and meticulously, his slaves piled up stones and wood faggots across moats, thousands getting picked off by citadel archers and catapults of ignited naphtha. The khan didn't really mind how long this took. His ordos and flocks could live off the steppe pasture indefinitely; the weapon of time served nomads well. As starvation set in behind city walls, he killed desperate defectors on the spot.

When the citadel of Otrar finally fell sometime in the winter of 1219–1220, the remaining population of the city was enslaved or slaughtered. This wasn't sadism. This bloodshed was rational, meant to relay a rational choice to the peoples of the other cities of Khwarazm: resistance is suicide; disobey your leaders; give yourselves up.[16]

Consequently, town after town on the path southward to the capital city of Samarkand simply surrendered. If everyone cooperated with an orderly plunder, then no one was hurt. Only places still fearful of the shah's power resisted at all, but these were few, and they were fewer still after word got out of their concomitant decimations. By late in the winter of 1220, most all the strategically important citadels and fortresses of Khwarazm had been occupied or destroyed. The Mongols were positioned to take Samarkand itself. The only remaining town, Bukhara, lay beyond the impassable Kyzylkum Desert, if one didn't take the road through Samarkand, and tiny Bukhara would fall quickly anyway once the capital city itself was seized.

So it was a surprise to the people of Bukhara when Chinggis Khan's army impossibly surfaced in the surrounding countryside. "His troops were more numerous than ants or locusts," says Juvaini, the best ancient historian of the conquest, "being in their multitude beyond estimation or computation. Detachment after detachment arrived, each like a billowing sea, and encamped around the town." As with other smaller towns, the citizenry of Bukhara surrendered immediately.[17]

The otherwise reliable historian Juvaini recounts a questionable story about this moment in the conquest. He says that while Chinggis Khan inspected the interior of the city of Bukhara and the walls of its citadel, he entered the central mosque thinking it was the governor's palace. Upon learning its true function as a place of worship, Juvaini says the Mongols dumped the Quran manuscripts on the ground to make flooring for what would be the new horse stables. He says Chinggis Khan then ordered local dancing girls and wine and improvised a little party in the mosque entailing a good deal of drunken Mongolian singing. But the episode is hard to believe, given Chinggis Khan's usual policy of respecting local religious authority and his typical efforts to win it over. Indeed, well before the invasion, Chinggis Khan had many Muslims in his own entourage, and by this time in the Khwarazmian campaign that number had certainly increased. Though on occasion he did raze a mosque along with the rest of a town, and he did bristle at the imposition of having to provide halal food to slaves, generally he had no special interest in insulting local prophets and gods.

More plausible is a speech Juvaini claims that Chinggis Khan delivered from the pulpit of the festival mosque just outside the town gate once he had finished making initial inspections:

> O people, know that you have committed great sins, and that the great ones among you have committed these sins. If you ask me what proof I have for these words, I say it is because I am the punishment of God. If you had not committed great sins, God would not have sent a punishment like me upon you.[18]

This is precisely what he had written initially to Master Qiu Chuji about the Jin and Song empires. Their leaderships had grown fat, and their peoples had allowed that to happen. The Mongol khan was the holy scourge itself. He acted not against the will of Heaven but in its name. His military nation represented the brutal and taut sacred order, the proper way of the world. The Mongols had come to return the world to its ideal state of domination by the lean, active, simple, and courageous. It was not the god of the defeated who had failed them; the people had failed themselves. This sounds more like the ecumenical voice of the khan.

THE GREAT THOROUGHFARE

Halfway through his journey, somewhere in the Gobi Desert straddling Mongolia and contemporary Xinjiang province in the westernmost corner of China, the old master stepped out of his carriage into the night. Most reasonable people of the world even then would have conceded that this very spot constituted the renowned Middle of Nowhere. The caravan had to travel at night. During the day, the sterile desert was uncrossable, yet it was the only way to get from Prince Tamuga's camp in Mongolia down to the villages along the foothills of the Tien Shan Mountains leading into contemporary Kazakhstan. That foothill path would put the group directly onto the road down to Samarkand. But now Qiu Chuji was in the dark Gobi Desert, and the caravan, including his own entourage of nineteen disciples, had stopped for a break. What would the master see in the heavens that night? Stars like no other place on earth; perhaps a huge moon. This desolate trail in the Middle of Nowhere hadn't yet become part of the Silk Road; Chinggis Khan had only just become the undisputed emperor of that great thoroughfare. But this modest path would soon become the Mongolian fork of the Silk Road, as more merchants made the trip up to the northern ordos, which were becoming increasingly wealthy and influential.

Qiu Chuji had endured worse than this. It's fair to suspect that, despite all his protest and procrastination, he was actually enjoying some of this adventure. As a young man, a similar spirit had overtaken him when he realized he needed to leave the lazy Shandong coast to find his own true way.

Sources are sketchy about Master Qiu Chuji's childhood. At age nineteen, however, he wandered into a local monastery on Mount

Kunyu, apparently looking for something more than what life and position had allotted to him.

There, in the monastery, Qiu Chuji met his own future master, though this would not be the abbot of the monastery. Rather Qiu Chuji came under the sway of a mere mendicant, a wandering beggar, who by chance had taken some days' refuge in the same place. He was a middle-aged brute of a man, described as having wild charismatic eyes. The initiates called him Lunatic. Well, some called him drunk, though to be fair Lunatic Wang Zhe's eccentricity could no longer be blamed on alcohol because by then he'd given that vice up.

At one time the peculiar monk had been the wine and liquor tax collector of his small hometown in Shaanxi province. Hagiographies say Lunatic had taken the civil service and military examinations to improve his lot, but no extant record of a career in either of those honorable vocations would indicate that he passed those exams. So Lunatic Wang Zhe soused his existential disappointments in the liquor he taxed and neglected his family, until one day, while imbibing in a saloon (probably while on the job), a group of holy immortals crashed the place and demanded a drink from Lunatic's own flask. This must have made an impression because at that moment Lunatic gave up the bottle, his job, and his family and set out to find the Way.

So Lunatic Wang Zhe left his home province of Shaanxi and, a year later, settled in Nanshi village near Ganhe and Huxian. Instead of building a home, he built up a dirt pile ten feet high and dug out a vault. There he lived, meditated, and perfected the inner alchemy. He called his earthen hermitage the Tomb of the Living Dead and put a sign at the door that said: "Here rests Lunatic Wang."[19] He had no students and took no visitors. He left the hut infrequently only to beg. After three years of solitude, textual study, sensory deprivation, fasting, and general drying out, his practice was perfected. He'd realized the Way.

The immortals had even taught him the inner alchemy. He traveled to the more populated coast to find students, which is where Qiu Chuji met his master, and half a dozen other disciples also came under the charismatic spell of Lunatic Wang Zhe and the mystery of the Way.[20]

One day Qiu Chuji overheard a secret conversation between Lunatic and the group's oldest disciple, Ma Yu. Lunatic seemed to be describing a special breathing technique, a rotation of vital breath, from the lower elixir field near the navel up through the upper elixir field in the brainstem. Qiu Chuji overheard his master instruct Ma Yu on how to allow the belly to rise and fall when breathing, and to let the skull bounce oh so gently on the tip of the spine as one drew in air. The secret inner alchemy! Qiu Chuji couldn't help but stay to eavesdrop. But once Master Lunatic spotted Qiu Chuji listening in he instantly became silent. Later Qiu Chuji pleaded with his friend to reveal some details of the teaching, but Ma Yu wouldn't say a word.

This eldest disciple Ma Yu was a rich man, a landowner, and a prosperous local business person. He'd built a monastery on his property for Lunatic's small group, which they called Quanzhen An, Hermitage of Complete Perfection. There Lunatic Wang and his band of seven students conducted retreats in solitary confinement. A disciple never left his hut for one hundred days. He had his daily meal of rice delivered through a sunless window. Wealthy Ma Yu did these hundred-day retreats as well. So did his well-to-do wife Sun Bu'er, who was also a disciple. When Lunatic declared that all initiates must be celibate, Ma Yu and Sun Bu'er divorced.

Especially harrowing was the day Lunatic prepared Ma Yu to go begging in the streets. Lunatic smeared rouge all over Ma Yu's respectable face and tied up his hair in the pigtails of a child. Then Lunatic sent him out, commanding this community elder to go beg, especially from his own extended family and in-laws. This humiliation was too much. Ma Yu loved his master; he'd paid for the Quanzhen hermitage; he didn't mind intense deprivation of any kind; he wished desperately to realize the Way. But Ma Yu couldn't abide the humiliation of begging in a clown outfit and told his master so.

Lunatic responded by beating Ma Yu continuously over the course of the entire night. From dusk to dawn Ma Yu endured random, vicious blows from his beloved teacher. Qiu Chuji witnessed the dark episode himself and received Ma Yu's broken body the next day to attend to his wounds. And it was Qiu Chuji who convinced Mu Ya not to flee from the hermitage. Master Lunatic must have had his reasons, Qiu Chuji counseled. Lunatic's violence couldn't be utterly senseless. Hadn't the master chosen Ma Yu especially to receive private lessons in the inner alchemy? That's what must have angered Lunatic. Their master would not have wasted his time beating a hopeless disciple. Ma Yu's realization of the Way couldn't be far off.

So, with Qiu Chuji's personal encouragement, Ma Yu decided to stay. And indeed shortly thereafter Ma Yu became the first disciple of the original seven to realize the Way.

What is the Way? What is the Way? The question frustrated Qiu Chuji the whole time he served Lunatic Wang Zhe. Lunatic wouldn't tell him a single word about the inner alchemy, as he'd told Ma Yu. For Qiu Chuji Lunatic assigned every conceivable privation and humiliation instead. Fasts, celibacy, isolation, poverty, sleep deprivation, and a daily agenda of excruciating and completely senseless tasks. *Senseless.* Every morning Lunatic had a new task for him. Roll a boulder up to the hilltop, then let it plunge down again and start over; cover the pots and pans in pig excrement, then clean them up; fill huge water buckets from the well, lug them to the hermitage, and dump their contents wastefully into the earth. When it was snowing, Lunatic had Qiu Chuji sit on top of the snowbank. When scorching, Qiu Chuji was to stand on one foot in the open sun. When it was beautiful, Lunatic charged him with a day in dark solitary confinement. Lunatic seemed to make these assignments up randomly each morning. *Random, senseless tasks. How could this be the Way?* "Since the time I began to follow the master," Qiu Chuji thought silently to himself, "I have been unable to understand what the Way is. Everything that he has taught me or made me do has had *nothing to do with anything.*"[21]

To explain himself, Lunatic would only smack or kick a student. When feeling magnanimous, he might grunt. Though at other times he might spurt out something from the ancient traditions. He liked Master Lao's Daodejing (Way and Its Power) and Master Zhuang's corpus (Zhuangzi), and he also talked about the more recent Qingjing Jing (Classic of Clarity and Stillness), but these scriptures hardly made any sense to Qiu Chuji. They certainly didn't make any sense out of the random violence of his master. They didn't reveal any meaningful order of things. They never indicated what, exactly, the Way *is*. They spoke only by negation, the way a teacher corrects a presumptuous student: *No, that's not it. No, that's not it. No that's not it. . . .* Master Lao famously began the ancient treatise on the Way with the impossible caveat:

"The Way that can be told of is not the changeless Way."

He also warned:

"Those who know do not speak; those who speak do not know."[22]

So maybe the whole thing was inscrutable. Or maybe it was a fraud.

Now out on this this rocky road of the Gobi Desert, a road so untraveled that it could barely be called a road, Qiu Chuji faced the impossible charge of explaining this ineffable mystery to Emperor Chinggis Khan himself. Maybe the conflation of the impossible road and the impossible charge reminded Qiu Chuji of some verses he studied in his youth about the making of roads:

> A road is made by people walking on it; things are so because they are called so. What makes them so? Making them so makes them so. What makes them not so? Making them not so makes them not so.[23]

ZHUANGZI

It hadn't made sense at the time, back when Qiu Chuji studied these verses at the feet of Lunatic. But decades later, as Qiu Chuji readied his old body to push back up into the carriage, once again to bump through the night toward the Tien Shan Mountains and then to Heaven-knows-where in Khwarazm, now these verses probably meant something more to him. In the end, he received his realization at the feet of his master. At Lunatic's deathbed, Qiu Chuji had received his one last lesson. It wasn't much. In fact Lunatic had revealed literally *nothing at all*. But those final empty words allowed Qiu Chuji just a glimmer of the Way, enough to keep him going all these years.

Lunatic's disciples gathered round their dying master. Of the original seven, only four remained. They'd all been on the road back to Lunatic's home province in Shaanxi, to build their permanent monastery, but Lunatic had taken ill along the way. On his final night, as Lunatic was about to ascend to immortality, he commanded Qiu Chuji to follow Ma Yu as the new master of Quanzhen.

Lunatic then turned directly to Qiu Chuji and spoke the last words before he died. "You have committed one great sin which you must get rid of," he told Qiu Chuji. "In the past you thought to yourself that everything that you had been taught had nothing to do with anything. You never understood that *that which has nothing to do with anything is the Way.*"[24]

So the caravan traversed its own abstruse way along a road that could only provisionally be called a road. Across seemingly unbounded miles of open steppe, Qiu Chuji often settled into his carriage and tried to clear his mind of thoughts. "I make myself identical with the Great Thoroughfare." Such had been sage Master Zhuang's advice so many centuries before.[25]

IN THE ORDO

When the Khwarazm shah heard news of the fall of Bukhara, he packed up the royal entourage and crossed back over the Amu Darya River in forfeit of his empire. The great city of Samarkand itself fell in ten days. The shah himself had not been in Samarkand defending his crown jewel; he chose to receive reports of events from a safer encampment further west. When he learned the news of Bukhara, he knew his empire was destroyed. By taking Bukhara, Chinggis Khan and his son Tolui had severed the Silk Road and cut off Samarkand from the rest of the

Khwarazm shah's empire. Samarkand would fall, there was no longer any way to protect it. So the shah headed due west to the Caspian Sea, to the familiar heartland of his father's old kingdom, escaping to a remote island. The empire was done. Shortly thereafter, he withered away from dysentery.

Medieval Muslim historians would generally lambaste the shah for losing the empire to barbarians. They would critique his crass diplomacy and unsubstantiated militarism. Those critiques were probably deserved. But then again, what rational person could have predicted the awesome intelligence, discipline, and might of the Mongol nomad nation? A mobile death machine; an empire needing only its horses, bows, flocks, and tents. The world had seen nothing like it.

While Chinggis Khan cleared away loyalist uprisings along the foothills of the Himalayas, Master Qiu Chuji finally arrived in the captured city of Samarkand in the winter of 1221–1222. How strange this city of Muslims must have seemed to his entourage of disciples from provincial Shandong Bay. His journey's chronicler was especially amazed to see a strange fowl called a peacock, and also huge elephants parading through the streets, "which come from India," he noted, "several thousand li to the southeast."[26] The association brought to Qiu Chuji's mind the Buddha and the traditions emanated to China from India. He took a moment to honor the Buddha by writing a brief verse:

> He surpassed birth and destruction,
> He entrusted himself to the turning of the cosmos.[27]

Qiu Chuji met Chinggis Khan's second son Chagatai and asked for the whereabouts of his father. Chinggis Khan was on

Snow Mountain, the son said. The khan would send word when he was ready for the master to come down and meet somewhere in vicinity of Kabul.[28]

Qiu Chuji's chronicler says that the master did not take kindly to this idea. "He'd heard for a thousand li to the south of the river there is no vegetable at all."

"My diet consists of rice, meal and vegetables," Qiu Chuji told the khan's son. He would very much prefer to stay and wait for the emperor in Samarkand.

In April of 1222 Qiu Chuji received the following message directly from the khan: "Adept! You have spared yourself no pains in coming to see me across hill and stream, all the way from the lands of sunrise. Now I am on my way home and impatient to hear your teaching. I hope you are not too tired to come and meet me."[29]

Liu Wen, the Chinese envoy and medical adjunct who had first told the emperor that Qiu Chuji was three hundred years old, also received an instruction from the khan: "I count on you to convey my message and persuade him to come," the khan had written. "If you are successful in this, I shall not fail one day to reward you with rich lands."[30] But would there be any penalty if the khan should be disappointed with this monk? Liu Wen must have wondered how old, exactly, aged Master Qiu Chuji actually was. He couldn't have looked three hundred years old. But then again, what should a tricentennial monk have looked like?

They crossed the Amu Darya in boats and then passed through the Iron Gate gorge. In the middle of May the envoy was finally greeted by a high officer of the khan, ready to lead them to the emperor's ordo. The camp consisted of the khan's honor guard of ten thousand cavalrymen. After a few inquiries, the khan's high officer showed the master and his disciples to their quarters in the camp. They barely had time to drop their luggage, because the khan wished to see Qiu Chuji immediately.

Did the master have any objection to this?

He did not. It was time to meet Chinggis Khan.

The two men greeted one another with due deference to their stations and relative powers. This was not the first throne room Qiu Chuji had walked across nor the first emperor he'd met. As for the khan, naturally he knew his own earthly power, but he was respectful of religion and did feel some admiration for the old master. The khan certainly knew how to use the charisma of religious clergy to his political advantage. But the khan's respect also came from something more than this. He seems to have been genuinely curious. No, he hadn't adapted too many of the religious traditions he'd come across before. He remained the servant of Tengri the Mongol sky god. But he was broadminded enough to suppose that maybe the Daoist monk had some secret to immortality, or at least to the prolonging of life. And the emperor still hurt from the arrow to the knee he sustained back in China. His back and sciatica now flared up more often than when he was young. He simply couldn't ride horseback as long as he used to. Almost sixty, the traditional age of Mongol retirement from the cavalry, the khan could feel for himself in his own joints and muscles a future in which his ability to command from horseback would be severely compromised. Maybe most of all he lamented that his hunting vigor had already suffered. The sacred autumn hunt, the Mongolian nerge festival, was still his favorite national ritual, but, alas, hunting was a young person's sport. Perhaps he wished only to enjoy it for a few seasons longer.

"Other rulers summoned you, but you would not go to them," the khan said. "And now you have come ten thousand li to see me. I take this as a high compliment."

"That I, a hermit of the mountains, should come at your Majesty's bidding was the will of Heaven," the master replied.

This delighted Chinggis Khan. He begged the master to be seated and ordered food to be served. Then he got straight to the point.

"Adept, what Medicine of Long Life have you brought me from afar?"

"I have means of protecting life," the master said, "but no elixir that will prolong it."[31]

That must have been quite a revelation.

How old are you? the khan may have wondered aloud.

Seventy-two, the master would have replied.

Would the khan have lifted an eyebrow? Seventy-two wasn't exactly ancient.

The khan wondered what was this immortality that Liu Wen had spoken of?

Qiu Chuji's friend Ma Yu had once written a poem when considering this very question.

The grain cart enters, and the manure cart exists.

They take turns coming and going.

When will it come to an end?

Even if people can cause their life to span over a hundred years.

This is only thirty-six thousand days.

The poem is called: "Lamenting That People Only Know How to Eat Food and Defecate Without Ever Assigning Their Minds to Their Nature and Life."[32] Qiu Chuji agreed with Ma

Yu. The group's founder, Lunatic Wang Zhe, was also of the opinion that one hundred years is the greatest limit from the womb until death.[33] Lunatic had explained:

> As for when I speak of leaving the ordinary world, I do not mean to say that the body leaves. In such cases I speak of one's state of mind. The body is like the lotus roots, and the mind is like the lotus flower. The roots are in the mud, while the flower is in empty space. As for people who have attained the Way, their bodies are in the ordinary world, but their minds are in the sacred realm. People nowadays who desire to be ever deathless and depart from the ordinary world are great fools who have not fathomed the Way's principles.[34]

The khan, being very much a political realist, may well have also appreciated this biological realism. The body dies. It cannot become immortal. At stake are the experiences of the *mind*, in the here and now, during the precious period of one's life. And there's something more to that experience than shoveling in gruel and pushing out excrement.

And so the teaching began. The khan found this all quite fascinating. But he still had some questions remaining regarding the issue of Qiu Chuji's age. Why did the Quanzhen group have a reputation for immortality?

Qiu Chuji replied that this was a very advanced lesson. Immortal wasn't a word he just threw around. It was liable to dangerous misunderstandings. He did not believe himself to have achieved immortality or even to have fully realized the Way. "I continue to encounter countless difficulties to this day," he said.[35]

The chronicler of Qiu Chuji's journey reports: "The Emperor was pleased with his candor, and had two tents for the master and his disciples set up to the east of his own." Qiu Chuji left the throne tent to unpack in his new quarters, but no sooner had he arrived than the interpreter of the khan came with an additional question:

"People call you 'Tangri Mongka Kun'[36]—'Holy Immortal.' Did you choose this name yourself or did others give it to you?"

Qiu Chuji answered: "I, the hermit of the mountains, did not give myself this name. Others gave it to me."

Soon after, the interpreter came to him again on the emperor's behalf and asked another question. "What," he said, "were you called in former days?"

Qiu Chuji replied that he had been one of four pupils who studied under Master Wang Zhe. The other three had all passed away, and only he was left in the world. "People," he said, "generally call me 'Senior.'"

The khan then asked General Chinkai, who had been the military attache on Qiu Chuji's envoy, what one ought to call the adept. "Well, some people call him 'Father and Master'; others, 'The Adept'; others, the 'Holy Immortal.'"

"From now onward," said the khan, "he shall be called the Holy Immortal."[37]

MASTER OF LIFE

Rebel insurgencies drew the khan away from his spiritual training. Qiu Chuji returned to Samarkand and stayed there until he received word, in September of 1222, to come meet the khan south of the Amu Darya as before. The rebels had been sufficiently routed and the khan was almost ready to return to his lessons. The emperor was now just finishing the autumn nerge, the Mongol sacred hunt, up in Snow Mountain in the foothills of the Himalayas east of Kabul. Afterward, teacher and student would travel together out of Khwarazm for good, and head back to China.

The birding during the hunt had been exquisite. The whole region was known for its excellent birding. The emperor returned through the valley paths and passages with carts and donkey packs loaded down with the lifeless carcasses of all kinds of native birds. The ducks and geese were especially good-looking and fine-tasting creatures: ruddy shelduck and wigeon, greylag and teal, mallard, pintail and shoveler. So many types of handsome animals lived by these cold mountain lakes.

Qiu Chuji's entourage followed a small river upstream for a ways, headed east and south. "We passed the great city of Balkh," writes the chronicler. "Its inhabitants had recently rebelled against the khan and been removed." "Removed," of course, meant slaughtered and enslaved. The khan had a policy of leaving no survivors after a rebellion. "We could still hear dogs barking in its streets."[38]

By the time Qiu Chuji found the ordo, the khan was already there. Once again the khan was anxious to see Qiu Chuji right away. When Qiu Chuji entered the throne tent, Chinggis Khan insisted that he not bow or kneel. They spoke casually and concluded the chat with a round of kumiss mare's beer for the entire Daoist entourage, which the monks gladly drank.[39]

The first day of the lectures soon arrived. The khan erected an imposing pavilion for the event. "To the left and right candles and torches flared," says the chronicler. After taking his seat, Qiu Chuji noted that Liu Wen and General Chinkai had taken extraordinary pains to see him safely across Asia. He wondered whether his kind chaperones might be admitted to hear the lectures. The request was granted. Qiu Chuji then began the first of what would finally be four formal discourses on the Way.

> The Way is the producer of Heaven and the nurturer of Earth. The sun and moon, the stars and planets, demons and spirits, men and things all grow out of the Way. Most men only know the greatness of Heaven; they do not understand the greatness of the Way. My sole object in living all my life separated from my family and in the monastic state has been to study this question.[40]

So began the illustrious lectures, with a brief cosmology of the unseen order of the universe. Encompassing both the celestial and the earthly world, controlling these spaces and all possible others, is the Way—the Dao. It is the principle by which creation occurs. What is the principle? Insofar as that can be articulated (which it can't), it is that creation occurs by mysterious alchemy in the interpenetration of opposites. Yin and Yang. Opaque and Clear. Dark and Light. Water and Fire. Female and Male. Earth and Heaven. Will and Fate. Action and Inaction. One should not think that these states are essentially differentiable. These literally create one another, and in doing so they create the world. In their pictographs, Yin is a hill overcast in shadows while Yang is the same hill bathed in sunlight. Opposites are merely two ways of looking at the same hill—with the understanding that the hill is itself created by being seen from these interpenetrating and inseparable points of view.[41]

But this idea was not primarily what Qiu Chuji wished to teach. The emperor was intelligent and broadminded and indeed expressed academic interest in cosmic principles, but what he had really asked about were the means of protecting life. So, with minimal general preparation, Qiu Chuji turned to a specific explanation of the life principle, *qi*.

What is qi? It is *life force*. Qi is the force of motility and change in the universe; it is the animating means by which the Way is enacted, for both animate and seemingly inanimate things. Guiding creation, "above" it, as it were, there is only undifferentiated qi—undifferentiated change and motility, undifferentiated chaos in motion. But, when qi coagulates by the principles of yin and yang (which, to say it again, are essentially principles of *perception*), in that interpenetration of opposite perceptions of undifferentiated qi *seeming stability* occurs; things *seem* differentiated into opposites, that is to say, creation occurs. Stable things appear to be.

Etymology may be a helpful way to understand this difficult concept. Chinese has a fascinating character for the life force qi: 氣. Its pictograph derives from two others. The first is the ancient symbol for rising steam, or vapor: 气. At times the picture also meant air, breath, and even spirit. The general meaning of this symbol is something like "invisible presence." Then, at some later point, writers of Chinese began to add an extra character to it, the symbol for rice. This transformed the qi character into a picture of steam rising from cooking rice. The pictograph then began to mean something like: "the invisible presence that is released from food." So qi means life energy, or life force.

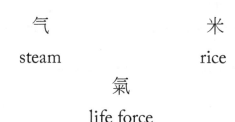

Fairly quickly, ancient Chinese science began to abstract the meaning of the word to all types of motility and change, both animate and inanimate. Yes, the "life" and food aspect remained. Indeed it was crucial to the understanding even of inanimate motion, because the mechanism by which change occurred in inanimate things (such as gravity) remained as much a mystery as the motile source in life. At the same time, in a seeming contradiction (if the Way didn't contradict itself it wouldn't be the Way), the life process was itself seen as a function of the motility of inorganic elements. Qiu Chuji's own master, Lunatic Wang, had often said: "Truly this body is a ball of mud and a clod of dirt. When gathered together, it becomes a body, and when it scatters, it becomes dust."[42]

Qiu Chuji knew that some Chinese scientists had begun to speculate that qi existed materially, as a separate physical energy. They called their science the outward alchemy. They had even tried to locate qi experimentally, as though the mystery of life could be isolated and corked up in a bottle. But this was not Qiu Chuji's opinion. He believed it to be a metaphysical force. In humans it was carried in the blood and put there by the breath. It was cultivated not by outward mechanical manipulations of the elements, as the outward alchemists believed, but by an *inner alchemy* of the blood and breath.[43]

Did the khan nod in recognition? Blood and air. These he certainly understood. The monk's ideas could only have been eerily familiar to a devotee raised in the tradition of Mongolian Tengri worship. The khan knew the mysterious power of the sky; he knew that in human beings this power was carried in the blood.[44] Qi! The alive feeling! He'd felt the pulse of this life force many times. Perhaps he considered all the objects of his desire. These included material gain, sexual releases, highs from his beloved kumiss mare's beer, and even subtle things like the rush of insight and learning he felt during these lectures. The qi experience certainly included lordship, power over other people. Perhaps he'd felt qi most in himself at exactly the moment he was ending its presence in another human being—the alive feeling of battle! The same feeling occurred with the first arrow shot of the sacred hunt. *Blood.* In the thrill of the hunt one could also feel the qi. The vitalizing power of it! So the khan had felt qi many times. There were days when he had chased after surges in the alive feeling all day long, and when his exhausted body couldn't take another minute he retired to sleep where he continued the quest, even in dreams.

Qiu Chuji regretted to inform the khan, however, that in fact following those urges, and using the life force toward the pursuit of outward objects, only depleted that very force. "If your eyes see colors, your ears hear sounds, your mouth enjoys flavors, and your nature follows your emotions," he said, "you will leak out your qi."

"You are like a ball filled with air," Qiu Chuji said. "If a ball is full of air, it is firm. If the air leaks, it is not firm. If people make their qi their masters rather than being masters over their qi, they will follow objects, give rise to thoughts, and their primal qi will leak like the air leaks from an air-filled ball."

Focusing one's life energy outwardly scatters one's fount of qi in the wrong direction. Though it may seem that we are becoming enlivened by the pursuit of external desires, Qiu Chuji seems to have been saying that we are actually depleting ourselves of this precious energy. One need not look to *outward* conquests to locate the precious alive feeling. Rather, what we should be doing is cultivating and guarding qi as a treasure that is already *within* us.

"If your qi is complete, you live," Qiu Chuji said. "If your qi is lost, you die. If the qi is vigorous, you are youthful, and when the qi declines, you age. Always cause your qi not to leak."[45]

"The Emperor was delighted with his doctrine," writes the chronicler, "and on the nineteenth, when there was a bright night, sent for him again."

The khan then believed he was ready. Could Master Qiu Chuji please explain the inner alchemy?

The principle was exceedingly simple, Qiu Chuji explained, but practice was difficult. One had to become a master of qi and not become mastered by it.

And what, precisely, did that entail?

There were preparations. Typically poverty and simplicity of domicile were necessities for finding the Way. After all, the entire process hinged on not becoming servile to outwardly directed impulses and conquests. As leader, however, his excellency had special responsibilities and may not have been able to enact these typical requirements. More than that, Qiu Chuji could see that the great khan, in his own way, was indeed also a simple ascetic.

The whole nation lived on simple rations and in simple roving tents. So his excellency already might not have been all that far from realizing the Way.

Qiu Chuji considered the question of what the khan might practice and decided that in the case of his excellency, given his particular set of weaknesses and strengths, it meant the khan should stop having sex.

"If common people," said Qiu Chuji, "who possess only one wife can ruin themselves by excessive indulgence, what must happen to monarchs, whose palaces are filled with concubines?"

The remark must have registered. The khan had over five hundred wives and concubines.[46]

"I learned recently," Qiu Chuji continued, apparently unaffected by the hubris of his suggestion, "that Liu Wen had been commissioned to search Beijing and other places for women to fill your harem. Now I have read in the Daodejing that not to see things which arouse desire keeps the mind free from disorders. Once such things have been seen, it is hard indeed to exercise self-restraint. I would have you bear this in mind."[47]

So the monk was still upset over having harem girls on the envoy. Was the khan bemused, amused, or both?

Qiu Chuji sharpened his point. When he served the Jin emperor decades ago, Qiu Chuji said, the man was so oversexed that he needed two attendants to hold him up as he staggered to the throne each morning. That emperor, according to Qiu Chuji, "completely recovered his strength and activity" by the same simple instruction: No sex.[48]

Qiu Chuji explained the utterly precious nature of sexual energy. There were specific exercises for transforming the enormous drive of outward sexual desire into the cultivation and purification of the inner qi. But these were complicated matters, and those sexual techniques were very advanced. The first step was simple celibacy.

"Try sleeping alone for one month," Qiu Chuji prescribed. "You will be surprised what an improvement there will be in your spirits and energy. The ancients said: 'To take medicine for a thousand days does less good than to lie alone for a single night.'"

"His Excellency has already produced a numerous posterity," Qiu Chuji concluded, "and can afford to husband his strength."[49]

The record does not indicate whether the recommendation had any effect on the khan's plans for the evening.

Once again Qiu Chuji passed through the flickering walkway of candles to the door of the grand interview pavilion. The khan had shown every indication that he was a thoughtful and appreciative student. He realized that the advanced inner alchemy might have been too difficult for a neophyte. Still, perhaps there remained simpler means a beginner might practice? Could Master Qiu Chuji please tell the khan: What is the inner alchemy?

Qiu Chuji was torn by the request. The inner alchemy had exceedingly powerful effects. Done incorrectly and without guidance, the simplest practices could lead to severe mental issues: perception fragmentation, dissociative states, even suicidal depression. He'd seen this happen many times. A good student, clearly on the way to realization, would suddenly crack up, having witnessed an operation of phenomenal innerspace that contradicted the stable world he thought existed, and so his world would fall apart. Even after years of his own study directly with Master Lunatic, Wang Zhe never consented to teach Qiu Chuji any element at all of the inner alchemy. Qiu Chuji had only gotten started after he spied his older colleague Ma Yu receiving strange lessons in breathing from Lunatic. The two had shut up as soon as they realized Qiu Chuji was watching. But Qiu Chuji took those few seconds of illicit instruction and pieced together his own practice. That's how he'd gotten started. Later, years after the death of Lunatic, Ma Yu finally consented to teach Qiu Chuji the system.

The khan reminded Qiu Chuji that his royal responsibilities would never allow him to study in a hermitage. Please pity a simple fool and teach him some element of the inner alchemy so that he might cultivate vitality on his own. The khan would contact the teacher should he come to substantial difficulties.

So Qiu Chuji agreed to teach Chinggis Khan the inner alchemy, with the caveat that these particular lessons could not be shared in the review notes the khan had ordered to be made of the lectures.

In terms of protecting human vitality, as was the khan's interest, the inner alchemy was a question of savoring one's relationship to breath.

Breathe gently. When you inhale, find the tension and subtle energy that stretches the belly outward just below the navel. Notice this. This is qi. Upon inhalation, also bring attention to the base of the skull. It too seems to flood with energy and tension. Notice this.

Now when you exhale, again bring attention to the lower region below the belly and also to the upper field of the brainstem. Follow the vital feeling as it courses through the rhythm of breath, up and down.

Now touch the tongue to the top of the palate. The tongue will comprise a bridge. When you inhale, follow that vital energy as it flows from the lower field up through the spine to its tip at the base of the skull. When you exhale, allow the energy to flow from the base of the skull across palate and through to the tongue downward by way of the chest. From there, qi will continue its circuit down to the lower abdomen where the cycle recurs.

Cherish the accompanying vitalizing sensations.

Repeat indefinitely.[50]

To always make your entire mind limpid, to remain alert and aware through the twenty-four hours of the day, to not let your actual nature become obscured, to make your mind stable and your qi harmonious, this is your true inner daily sustenance.[51]

QIU CHUJI

The emperor couldn't help but wish to know, what would this achieve?
Clarity and stillness.
Spirit purification.
Emptiness.
Immortality.

The lesson was ponderous indeed. Qiu Chuji warned that if the khan chose to proceed, he should work slowly and with caution. Spirit immortality—*shenxian*—was no game.

So concluded the lecture on the inner alchemy and the preservation of qi. To those present the khan said: "You have heard the holy Immortal discourse three times upon the art of nurturing the vital spirit. His words have sunk deeply into my heart. I rely upon you not to repeat what you have heard.'"[52]

GIVING UP THE HUNT

At the end of the final discourse, Chinggis Khan made an announcement: "I have received your earnest instructions and listened respectfully to your advice. These are all things difficult to practice; however, I shall certainly act in accordance with the Immortal's instructions and diligently put them into effect."[53]

The khan ordered his Chinese scribe to write up notes of the lectures, excising, of course, all details regarding the secret practice of the inner alchemy. The interlocutors traveled north together through Khwarazm. The khan was headed to a national meeting to be held in the Kazakh steppe where he and his brothers and sons would decide what to do next about the recent Tangut rebellion in central China and the remaining Jin empire in the far east. His outpost in China, General Moquli, had died suddenly, so conditions had recently deteriorated. For his part, Qiu Chuji was going home, back to Beijing and then Shandong Bay. The two chatted along the way. "During the remainder of the Imperial Progress to the east," writes the chronicler, "the Master constantly discoursed to the Emperor concerning the mysteries of Way."[54]

Still, it was something of a surprise to Chinggis Khan's advisers when his majesty made a sudden announcement: He'd given up hunting.

The Mongol emperor had *given up hunting?* But why? By all accounts this most important ritual of the empire was also the emperor's own greatest love. The proclamation made no sense. Why would the khan give up the hunt?

Perhaps it was because Chinggis Khan had finally decided to cherish the life force.

What about the ascetic monk had so gripped the most powerful man on earth? Was it that the old master charmed the emperor? Or amused him? Or did the emperor find something genuinely intriguing about the Way? One can almost imagine him sitting alone in his throne room, cleared of all attendants, and closing his eyes to try out the inner alchemy. Breathe low. Breathe high. Breathe low. Breathe high. If he did this for any time at all, he certainly would have enjoyed a glimpse, no matter how elementary, of the operation of the Way in phenomenal space. That itself is the beginning of spirit purification; that itself is realization.

We can only wonder. We do know for sure, however, that the emperor had a more immediate incentive. He was flat out feeling old. In March of 1223, as the ordo moved north, he was hurt during a short springtime hunting expedition. He'd shot a boar, but at that very moment his horse stumbled and the khan fell to the ground. The boar stood still. It didn't rush, apparently afraid to approach. In a split second, the emperor's military attendants brought a fresh horse and evacuated the emperor. The hunt was canceled. They all returned to camp.

"Hearing of this incident," writes Qiu Chuji's chronicler, "the Master reproached the Emperor, telling him that in the eyes of Heaven life was a precious thing. The khan was now well on in years and should go hunting as seldom as possible. His fall, the Master pointed out, had been a warning, just as the failure of the boar to advance and gore him had been due to the intervention of Heaven."

"I know quite well," replied the emperor, "that your advice is extremely good. But unfortunately we Mongols are brought up from childhood to shoot arrows and ride. Such a habit is not easy to lay aside. However, this time I have taken your words to heart."

Upon saying this, the emperor then turned to his attendant, proclaiming: "In the future I shall do exactly as the holy Immortal advises."

On a later occasion, the khan summoned those of his sons traveling in the ordo, as well as other princes, high ministers, and officers, and said to them: "The Chinese reverence this holy Immortal just as you revere Heaven; and I am more than ever convinced that he is indeed a Being from Heaven!" The khan then proceeded to repeat to them everything the master taught him on various occasions, adding: "Heaven sent this holy Immortal to tell me these things. Do engrave them upon your hearts."

The chronicler records: "It was indeed two months before he again went hunting."[55]

The khan pleaded with Qiu Chuji not to begin his trip back to Beijing alone. They could travel together. Wouldn't Qiu Chuji like to travel with the camp back to China? The master and his entourage might enjoy the ordo's conveniences for some further miles along this difficult thoroughfare. But the master declined. His excellency had promised Qiu Chuji he would be home in China within three years, and that time had come. China was still war ravaged. The Jin had not yet given up. Hunger and decay still ruled. Starving young people needed the protection of his monasteries. He was needed at home.

"My sons," said the khan, "are soon arriving. There are still one or two points in your previous discourses which are not clear to me. When they have been explained, you may start on your journey."[56]

The khan wanted to make a final present to Qiu Chuji of oxen and horses for the trip, but Qiu Chuji refused. So the khan asked his minister whether Qiu Chuji had a substantial number of disciples in China. Indeed he had, said the minister. The emperor then directed that the master's pupils should henceforth be exempted from taxation and military enslavement, and he published an edict to the same effect, sealing it with the imperial seal.

Some in the Daoist church later reflected that this was Qiu Chuji's greatest contribution to Chinese history. He used the edict to protect thousands upon thousands of young initiates who otherwise would have been drawn into the final episodes of the Mongol-Jin war. Others said Qiu Chuji's contribution was really his extraordinary evangelism. In effect, he had refounded Daoism as a formidable religious movement nearly a millennium after it ceased to be relevant at the popular level.[57]

Still, one could argue that Qiu Chuji's greatest gift was to the recollection of the life force itself. Too often a person overlooks the fount of therapeutic energy that already resides within and rather prefers the substitute of external excitements and conquests. Qiu Chuji taught the khan that those external conquests—particularly violent and sexual ones—often amount to distractions. Therapeutically speaking, these are but fleeting excitations, bringing but transitory relief before they recede and leaving us in search of the next distraction. The impotence of constant acquiescence to limbic expectations is all too noticeable to anyone who has ever become stuck in that cycle.

The limits of external distraction become even more obvious when one is introduced to the seeming volcano of energy theorized and cherished by Qiu Chuji. To feel this special interior force, so different qualitatively from the experiences attached to the outward drives, Qiu Chuji taught that one need only notice and savor the vitalizing somatic flow attending the journey of one's own breath. Start to cherish this breath as a gift and treasure. Then, once one has some capacity in recognizing the operations of the Way in this limited arena, the flow of vitalizing qi soon becomes apparent in the experience of each and every phenomenon.

Today, cutting-edge research in the neurology of spiritual experience appears consistent with Qiu Chuji's Daoist explanations of the inner alchemy. The ascetic privations taught to Qiu Chuji by his master Lunatic Wang Zhe—such as celibacy, fasting, and discomfort from the natural elements—are all pre-dominantly frustrations for the limbic system of the brain, the seat of primary, innate, preorganized emotions shared with so many animals. This is the arena of basic instinct and drive, gen-erating strong and direct influences on autonomic function, which makes their impulses difficult to ignore. In most animals, those limbic activities go directly to the brain stem and out to the body, stimulating immediate instinctual actions.

Yet, in primates such as ourselves, elaborate network connec-tions have also developed between regions of the limbic system and those of the prefrontal cortex, the most recent addition to mammalian brains. These prefrontal cortex regions (set in our foreheads just above our eyes) are especially developed in pri-mates and function as the seat of abstraction, executive func-tion, planning, and contextualization. When these activate in consort with limbic activities, the effect is often a tempering of the limbic system. Studied with PET scans and fMRI, these tempering connections between the prefrontal cortex and the limbic areas appear to be among the most primary networks of spiritual experiences.[58]

From a cognitive view, the affects produced through limbic tempering practices (asceticism) can be therapeutic, powerful, and permanently transformative. In some times and places these affects have been called awakening or enlightenment, in others nirvana or self-annihilation in God. In the case of medieval Daoist theory, Qiu Chuji preferred to call this activity *spirit puri-fication*. No matter the nomenclature, by exercising the limbic and prefrontal cortical connections together, one's limbic system seems to be able to find calm, temperance, and even comfort in an often cold and frustrating universe.

Earlier Daoist practitioners, from the millennium before the common era, once called this subtle inward transfer of one's attention the Inner Work (*neiyeh*).[59] Then, of course, Master Zhuang himself had written the magnificent Inner Chapters, mapping these operations on all phenomenon. In the footsteps of this ancient tradition, Lunatic Wang Zhe and his most successful founding student Qiu Chuji introduced the Inner Alchemy. The Quanzhen group took the philosophic and poetic insights of earlier masters and made a positive psychology of them: a science of nurturing and savoring a life energy we each already store within ourselves but barely think to notice. Perhaps the Quanzhen group helps us remember only this: the vitality we already hold is treasure enough; our life's work is but the struggle to remember and cherish what is already ours.

Chinggis Khan seems to have learned this. The record indicates that the khan himself had hardly exhausted his own interest in these vital interior energies at the time he and Qiu Chuji parted. Letters from the emperor kept catching up with Qiu Chuji all the while he traveled home along the Silk Road. He received a downright chatty letter from the khan in October of 1223:

> You left me and set out on your travels in the spring and were still on the road during the great heats of summer. I hope you have suffered no inconvenience and were well supplied with post-horses. I hope that you were always provided with plenty to eat and drink and were never stinted. . . . I hope that the common people came to hear you. Are you well and in good spirits? Here I am always thinking about you, O Holy Immortal! I have never forgotten you. Do not forget me.[60]

Arthur Waley, the greatest European scholar of Asian religion of the last century and the translator of Qiu Chuji's travelogue, notes the simple and colloquial nature of these sentences and wonders whether they may have been personally dictated by Chinggis Khan *in Chinese*.

Qiu Chuji received a similar message in January of 1224, and from there the record of their relationship ends. Who knows for how long Chinggis Khan went on to consider the Way? Historians record that, in the year 1227, while wrapping up his final campaign against the Tangut in central China, Chinggis Khan fell from his horse while hunting. He succumbed to a fever brought on by the accident on August 18 of that year.[61] His empire lasted until gunpowder and ocean trade ended the dominance of the steppe nomad, though his brilliant cavalry caracole would be studied and resuscitated by both Allied and Axis tacticians in the tank battles of the Second World War.[62]

There is no evidence that the khan ever seriously considered giving up the enjoyment of his harem. Genetic estimates claim that Chinggis Khan has sixteen million current descendants.[63]

And Qiu Chuji never learned of the terrible accident that finally killed the immortal Chinggis Khan, for Qiu Chuji himself went on to join the immortals later that same week, at the advanced (though credible) age of seventy-nine.

The chronicler records that as Qiu Chuji had approached the end of his journey home along the great thoroughfare of the Silk Road, he came to town upon town with populations extraordinarily excited by his return. As spiritual adviser to the emperor, Qiu Chuji had become famous. Thousands came to be blessed by him and to spend some few precious moments in his presence. Finally when he reached Shaanxi Province and its city of Datong, the huge numbers of admirers having come out to glimpse the master could no longer be controlled. The chronicler records that, after a week of trying to calm the crowds, the regional governor decided to hold a formal ceremony recognizing the authority of the old monk and his new Quanzhen sect. He presented the master with a gift of three exquisite wild geese captured in the province.

The next day, Qiu Chuji took the birds with him on his habitual daily walk along the outskirts of town. When he reached a neighboring lake he borrowed a small boat and took the birds out. Then he set them free. "He watched them for a little while dart and play amid the windy waves," says the chronicler, "in manifest delight at their freedom." There in the boat, as the birds crossed over the horizon, a subtle energy coursed through the old master, and so he wrote a poem to capture the vital spirit of the moment:

> They tended you to no purpose, save to bring you to the kitchen;
> And only my kind intent saved you from becoming a meal.
> In light skiff I took you out and set you among the huge waves
> There to wait, till at autumn's end your wings are fully grown.[64]

6

MARY LOU WILLIAMS

Jazz for the Soul

Praise him with trumpet sound;
   praise him with lute and harp!

Praise him with tambourine and dance;
   praise him with strings and pipe!

Praise him with clanging cymbals;
   praise him with loud clashing cymbals!

Let everything that breathes praise the Lord!
   Praise the Lord!

—Psalm 150

LOVE

There is a plethora of great Christian confessional literature, from Augustine who initiated the form, to Margery Kempe, Teresa of Avila, Cardinal Newman, and even Leo Tolstoy. However, when I remembered that Mary Lou Williams walked off the jazz bandstand at age forty-four, suddenly and at the very height of her fame,

improvisational ability, and compositional authority, I was viscer-
ally reminded of the panic and self-loathing that could make just about
anyone want simply to exit the stage. Therefore in this case the mas-
terpiece under consideration is not a book. It is music composed to
accompany a liturgy, Mary Lou's Mass. *Williams wrote it to cap-*
ture her feeling of suffering—and its apotheosis.

    Central to this story is the swing rhythm itself. When locked into
this rhythm, one's whole body follows the pattern of a wave—over a
curve, crest after crest, building up and letting go, and always pro-
pelling forward. It can create this oceanic pull in a crowd all at once,
together, everyone riding the same wave, everyone rising and falling
to the same pulse. It's powerful. Mary Lou Williams was recognized
even in her youth to be among the greatest masters of this rhythm. In
her maturity she decided to harness the power of that group feeling for
a higher purpose—to remind people to take care of each other.

NIGHTLIFE

When Mary Lou Williams was seventeen years old, Fats Waller
declared her to be a stride piano genius. At twenty-seven she was
recognized among the greatest jazz pianists of the swing era. She
also wrote and arranged for the biggest bandleaders in America, including Benny Goodman, Duke Ellington, Count Basie,
Earl Hines, Louis Armstrong, Gus Arnheim, Glen Gray, and
Tommy Dorsey. At age thirty she became teacher of the bebop
generation, especially the towering pianists Thelonious Monk
and Bud Powell. At thirty-six she conducted players of the New
York Philharmonic at Carnegie Hall for her own jazz masterpiece, *Zodiac Suite*, and consequently became part of the American musical canon. Then at forty-four she fell apart.

    "I was in Paris," she remembered. "I was in my hotel room
alone and all of a sudden it seemed as though everything I had

done up to then meant absolutely nothing. I was despondent because everything seemed meaningless and useless."

Behold the story of an apogee among the twentieth century's greatest masses, composed by an African American woman from Pittsburg who would not squander her gift.

"I haven't the least idea what I'm doing in Europe," Mary Lou Williams wrote in her diary from Paris in 1954.[1] Yet she knew all too well. She'd gone there scrounging for work.

It had been two years since she'd seen her beloved Harlem apartment, once the very epicenter of the bebop revolution in jazz harmony. She could remember her Harlem living room exactly. It had three primary features: an upright Baldwin piano; a phonograph player; and a white rug where she encouraged guests to lounge without shoes. Back in the old days, especially during World War II, Mary Lou's cozy living room had been a salon in which to reflect on the deeper structures of music, namely harmonic development. Very significant changes had been occurring in this regard, one could hear it all around—on the radio, in phonograph recording, and also in film scores. After their regular gigs with big band orchestras let out early each morning, Mary Lou's friends would all come over to her Harlem apartment to gather on her white rug. "The guys used to come to my house then," she remembered. "Miles, Mel Tormé, Sarah Vaughan, Dizzy—all the boppers. Even Benny Goodman."[2] They'd listen perhaps to Stravinsky, Schoenberg, Delius, or Bartók just as soon as they'd play the latest Duke Ellington compositions. Often Ellington's own arranger Billy Strayhorn was there to give comment about what he was hearing and what the Ellington band was doing. Dizzy Gillespie typically showed up with his arranger Tadd Dameron. Then they'd all go over to the piano and figure out whatever figure, chord, or rhythm may have intrigued them from their listening. Dig the new tritone harmonies and atonalities. How could one even *use* those new ideas, let alone *utilize* them?

Also ever present in Mary Lou's apartment, though rarely along with others during her salons, were two shy pianists who played Minton's Playhouse in the Cecil Hotel. "Bud Powell, Monk, and I were inseparable," she remembered. "During the 40s that was every day, every night, all of the time."[3] They'd come by even after the Minton's after-hours party closed, when the rest of New York was already up and going to work. Mary Lou turned over in bed one morning to see a fully clothed man sleeping on the twin mattress next to her. She screamed. He fled into the closet. Her dresses fell from the hangers all about him. It was Thelonious Monk. Her last guest had left the apartment door unlocked so Monk just let himself in. He had a new musical idea he wanted Mary Lou to hear. Then of course he didn't want to wake her and so he himself nodded off on the twin bed. They laughed about that one for years; it was one of Mary Lou's favorite stories.[4]

Back then Mary Lou and Monk especially enjoyed trying out "Zombie Chords" together, what Mary Lou had taken to calling the strange harmonic extensions they heard in the atonality of contemporary horror film scores. Monk was really adept at using these. Often one couldn't anticipate what sort of chord Monk might choose next, he might go in any direction at any time.

"Thelonious is a nice guy," she later told an oral historian from Yale. "He's odd. He doesn't talk much at all."[5] The other Minton's pianist, Bud Powell, was like that when he was melancholic. Frustrated stage managers sometimes couldn't even get him to play. But sometimes he was manic, and that's when Bud Powell bopped. He could get fired up and display incredible charisma. Bud Powell might play a few breakneck bars of Chopin's "Minute Waltz" and then suddenly stop. And then start again. And stop.

And look around the room suspiciously. Audiences loved his energy. He could be manic in expressing his romantic interest in Mary Lou, as well, although he was fourteen years her junior. He called her Baby Doll, but she expressed no return interest except familial love. "I have been sister and mother to many musicians," she later said of their relationship.[6]

Bud Powell, when Mary Lou first met him when he was sixteen, was still predominantly a right-hand player, like his piano hero Art Tatum. At Minton's, and elsewhere after hours, he played mostly lead keyboard improvisation at the same breakneck bebop pace as a horn. Mary Lou could hear Bud's talent— just incredible touch even at his young age—but she herself, of course, was a master of the rhythmic left hand. In her early career as a big band pianist, Mary Lou had swung the whole orchestra from those low notes, and rhythms would always constitute the foundation of her pianistic voice. She thought Bud needed to develop his. A friend remembered a typical lesson in Mary Lou's apartment. "She had a little ruler in her hand and she used to hit Bud on his hand and say, 'Left hand, Bud, left hand.'"[7] Bud finally did figure out the rhythmic voice of his left hand while working at Mary Lou's Baldwin piano. It arrived suddenly, after weeks of work. When it came, he yelled out to Mary Lou in the bedroom. Had she heard? Had he gotten it right? Yes, she called back. She'd heard. She'd been monitoring his progress. Indeed the great Bud Powell found his left hand in Mary's Harlem apartment.

Then the whole music scene decayed rapidly after the war. In New York, 52nd Street turned into an all-night party, black and white. Filled barrooms and clubs made many players flush with cash and fame, and the combination did not always suit their mental health. At the same time, heroin flooded American ports, fed by the free peacetime flow of traffic, now global. Police in all American cities increased their already copious racial profiling procedures.[8]

Perhaps the seeds of Mary Lou's Parisian breakdown in 1954 can first be marked by the beating of Bud Powell in 1945. Orchestra work brought him to Philadelphia, where police found him after hours wandering and intoxicated along Broad Street. They beat him viciously, especially his head. Ten days later and back in New York, his mother sent him to Bellevue Hospital, still crazed but now complaining of headaches. Doctors ordered two months observation at a psychiatric facility. He was twenty-one years old.

Shortly thereafter, in the summer of 1946, Charlie Parker ended up missing Mary Lou's Carnegie Hall performance of *Zodiac Suite*. She was approaching the height of her career, conducting members of the New York Philharmonic through her most mature and enduring jazz compositions and arrangements; but her friend Charlie Parker was strung out and living in Los Angeles at the Civic Hotel in Little Tokyo. On the night of his arrest, he'd come down to the lobby naked, twice, and upon returning to his room set it ablaze. Police beat Parker before they locked him up, but a merciful judge assigned him hospice instead of jail time, a six-month stay in the Camarillo State Hospital.[9]

Around this time Mary Lou had been running around New York with Billie Holiday and Holiday's boyfriend Joe Guy, a trumpeter. Billie Holiday partied hard. Some remembered her shooting up nonchalantly over the kitchen sink at apartment parties. But the Federal Bureau of Narcotics had agents infiltrating the music scene. Holiday and Guy were arrested in Holiday's apartment in May of 1947. When police strip-searched Holiday there, she is said to have protested by urinating on her own floor. She was jailed for eleven months in Alderson Federal Prison

Camp in West Virginia for heroin possession.[10] Eleven days after her release she played to a sold-out audience at Carnegie Hall. But even Billie Holiday couldn't play Carnegie Hall every night, and any venue with a bar was now closed to her (and would be for the rest of her life) since her New York City Cabaret Card was suspended along with the heroin conviction. Mary Lou tried to find her work, but to little avail.

Then in November of 1947 Bud Powell wound up in a fight in Harlem. Due to his psychiatric record, a judge sent Powell directly to Creedmoor Psychiatric Center in Queens, which utilized electroshock as Powell's primary treatment and charged his mother for the procedures. Perhaps he was lucky not to have been prescribed lobotomy, then in its heyday. Released eleven months later, Mary Lou found Bud Powell a few gigs where she worked, at a club called Café Society. But after his incarceration at Creedmoor Bud increasingly just sat at the piano stool morose. "He just sat there and looked at people," she remembered.[11]

Mary Lou had her own problems. Although she avoided liquor out of fear of following her mother into alcoholism, she kept getting fired from her regular piano gig at Café Society for using marijuana in the changing room (she called it "smoking tea"). Experiments with Benzedrine tablets and coffee never ended well either.[12]

Perhaps the final blow came on an evening in August of 1951 while Thelonious Monk was visiting his mother, caring for her during her cancer treatments. Bud Powell brought some friends over to keep Thelonious company. Instead of disturbing Mrs. Monk, Thelonious chose to come out to the street to sit in their car. A narcotics squad approached and shook them down. An envelope of heroin appeared at Monk's feet. They convicted Monk and everyone else in the car of heroin possession. Monk claimed it wasn't his. Monk's past marijuana conviction mandated jail time and, even more damaging a penalty, the loss of his New York City Cabaret Card. Like Billie Holiday, Monk could no longer play clubs serving alcohol in New York. Given Bud Powell's psychiatric record, a judge hospitalized him for nearly a year and a half, through to 1953. There he was medicated with a new drug, Largactil, made of chlorpromazine. It had been invented the year before as a blunt pharmaceutical alternative to electroshock and lobotomy. Largactil, in effect, was a chemical lobotomy in pill form.

Sometime during those dark days, Bud Powell handed Mary Lou a poem he had written for her, which he titled "The Great Awakening:"

> I was sitting in the garden one late afternoon
> And out of the sky a feather fell
> And not a moment too soon.
> I didn't stop to regard from what source it came
> I only know it lifted me out of the depths of shame.

After several verses of tormented confession about his life misled, Powell realized that God had sent a dove to watch over him, which had dropped the awakening feather.

Mary Lou put down the following comment in her notebook: "I pray that some day Bud will know how straight he was when he wrote that."[13]

So Mary Lou had fled the New York scene, first to London and then to Paris. She was not quite alone in Paris. She knew people in town—Garland Wilson, James Baldwin, Hazel Scott, Mae and Mezz Mezzrow, and Inez Cavanaugh—but she wasn't living well there. Her hotel room was small and uncomfortable. It had no private bathroom. In 1954, it had been two years since she had even touched her beloved Baldwin upright piano or white rug, both collecting dust in her Harlem apartment thousands of miles away. She constantly had to hustle for money. In her diary she wrote down all kinds of apprehensions about herself and about her friends. She had terrible premonitions about Charlie Parker and was certain something awful was about to befall him.[14] And then one day her closest friend in Paris, Garland Wilson, who played piano in the gay clubs and sometimes shared a hotel room with Mary, broke down crying at the keyboard during his gig at Le Boeuf sur le Toit. The man sobbed so uncontrollably that Mary Lou could barely get him to his feet to go back to their hotel. "Deep down inside I felt something was wrong," she wrote. "All these strange things happening to me—wow! I cried inside also."[15]

Garland partied hard, but had it really been all *that* hard? Had Garland been out any more than Mary Lou? Could it have been his drinking? *Mary Lou* had in fact started drinking—after a lifelong phobia of turning into her alcoholic mother. "I was much high practically every night off champagne, my favorite drink."[16] Often she just brought her champagne back to her room, preferring to be alone. She'd been drinking when news reached her around two o'clock in the morning that Garland Wilson was in the hospital. It was too late to visit him there. She went to bed, not able to sleep. "The phone rang—my heart missed a beat—he's dead I said to myself." And indeed it was true. Her best friend in Paris was dead, a great American pianist and Mary Lou's contemporary in age.[17]

Days later, after burying Garland Wilson, an inkling of clarity finally came to her. Her entire existence had to change. She had to leave Paris. "Made up my mind then and there, and thank *God*, for I'm sure I was on my way for a real crack-up."[18] She was particularly forthright about coming to this moment when she confessed to fans and other readers of the African American magazine *Sepia* in a remarkable article that itself deserves inclusion in the canon of great American spiritual documents:

> I had been just about everywhere and done everything on the after-dark beat as a musician. And then suddenly all of this seemed unimportant, even the money. . . . I found the need for spiritual peace, the need to be able to live with myself. . . .
>
> I was in Paris. I was in my hotel room alone and all of a sudden it seemed as though everything I had done up to then meant absolutely nothing. I was despondent because everything seemed meaningless and useless.
>
> Even my beloved music, the piano I played, all seemed to have lost their appeal. So had my former associates in show business, the musicians, the night club owners and the wealthy men and women who were my patrons and who had been dining and wining me—none of them seemed important any more. . . . It was just despondency based on the fact that I felt everything I had been doing was no good.[19]

And so at age forty-four, while playing from her friend Garland Wilson's old piano stool at Le Boeuf, she let it all go. She'd exhausted all options. The need for change was too urgent to wait for a plan. The stresses and temptations of the nightlife—since childhood her only known world—had finally crushed her.

"I walked off the bandstand," she said. She told the club manager to keep her outstanding salary. To her mind she was never going back.[20]

Charlie Parker died in 1955, age thirty-four.
Art Tatum died in 1956, age forty-seven.
Billie Holiday died in 1959, age forty-four.

Joe Guy died in 1962, age forty-two.

Tadd Dameron died in 1965, age forty-eight.

Bud Powell died in 1966, age forty-one.

RETREAT

The several years Mary Lou spent back in Harlem while recovering from her Parisian breakdown she later explained guardedly. "I just stayed in the house for two years; I turned the radio on once, heard Art Tatum had died, and turned it off again."[21]

Art Tatum had been Mary Lou's contemporary at the piano, and the loss certainly struck her. Yet her first years back in Harlem, nursing what appears to have been major depression, hadn't ensued quite so simply. In fact, it had taken a good deal just to get Mary Lou back to the States at all. When she walked off the stage of Le Boeuf, she did so without a clue about her future. She no longer had any vision, no basic daily plan, let alone a purpose for her life. In fact, to her mind she had certainty of just one thing: *Music had failed her.* Surely she had pursued the art to the very precipice of her considerable talent, intellect, and human energy. What had it achieved? Apparently it had led to an alcoholic breakdown, while similar musical energies were leading a preponderance of her colleagues and friends to early deaths. The music they had all so adored and served to the point of veneration had failed Mary Lou as it seemed to have failed most everyone around her.

She'd only gotten back to Harlem at all through the considerable support of her closest friends. Pianist Hazel Scott, Mary Lou's best friend from the Café Society circle and visiting Paris that summer in 1954, after months of searching finally located Mary Lou holed up in the suburban home of a young Parisian boyfriend who still lived with his grandmother.[22] There Hazel Scott accomplished two things that saved her friend's life.

First, she arranged Mary Lou's fare home to Harlem from a wealthy European jazz patron.[23]

Second, Hazel Scott told Mary Lou to start praying. Specifically she told her to start reading Psalms.

"Bless you Scott may you wail until . . ." had been the unfinished benediction Mary Lou wrote down for Hazel in her diary while still living in the Parisian suburb with her boyfriend. "This great and wonderful talent introduced me to what really saved me—*God*—that is what I was searching for."

"Had always kept a Bible around," Mary Lou explained in these initial notes of her realization, "but obviously could not reach Him—allow me to say He is the greatest and in pure musician's language the grooviest."

"Just think," she'd concluded in these initial notes, "one can still have as much fun—yet observe 10 commandments, etc. By all means try to love, even love your enemies for 'God is Love.' Just think He sent me a messenger and I tried to turn my back on Him—but the guy was patient."[24]

That had been Mary Lou's immediate report of her awakening. It had happened suddenly. Before this there had been just inklings brought on by tourist visits to cathedrals throughout Paris as well as some private investigations into occult books. But Hazel Scott's visit and counsel to pray launched an abrupt beginning for Mary Lou, a veritable new life.

Of course, sudden inspiration did not constitute the final realization of her new spiritual composition, but could only offer a few notes and phrases toward a beginning. Mary Lou would soon come to consider this initial inspiration as the right first step down a long and still difficult path. "It was torture as I groped there in the dark trying to make contact with God," she explained to readers of *Sepia*.

> Slowly, however, the deep spell of despondency that had held me in its grasp for days began to lift and I saw things I have never seen before in my mind's eye.
>
> Bright things, clean and pure . . . beautiful things, people— not ugly, drab and sinful as I knew them, but people who were living and acting as they should—as children of God.
>
> In my efforts to get through to God, I felt great relief. For the first time in days, the cloud lifted and I began to feel like living again. I asked God which way I should go.[25]

Now Mary Lou could hope with some confidence that her path might be long, that she need not necessarily suffer the same miserable demise of so many friends and colleagues, and that finally she might still do something significant with her life. Although no longer trusting her music, she still didn't know what her purpose could be.

Her divine messenger, Hazel Scott, managed to get Mary Lou back to Harlem and settled in her old apartment. It still held her white rug and beloved Baldwin, though Mary Lou now barely acknowledged the instrument. The keys no longer held any attraction for her, still symbolizing as they did the instrument of her demise. So she left the piano there in the living room untouched. She didn't have people over anymore either, not like in the old days. She just stayed at home and meditated and prayed or sometimes walked about the neighborhood. She later rightly acknowledged these years as a period of retreat and of self-treatment for depression.

In its earliest days, Hazel Scott came around each Sunday to gather Mary Lou for prayer at the Abyssinian Baptist Church, Harlem's great Gothic and Tudor revival edifice on 138th Street. There Hazel Scott happened to reign as first lady, the wife to Reverend Adam Clayton Powell Jr., also Harlem's delegate to the U.S. House of Representatives. Hazel Scott herself was Trinidad born and still Catholic, though she attended her husband's Baptist ministry most often. Mary Lou participated fervently from the pews, often lingering after services to continue reciting Psalms or to offer her own direct words of prayer.

Then one weekday, when the Baptist church was closed and the people of Harlem bustled through the business of the day, Mary Lou found herself simply wandering the streets. She did not exactly go about aimlessly, but rather she looked for some meaningful venue in which to perform her life. Then, on 142nd Street and Seventh Avenue, she made a fateful and inspired discovery. She saw the open doors of Our Lady of Lourdes Church and was drawn to peek inside. "The Catholic Church was the only one I could find open anytime of day," she later said.[26]

There, in the strange Catholic pews, Mary Lou Williams had an insight once shared by one who would become a patron saint of Europe, St. Teresa Benedicta of the Cross. Edith Stein, too, while in Frankfurt on vacation from her philosophical studies at the university, had also walked by a local Catholic cathedral to discover open doors and a curious gravitational pull to look within. There Edith Stein saw what Mary Lou Williams also observed: people talking to God privately, personally, as though just come in for an informal chat in the middle of the busy day. The potential for this kind of intimate relationship with divinity impressed each of these women so deeply that both observers began feeling the pull to visit to the cathedral as often as possible. Each found herself there most every day, remaining for hours of intimate conversation. They had each discovered the special quality of the Catholic cathedral to induce calm and meaning, especially through private prayer.[27]

For both women, the young German Jew of 1916 and the middle-aged African American of 1955, the *feeling of prayer* would become the shared arena of their spiritual contribution. It is not at all gratuitous to invoke the saint's name in comparison to the insights that would soon be contributed by Mary Lou Williams herself, which is the amazing bloom and fruition of spiritual genius we will now observe.

Mary Lou admitted that her novitiate days in the Catholic church had been enthusiastic and unsubtle, to say the least.[28]

To help her in these early Catholic investigations, she located a willing partner, Lorraine Gillespie. Besides Hazel Scott, Mary Lou found in New York upon her return an especially warm pair of friends in the Gillespies, Dizzy and Lorraine. Of all the musicians who had survived the bebop years, Dizzy himself was perhaps the most professionally and emotionally stable. He and Lorraine both, very early in Mary Lou's withdrawal and retreat, insisted on visiting their old friend in her apartment, often bearing gifts of food and valuables. While Dizzy himself at that time was not interested in pursuing any formal spiritual interests (he would become Baha'i in 1968), Lorraine was curious. She and Mary Lou became a set for the next several years as they went to Eucharist services at Lourdes Church, attended Jesuit classes at St. Ignatius Loyola Church on Park Avenue, and otherwise stopped by cathedrals and chapels throughout the city for more private rounds of silent prayer and divine conversation.

Soon enough, each of the women had gained the vigor of the novitiate, but especially Mary Lou. "I got a sign that everybody should pray everyday," she explained. (She said the sign came to her in the form of "sounds," but otherwise did not clarify what she meant by this, whether as words or perhaps as music).²⁹ She rounded up everyone she could possibly bring with her to Lourdes Church services, including Bud Powell, Thelonious Monk (said to have fainted from fright upon entering the cathedral), Dizzy Gillespie when willing to appease his wife Lorraine, Lucille Armstrong (Louis's wife), and really anyone Mary Lou could corral.³⁰ Miles Davis teased her gently by calling her "Reverend Williams." He kept asking her to record with him, but she still wasn't going anywhere near the piano.³¹

Mary Lou owned a Royal typewriter that saw far more use in those years than her Baldwin upright piano; she constructed and mimeographed elaborate prayer instructions for distribution to friends and even offered these openly on street corners. Her notes included the following: "Prayers to be read every night before retiring"; "Prayers to say at the crucifix everyday"; "Daily Routines for praying." She constructed lists of dozens of saints and their purviews of therapy and inspiration: for "writers"; "musicians, singers, television"; "orator, teachers, scholars"; "skin diseases, hospitals, invalid, headaches, insanity, nervous disease"; "lovers"; "impossible things"; "servants"; "retreats." She wrote directions for moving effectively about the many altars of the church while meditating. Her recommended cycle of prayer was thirty-six days, four times the length of the standard Catholic novena retreat period. She also advocated fasting.

"*Important*," she warned. "Start All Prayers Between 6 and 7 a.m. Christ arose around that time."

"*Urgent*: Read set of Psalms before retiring."³²

For herself, Mary Lou constructed her own private liturgy, typing out hundreds of numbered and collated names of family and friends to pray for. Her list covered her first husband John Williams and second husband Shorty Baker; old band leader

Andy Kirk; Josh White, Paul Robeson, and Lena Horne from Café Society; Bud Powell and Thelonious Monk (of course); the Gillespies; the Armstrongs; Hazel Scott and Adam Clayton Powell Jr.; Billy Strayhorn; Billie Holiday; Tadd Dameron; Mae and Mezz Mezzrow; Teddy Wilson; Duke Ellington; as well as Charlie Parker and Art Tatum while they were alive and then their souls after they passed suddenly in 1955 and 1956 respectively. Also on her list were the individuals and families of Cab Calloway, Ella Fitzgerald, Eartha Kitt, Joe Louis, Ida James, Rose Murphy, Nellie Lutcher, Bea Ellis, Nat King Cole, Roy Eldridge, Max Roach, Errol Garner, Oscar Peterson, Oscar Pettiford, Pearl and Bill Bailey, Johnny Hodges, Ben Webster, Billy Taylor, Sarah Vaughan, Stan Kenton, Nipsey Russell, her sister Mamie's "next door neighbors," "Joe the drummer," "the Palace Market guys," "the Amsterdam Bank messenger and family," and many more. Mrs. Eleanor Roosevelt somehow also made it into Mary Lou's prayers.[33]

And always she prayed for the soul of Garland Wilson, her friend departed in Paris.

"What were you praying for?" a reporter asked her about those novitiate years.

"I was praying for people," she said. "I was praying for the world."[34]

REBIRTH

In December of 1957 *Ebony* magazine reported on the existence of 550,000 black Catholics in America, including 57,000 in New York. By then, Mary Lou Williams and Lorraine Gillespie were among them, having converted together on May 9, 1957, the day after Mary Lou's forty-seventh birthday.[35] Their mutual confessor, Jesuit Father Anthony Woods, had overseen the baptisms.

Baptism itself seems to have curbed Mary Lou's novitiate enthusiasm to evangelize so boldly and erratically. She then turned her attentions more directly to the first cause of her heart, victims of the nightlife she once knew so well. She began collecting indigent and needy musicians from around Harlem into her apartment, "dope addicts and alcoholics," she called them, and offered temporary housing, clothing, and food, especially during periods of attempted recoveries.[36]

When Mary Lou relayed her reasons for returning to America in the first place, she always told people it had been her haunting premonition in Paris of the demise of Charlie Parker. Just months following Mary Lou's return to New York, Charlie Parker finally did die, at age thirty-four, while sitting on a couch watching daytime television. Mary Lou joined a steering committee along with the Gillespies to raise funds for Parker's burial expenses and bereaved children. The successful fundraising episode gave Mary Lou the idea to open her own charitable organization for the recovery of musicians from drug and alcohol abuse, which she named Bel Canto. Her idea was to run thrift stores stocked with gifts from New York department stores as well as from wealthy friends. She opened two storefronts for the organization over the ensuing years. She also began keeping her home open for needy musicians who were serious about recovery.

She still felt no inclination and had no inkling of when she might go back to the piano. "My music was dead to me. Completely." "I also got the feeling at that time," she said, "that I would never play jazz again nor would I return to my old life."[37] Her new spiritual pursuits—of charity and prayer—took up the endless hours she had spent with music. Given her genius and her exceptional drive, it is little wonder that she soon became talented in her new skills, especially in prayer. When not out on her corner trying to inspire young passersby neighbors to achieve for themselves (she especially loved children) or harassing managers of Macy's and Bloomingdale's for donations, she spent her time in church, typically alone.

Her schedule during these years was simple and repetitive. After attending three mass services in the morning back-to-back from seven o'clock until noon, Mary Lou would get home quickly to prepare lunch for her needy house guests and then return to the empty cathedral for a full afternoon of solitary prayer.[38] Perhaps Father Anthony Woods had introduced Mary Lou to the silent prayer and meditation techniques of St. Teresa of Avila, or perhaps Mary Lou discovered these for herself, but over the years she relied less on her typed sheets and mimeographed instructions and focused more on the opening of her heart to the suffering of her Savior.

Many times every day she walked through the articulate architecture and purposeful lighting of the cathedral, directing, as all cathedrals do, one's visual attention *upward*. She then traversed a central processional path through reverential pews, leading her to the cathedral's primary visual communication: a gruesome depiction of Jesus, nailed with iron spikes through bloody stigmata to a cross.

The entirety of the silent building declared a story of suffering and its apotheosis. So many times over these years in conversion classes with Father Anthony Woods she had reviewed St. Paul's understanding of that mysterious apotheosis: "Let each of you look not to your own interests," Paul had preached to the Philippians, "but to the interests of others." How was one to achieve this? By following the example of Jesus.

> Let the same mind be in you that was in Christ Jesus, who, though he was in the form of God, did not regard equality with God as something to be exploited, but emptied himself, taking the form

of a slave, being born in human likeness. And being found in human form, he humbled himself and became obedient to the point of death—even death on a cross.

PHILIPPIANS 2:4–8

The lesson church elders had since called *kenosis*, of emptying oneself, of giving one's life gifts even unto death, was not only expressed in Paul's epistle. The artistry and structure of the entire Catholic cathedral reflected a truth Mary Lou now knew personally, experientially. This was a story Mary Lou herself had lived. She had known suffering all her life—from her birth out of wedlock to an alcoholic and uncaring mother, to poverty, to a life lived since adolescence in pitiful hotel rooms, to a career controlled by powerful and often abusive men, to a society organized by violent racial hierarchies, to her own corrosive turn to drugs and alcohol—finally to the breakdown of any existential meaning at all—and she had discovered how to get through this. *Even in suffering, attend to the suffering of others. Give and love and pray. So will suffering make its apotheosis. God is Love.* Little wonder that, sometimes, through her hours of silent prayer in the silent church, she found herself talking less and listening more.

"It was so peaceful and quiet I could think," she said. As she became increasingly adept in spending long periods in the comfort of silent meditation, attuned to the suffering of her Savior and the world, she began to notice interior sounds which truly confused and surprised her. "I began hearing the greatest musical sounds while praying. It was inspirational for me musically to pray in the quiet church." Also, "I heard the greatest sounds while meditating."[39]

Still convinced that music itself had been her downfall, especially jazz music, she treated these sounds suspiciously. Perhaps she mentioned the affect to her friend Lorraine Gillespie, who in turn may have said something about it to Dizzy, for Dizzy then went and located a saxophone-playing priest who convinced Mary Lou that what she'd come to believe about jazz music was nonsense. Her musical tradition held no essential ingredient of waywardness or sin. "You play that music and offer it up as a prayer for others," the priest advised.[40]

From that moment on, Dizzy Gillespie would not let up. "After a while I had to get back to my piano playing," she told a Yale historian. "Everybody was worrying me to death including Dizzy Gillespie. 'C'mon, let's get goin'.'"[41] He harangued Mary Lou to perform some of her pieces from *Zodiac Suite* with him at the Newport Jazz Festival that summer after her baptism. She agreed. She did not particularly admire her own playing for that performance, but it brought her back to the piano, and within some several months of playing about town (Dizzy and Lorraine had signed as her personal managers) not only had she gained her old talent back, but now she felt she exceeded her considerable earlier capacity. "I suddenly felt that I had at last reached my highest plane in music, for everyone said that I was playing as though inspired. To those who would listen, I told them that the reason I was playing that way was because I had at last found God and that He was my inspiration and guidance."[42]

Later in life she stated the inspiration more succinctly: "I figure now that when I play it is a form of prayer."[43]

BLACK CHRIST

Fortuitously in 1959, the impish new pope, John XXIII, often photographed with a lit cigarette and grinning, himself initiated a radical conversation among Catholic communities worldwide. In the aftermath of World War II and in a period witnessing the death pangs of European colonial rule, the pope proclaimed that many traditional facets of the Catholic church needed updating. He called a council of all cardinals, archbishops, and bishops, over three thousand clergy, the largest such gathering in the church's history. Together they were to extend "a renewed cordial invitation to the faithful of the separated communities to participate with us in this quest for unity and grace, for which so many souls long in all parts of the world."[44] For, in fact, the world had just recently suffered the unnatural deaths of over forty million of its human inhabitants, and fearsome technology now existed that could wipe out many hundreds of millions more. This pope wished to offer his Church to the world as a means through which people everywhere might move forward together, "in this quest for unity and grace," as the pontiff had so beautifully phrased his hope for Vatican II.

Yet change is always difficult, even in the face of a potential worldwide failure of the old ways. Over the next decades, through all four autumn sessions of Vatican II (1962–1965) and well beyond, conservative European understandings of Catholicism resisted the new global reality. Besides debate about the role of Jews in world history (itself a related battlefield of meaning we must reserve for another time), it was *prayer* that would face the most resisted postcolonial overhaul of them all.

It could not have been entirely with naivete that just before the first meeting of the contentious council, in the fall of 1962, John XXIII pushed through the offices of the Holy See the canonization of a South American of African descent, Martin de Porres. There had been African saints before. Indeed Augustine was African. But African American was a more recent category, increasingly with its own symbolic significance worldwide. So the Pope found an African American saint in the Blessed Martin de Porres. Born out of wedlock in 1579 in Peru to a Spanish noble father who abandoned him and a freed African slave,

Martin de Porres never achieved ordination by the Dominican brothers in his own lifetime. But by 1837 the memory of Martin de Porres had realized such acclaim in the Americas that Pope Gregory XVI declared his beatitude, a step removed from sainthood. This story of an African-descended "lay brother" of the Dominicans, who traveled through the impoverished Peruvian countryside to serve his beleaguered kind, building hospitals and orphanages wherever he went, Saint of the Broom, as he would soon be named, resonated profoundly with diverse Catholic communities, not least in the United States.[45]

In the spring of 1962, when Mary Lou's confessor Father Anthony Woods heard the papal announcement of the impending canonization of Martin de Porres, the Jesuit contacted Mary. He had a wonderful idea. He truly hoped Mary Lou would consider it, although he approached her cautiously. As always Mary Lou remained protective of any interventions in her music. It had taken considerable effort even to have gotten her back to playing out at all. But, the priest wondered, would Mary Lou just perhaps consider composing something to play to honor the inaugural feast day of the new saint?

Mary Lou agreed instantaneously. Of course. It made perfect sense, musically, historically, spiritually. Here finally was a vehicle for the sounds she had been collecting for all these years during liturgical prayer as well as in her silence. This composition about the African American saint—himself descended from slave grandparents like Mary Lou—would comprise her first sacral articulation. It would relay the *reality* of black suffering. It would direct listeners to the *means* of its apotheosis. And most important, for Mary Lou as an artist, it would encapsulate in composition her own feelings while in prayer. And prayer meant *so much* to her. She had to get to work right away. Canonization was scheduled to conclude the first session of the Vatican

Council in the fall, and for Mary Lou this would be a complex project. She hadn't written anything as personally meaningful to her in twenty years, not since *Zodiac Suite*. But the sounds of prayer! How could she *demonstrate* these?

Into her mind flooded all of her thoughts about church music—Palestrina and Mozart—and mysterious modern music: even Frederick Delius's Nietzschean inspired choral *Mass of Life* and Schoenberg as well. It would be choral, she decided. Except for forty seconds of dug-in swing at the piano, the six remaining minutes of the piece, its basic content and framework, would be in essence a concertato for chorus, in the manner of Heinrich Schütz or Bach. Only Mary Lou's counterpoints and harmonies resolved in ways much further "outside" than the contrapuntal polyphony or triad harmonic structures the old masters had worked with. Her harmonies owed far more to Thelonious Monk, utilizing the "Zombie chords" and strange resolutions the two had coined together in the old bebop days.

Members of her classically trained chorus had a terrible time trying to follow these unorthodox harmonies. But Mary Lou was stubborn. Were these mysterious bebop extensions and substitutions what she heard at the silent alter while alone in prayer? Then that's what she would write and that's what the chorus needed to perform. It was her own feeling of prayer. Really, what better way to articulate the confusion and beauty of the divine mystery felt while kneeling before the sacrifice of one's Savior? Those old bebop harmonies were in fact *perfect* to represent the feeling Mary Lou had while praying.

Most important, Mary Lou needed the music to convey the life lesson of St. Martin de Porres, Black Christ of the Andes: black people, white people, mixed people, all people—make a Christ of yourself. *Take care of one another.* She was totally satisfied with the result when she came to perform it at the canonization festival of St. Francis Xavier Church on 16th Street in Greenwich Village, only blocks away from the old Café Society where she'd first toyed at the piano with the themes of *Zodiac Suite* and felt her first compositional maturity. She knew she'd hit that high mark once again and eventually became extraordinarily proud of what she would achieve phonographically when she created Mary Records in order to oversee all aspects of this special music's recording, production, and even marketing, including the commission of its beautiful cover art, a simple line-drawn rendition of her own hands folded in prayer. At first she thought to call the complete album *Music for Disturbed Souls*, though ultimately she decided to frame the work more hopefully, naming it *Mary Lou Williams Presents Black Christ of the Andes*.[46]

The critics didn't understand it. Neither classical nor jazz ("neither fish nor fowl," according to one typical review), they didn't know what to write or say about it. Mary Lou actually agreed that it was neither of these. *It was what she heard when she prayed*.[47]

Despite the tepid reviews, she knew she had achieved another masterpiece, this one more profound than her first with *Zodiac Suite*. Her colleagues agreed. A year later Duke Ellington followed suit by performing and recording his *Concert of Sacred Music* in a San Francisco cathedral. John Coltrane, an especially perceptive young saxophonist around that time, produced what became perhaps the spiritual recording of the century, *A Love Supreme*.[48] Duke Ellington then came out with his second venture into sacred music, his *Second Concert of Sacred Music*, which Mary Lou preferred to the first.[49] Later also came the Mahavishnu Orchestra and many other great endeavors to make a spiritual music of jazz sounds. Mary Lou Williams did this first. *Mary Lou Williams Presents Black Christ of the Andes* has not been superseded because masterpieces of the spirit can't be. But neither would it constitute Mary Lou's last word on the matter. Hardly.

MARY LOU'S MASS

It was two years after the apocalyptic Cuban Missile Crisis and less than a year since the assassination of John F. Kennedy when Dizzy Gillespie decided the world had gotten very much out of hand. He declared his own candidacy for America's highest office in 1964 with the simple slogan: Dizzy Gillespie for President. The bumper stickers and pins are still valuable among collectors. But Dizzy could be dizzy and Dizzy could be serious, and in his performances of highest genius he was both. What did his presidential campaign really mean? With regard to steering the world's direction, a trumpeter could do a better job.

Mary Lou agreed entirely, and not just because Dizzy had named her as his choice for ambassador to the Vatican. The jazz musician, she felt, had a much better chance of bringing some healing to this world than could the visions or actions of any politician or business impresario she had come across in her considerable travels and dealings. The world was nervous and neurotic. She said this to interviewers constantly. She started writing notes toward an article on the subject (going through several formal drafts, never published, but still fascinating).[50] Basically people needed to chill out—people needed to relax. People needed to love one another. People needed to *swing* together.

Swing *together.*

This possibility seized Mary Lou. What better venue to induce swing's unifying rhythm than during the Catholic mass itself?

What better way to invoke the therapeutic power of love and communion than with a single musical wave, floating all participants upward and higher—*together*—each communing singer buoying up the next, all the auditory and visual cues of the cathedral directed together in the meaning that *God is Love?*

As soon as the idea of a swing mass came to her, she knew its production could be her only calling. She wrote three such masses, each improved over the last, all ranking with any mass in the Christian musical canon. Each combined all the elements of her love and expertise, including especially the tutelage of children, for she intended all of her masses to be performed first and foremost by the youngest members of the Catholic community. And so school children ("1,000 kids!" Mary Lou exaggerated to a confidant) performed her first mass in her hometown of Pittsburg at St. Paul's Cathedral during the Summer of Love and Riot 1967.[51] Conservative protesters picketed outside the church.

Resistance and racism did not dissuade Mary Lou from her final purpose, to lead a mass in the Vatican itself. After she had composed and performed a second mass for the lenten season of 1968 at St. Thomas the Apostle Church in Harlem, she felt ready to approach the Holy See. But by the late sixties tides in the Vatican no longer pulled in the direction of ingenuity and change. The great outsider pope John XXIII, upon his death during the first year of the Vatican Council in 1963, was replaced by a Vatican insider, Paul VI. The new pope utilized the council's remaining sessions mostly to consolidate gains by paring away items of continued controversy. Among these contentious items was the inclusion of drums and cymbals in the liturgy. Though John XXIII had wished at the time of his death that the Vatican Council would move forward in allowing these, the final interpretation favored by Paul VI of the *Council's Pastoral Constitution on the Sacred Liturgy* was otherwise. The chief architect of the document and an expert on liturgy, the Reverend Annibale Bugnini, clarified the matter by noting that percussive instruments violated the necessary "decorum in the house of God" set down by Pope St. Pius X in his *motu proprio* on sacred music of 1903.[52]

Could it have been accidental that these instruments—drums and cymbals—originated in Africa and India and Persia and the Americas and the Middle East and everywhere now increasingly slipping from European dominance?

Perhaps it is more generous to suppose the learned church elders had not recently refreshed themselves with the words of David's Psalm 150.

> Praise him with clanging cymbals;
> praise him with loud clashing cymbals!

Whatever the reason, when in 1969 Mary Lou finally did go to the Vatican herself with the clear purpose of meeting and persuading the pope, during a remarkable formal audience she stepped out of protocol to request, face to face with His Holiness, permission and blessing for her to perform a jazz mass in the Vatican itself. Naturally, she would compose and conduct it.

Are we surprised to learn the pope stood speechless at the request? That silence was met by Mary Lou and by her supporters as tacit approval, for indeed she had many Catholic supporters in this mission. The Benedictine abbot of Rome agreed for his house and seminarians to learn and perform her mass as a ritual part of the Eucharist service itself.[53]

But the Benedictines were thwarted from above. The AP wire reported on February 2, 1969: "Roman Catholic church officials today canceled the first jazz mass ever scheduled for a church in Rome."

Instead, "Miss Williams took a combo and choir of seminarians through the music as a concert after a low mass." The AP further reported: "The atmosphere of the low mass was subdued. . . . The concert after the mass was not subdued. Soon the chapel was filled with the music of a piano, bongo drums, electric guitar and a string bass."

"It was a jumping, joyous rendition. . . . The congregation joined in and clapped for encores."[54]

(Heaven forbid).

After her failures and successes at the Vatican, nothing could stop Mary Lou from performing her mass during an actual Eucharist ritual at her own personal epitome of a cathedral, St. Patrick's on Fifth Avenue in New York, attended, in Mary's words, by "millionaires and everything!" For this purpose she hired as her manager a young Jesuit priest and jazz devotee, Father Peter O'Brien, then age thirty, who indeed deserves mention as a great champion of this profound Catholic event. O'Brien named the Vatican composition *Mary Lou's Mass* and convinced dance director Alvin Ailey to choreograph and perform it in 1971. Later, after her death, Father O'Brien personally collected the documents and resources that would become the Mary Lou Williams Archive held at the Institute of Jazz Studies, Rutgers University of Newark.

It was also Father O'Brien who arranged for the musical performances of *Mary Lou's Mass* by Catholic schoolchildren—always instructed and conducted by Mary Lou herself—in cathedrals and chapels nationwide. Along with these, Mary Lou also created a lecture on the history of jazz in which she described spirituals, blues, swing, bebop, and modern jazz, with her own musical examples at the piano. Totally committed to keeping alive the memory of the African American musical tradition, she performed this lecture on college campuses across America. Eventually Duke University offered her an appointment as artist in residence, where Mary Lou spent her last days, teaching and swinging and gigging to the very end.

Her performance of *Mary Lou's Mass* as part of the Eucharist service in St. Patrick's Cathedral on February 18, 1975, however, marked her own sense of the epitome of her career. There wasn't a lick of Palestrina, Schütz, Bach, or Mozart in it. Mary Lou's entire concelebration now consisted entirely of African American rhythms and forms, from its procession through its Kyrie Eleison and Gloria and Credo finally to its concluding psalm— the mass swings to such heights, I have insufficient words to say. Please do try to locate a recording.[55] The Kyrie Eleison alone must surely rank among the greatest ever composed. "You might call it a mass for a musician's revival meeting, a celebration of peace," said the *New York Post*, "the score embodies the whole range of Black Music." "Never is it music that calls attention to itself," noted *Newsweek*. "It reflects the self-effacing style of Mary Lou Williams, both as a musician and as a woman, as well as the persuasiveness of her spiritual conviction."[56]

If I may say so, *Mary Lou's Mass* performed as it was intended in concelebration, to bring hurting and impoverished people together in love, in the end achieves the apotheosis of that love. Augustine named this feeling *caritas*—loving care. Like Augustine before her, Mary Lou Williams hit darkest despair and then chose to pay her gifts forward. She did this by raising the affect of caritas in others. She used all resources of culture and spirit available to her to achieve this. And so she too, like Augustine in his confessions, composed a masterpiece of spiritual therapy. Even so, Mary Lou acknowledged to reporters only what she'd been saying with perfect simplicity for decades: "To me, jazz is a way of praying," she insisted. "That's what the folk who created it were doing, praying."[57]

Perhaps her old friend John S. Wilson at the *New York Times* captured the triumph at St. Patrick's Cathedral best after his own stunned witnessing of Mary Lou's capstone achievement. A congregation of more than three thousand concelebrants packed the pews, he said, "and stood four and five deep along the sides and at the rear of the huge edifice." Approximately a hundred excited students drawn from four Catholic schools across New York City composed the choir, mostly African American and Latino children of color. Mary Lou had gone into each of their classrooms and personally trained them.

Miss Williams, seated at a piano on the main altar, with her bassist, Buster Williams, and her drummer, Jerry Griffin, conducted the choir from the piano while she played and her Mass was celebrated.

The singers were split into two groups . . . they sang responses to each other and also coalesced as an ensemble.

Miss Williams led into each section of her Mass with an introductory piano passage that established the mood and the rhythm and, as the singers came in and the string bass and drums took up the beat, she supported the singing with light, flowing lines that danced along under the voices. Occasionally Mr. Williams or Mr. Griffin played a brief, subdued solo, Mr. Williams plucking somberly on his bass and Mr. Griffin employing his brushes lightly and deftly.

Despite the overflow attendance, churchly decorum was maintained throughout the service. When Miss Williams concluded her Mass with a driving, joyous performance of her setting for the 150th Psalm, "Praise the Lord," however, her listeners burst into spontaneous and extended applause. Miss Williams threw kisses.[58]

Praise him with trumpet sound;
   praise him with lute and harp!

Praise him with tambourine and dance;
   praise him with strings and pipe!

Praise him with clanging cymbals;
    praise him with loud clashing cymbals!

Let everything that breathes praise the Lord!
    Praise the Lord!

III

A RECENT CASE

7

BOBBY SICHRAN AND THE
DIVINE PRESENCE

The enlightened will shine like the radiance of the sky.

—Daniel 12:3

*T*he Zohar says that God's presence penetrates into the
world sometimes. God doesn't descend in his entirety, but
some small part takes the form of a light that illuminates
*a world otherwise dark and inscrutable. Kabbalists call this light the
Shechinah. Ideas can have that aura of divine presence, like the light of
truth. Places can have that aura, like a mountain vista or a riverbed
or even a lonely road, locations where for a brief moment the world
seems to be turning in perfect order. When this aura descends on a
person, it's really something special. Medieval paintings get their ico-
nography of a halo from this idea, I think. My point is, some people
seem to carry with them the Shechinah, the divine light, even as they
navigate the turmoil of their own messed up lives.*

My friend Bobby had this aura. At least he did for me.

*Why have I tried to record some memory of my friend? Because
what he taught me during personal crisis exceeded any of the wisdom
recounted in the previous cases. And also because I loved him.*

WINTER 2013

"Mickey Bones!"

It was Bobby on my voicemail. This was the second or third time he'd called since the New Year of 2013, but again I hadn't picked up. I'd see his name on the screen and push the call to messages. I couldn't talk to him; things were too hectic. January was always crazy at the beginning of the semester, and, besides, I was still decompressing from having spent family vacation at parents' and in-laws' homes in Florida. Cathy and the kids and I had endured the past two weeks living in retirement communities with draconian children's regulations, so when we landed back home in Los Angeles in the New Year, between the kids still being stir-crazy and Cathy being upset because her mom hadn't looked so healthy and my own relationship with my parents and brother having been on autofocus for the past two weeks, I think in the middle of my own family issues I just couldn't get myself to pick up the phone.

Then I'd forget Bobby's calls or sometimes I simply avoided calling him back. Bobby could take up a lot of time. Over the past fifteen years, while I barricaded myself completely in my ever-developing domestic chaos, Bobby had remained a bachelor. I thought there was no way he could understand how time-consuming my family could be, and I also thought he could never understand how complicated a marriage could be. Basically I didn't want to hear Bobby sound off about my domestic troubles. He was capable of doing that, getting himself involved in areas I was quite desperately trying to seal away out of sight. So January became February, and I never picked up the phone, and eventually he stopped calling.

In March one morning, just past midnight, I suddenly woke restlessly. I was having yet another dark night of the soul. This time the immediate matter on my mind was that I still needed to call Bobby. I heard clicks from Cathy's computer keyboard coming from her office where I could typically find her even at this hour. There she sat as usual, typing away, consumed by some intricate project.

"I forgot to call Bobby again," I said.

Cathy looked up. "How's he been?" she said.

"I think probably great. He should be, he's a newlywed."

This surprised Cathy. "He's married?" she said.

"He and Tamar got married over the summer."

"Really?"

"Didn't I tell you?" I said. "They had it in Fort Hamilton where his guard unit is based. Everybody wore officer's blue—Bobby too. So he had the military parading around. And of course, Bobby being Bobby, he had some ultra-Orthodox sect from Brooklyn officiate the thing. So the army base was swarming with black hats and women in wigs. Only Bobby could bring together Hasidic Jews and the U.S. military. I'd have paid to have seen it."

"We weren't invited?" Cathy asked.

I felt my viscera tense up.

"I haven't exactly kept close," I said.

I didn't need to say more. Cathy had known Bobby for as long as she'd known me, almost two decades. I'd known him for ten years longer than that. I still loved him, but the guy was certifiable. Thirty years had been an awful lot of Bobby.

"Sometimes people grow apart," she said.

Could it be? This was my very best friend from high school. For whatever set of reasons, it was me who had been letting the friendship cool. Maybe this was what I wanted.

"You can also call tomorrow," Cathy said.

I nodded in agreement. Cathy was right, and her words helped. I wanted to tell her so. I felt like I needed to spend a little more time with her before I returned to sleeplessness and she turned back to work. But for some reason I didn't know how. I felt this way a lot, actually. Stuck. Just stuck and incapable of opening up even to my own wife. So not knowing what else to say I went back to bed. Cathy turned back to her keyboard and again started clicking away.

It was April before I managed to call Bobby back.

"Mickey Bones!" he said when he picked up.

"Is this Bob O'Bedlam?" I asked.

"Speaking."

What a great accent. Bobby had an accent from the New York of another generation, as though he were on the set of one of those Cassavetes movies from the seventies that he loved. He'd have fit in right along with Peter Falk and Ben Gazzarra.

Come to think of it, his plans and capers typically made about as much sense as a Cassavetes film, which is why I had taken to calling him Bob O'Bedlam. Bobby had dropped out of college to become a rock star. Good solid plan there. Then he went back to school to get a degree in film. Another sure thing. Then, at age thirty-seven, he joined the army. Oy vey. Then he became fascinated with what he called "natural eyesight" and started supporting himself by giving lessons in how to see without glasses. I wasn't convinced that Bobby could see this way himself (he squinted a lot), but he was really into it. He had taken this latest stage of his career extraordinarily seriously, even managing to get himself accepted in a terrific doctoral program in psychology at the University of California at Irvine. He also continued to take his military career seriously, holding officer's rank in the U.S. Army Reserve. And now he was married. In point of fact his life had actually become much more grounded, but I'd been slow to recognize the changes in my friend. Our lives had finally grown back together.

"I want to get together," I said. "Are you down in Irvine? How's your Ph.D. program going?"

"I'm actually in New York," he said.

"Visiting your folks?"

"I was. Right now I'm in the hospital." His voice didn't indicate a shred of concern.

"The hospital? What's going on?"

"The doctors don't know exactly," he said. "I was walking down the street in Brooklyn and suddenly I fainted, so now I'm here. They're doing a bunch of scans and other tests. They won't find anything. It's nothing."

I told him that I had a good friend from college who was a brain surgeon, so Bobby should be sure to let me know about developments and I'd pass along all the information. Bobby wasn't interested. "It's nothing," he repeated. "Don't worry about it. Listen, I have bigger news for you."

"What?" I asked.

"Tamar's pregnant."

"No kidding?" I said, changing subjects in my mind. "Congratulations! How pregnant?"

"Six months. She's getting big."

I ran through the dates quickly in my head. This is what he must have been calling about months ago. Tamar had then just passed eight weeks, probably they'd just seen the heartbeat. And look at me, I hadn't even picked up the phone to allow him to share the life-changing news. Nice friend.

"All the pieces are starting to fit," said Bobby.

"You're going to be an amazing dad," I said. "Dogs and kids, same thing."

"Yeah?"

"Sure, you'll see for yourself really soon. Three months is nothing. You'll be a dad!"

"I can't really wrap my head around it," Bobby said.

"I know," I said. "For the mom, it's real right away. They've got that physical connection. First they're sick and then the kid is kicking away. But for us it's all theoretical until you see that little head pop out. Then suddenly it's *real*. At least that's how it was for me."

"I can't wait," he said. "I wonder what it will really be like." The conversation paused as we both imagined Bobby's forthcoming fatherhood and future. For some reason just then my mind turned backward in time and I grew nostalgic for my old friend, the crazy one, the one without a serious career and family responsibilities. Suddenly I wanted *that* Bobby back for a little while, maybe so I could go back too.

"Do you remember that script you always wanted us to write together?" I asked.

That had been yet another one of Bobby's crazy ideas. Back in high school, after he rented *My Dinner with Andre* on VHS, Bobby decided that he and I should do the same thing. But, in our case, Bobby said we'd just compose a script on the spot. His idea was for us to find a booth in some Long Island diner, plunk down a cassette tape, forty-five minutes a side, and press start. Ninety minutes later we'd have a script. Just like that. Of course the world would be utterly compelled by each improvised teenage bon mot. It was crazy; maybe it was adolescent; but Bobby continued to talk about this idea years later, even when we both found ourselves in our thirties and in California. The only change in his plan had been to move the diner to Los Angeles. For some reason, the old hairbrained scheme now came to my mind, this time seeming less silly.

"Sure I remember," he said. "We could never find time to do it."

"We should do that script already," I said. "What do you say we set it up when you get back to California? My classes will be out—yours too. We can talk about life, women, music, Jews, all that stuff we're always going on about."

"Like the old days," he said. "We can grab a bottle of whiskey and bang out the thing."

"Exactly."

"Before the baby comes out."

"As soon as you get back from New York," I said. "After you get better."

THE BRIS

After that we talked a few times on the phone, but the next time I actually saw Bobby was for the ritual circumcision of his son Benjamin. By then I knew that Bobby had a diagnosis of glioblastoma, what my neurosurgeon friend told me was the trifecta of all known human diseases. It's a brain tumor that comes from nowhere; reacts to no surgeries or therapies except to regrow exponentially; blows out the entire neurological system so that the end comes by having no communication from the brain to the rest of the body; and is rarer than picking all three horses in the Belmont Stakes. Average time to mortality after initial diagnosis is something like eighteen months, although around twelve is also common.

I pulled my gray Toyota up into the parking lot of Irvine's Lubavitcher synagogue, located in a strip mall like most buildings in that city. I parked and turned off the engine, but despite the August heat I didn't get out of the car. I couldn't. What was I supposed to feel in this situation? Sad? Guilty? Was I really supposed to feel happy? That wasn't going to happen. My mixture of emotions and thoughts were so confusing that I just sat there in the car immobilized. I'm a person who hates being a minute late, but I let my watch pass 9:30 a.m., then 9:35, then 9:45. I knew I had to go in.

Bobby's brothers Steve and Dave were already there. At the very least, I was glad to see them. I'd bumped into Steve here and there in Los Angeles since by chance we lived in the same neighborhood. We had always been able to talk, and now I knew his wife and kids. I hadn't seen Dave, though, since graduating high school.

After initial greetings and moderated smiles (given the circumstances), I asked the brothers how their parents seemed to be handling things.

"The family has regressed back to exactly 1983," said Steve. "It's as though each primordial role we had then has just been waiting for us to step into again."

I could actually see those primordial interactions. I'd spent so much time with Bobby I knew his family back then as I knew my own. I won't even go into the details here. Tolstoy famously said that each family is messed up in its own unique way, but I don't think I agree. I think the details are largely interchangeable. At least those of us on Long Island were messed up pretty much the same. As I looked around the synagogue in Irvine before the circumcision ceremony, I could see in Bobby's gathered relatives my own cousins and my own crazy aunts and uncles. They all shared the same shtick. They ate the same nasty gefilte fish twice a year after synagogue services they rarely attended. They came from the same dirt roads in Moravia, Latvia, Lithuania, and Ukraine. The latest advances in population genetics even told us that we Ashkenazic Jews descended from the same three hundred families. So when Steve said his family had all regressed to 1983, I knew the scene exactly.

"Families are a disaster under the best of circumstances," said Dave, always the most levelheaded of the three siblings. "And these are not the best of circumstances."

"I get that, little brother," said Steve. "I get that very much."

Across the room, Bobby's wife Tamar looked beautiful. I don't mean she had the glow of motherhood that descends on a woman in pregnancy and birth, although she had that too. I saw her, dark Israeli eyes and hair, seated among her family and holding fast to the baby in these last few minutes before the ceremony. Someone I took to be her mother was trying to wrest baby Benjamin away, but Tamar wasn't having it. She looked gorgeous during this loving spat with her mom.

I'd known Tamar now for a few years, though not very well. She'd been over for Thanksgiving two years before when they had started dating, and maybe after that we'd had a lunch here and there, but that was about it for my contact with her. Bobby had often talked to me about her on the phone though, so I had a mental picture of her painted by Bobby. She was a computer science professor at my own school, actually, with a Ph.D. from Stanford in computer science and math, which impressed me. Still, I thought of her as one of Bobby's girlfriends, even when they grew more serious, and whatever beauty I had seen in her had been in a girlfriend sort of way and not as a Bobby's partner in life. Now as I looked over at Tamar and her mother at the next table, especially as I saw Tamar swaddling her baby in these last seconds before the ceremony, she had a kind of complete and serene beauty, a woman of valor, as the Proverbs say. For a moment I completely forgot about Bobby's health and only felt pure happiness for his having finally found a family.

Bobby also had changed substantially in appearance. I saw him chatting near the dais with the rabbi and mohel who were about to start the ceremony. Bobby was mostly nodding, registering instructions. He now wore a black fedora in the style of the 1940s except it had an exaggerated brim which marked the garment as ultra-Orthodox. The new clothing jarred against my memory of his grungy music career outfits from the nineties. Bobby now also moved with some awkwardness, which was so different from his usual physical grace and balance. His movements now seemed more intentional and thoughtful, a result of the tumors and two surgeries he had already undergone.

But the main thing I saw that differed from my old friend Bob O'Bedlam was something akin to the change I saw in Tamar. Despite his physical spasms, somehow he appeared more *in* balance than when he had held his full physical capacity. As I saw him nodding to the rabbi and taking instructions regarding the fate of his newborn son, I saw Bobby excited, in the zone, alert, confident, in his element. He, too, now seemed filled with purpose.

Minutes later, during the ceremony, he confirmed this sentiment in his speech. He only could talk for a few minutes. His language capacity had been the greatest victim of the brain cancer. Over the past few months, after each episode and surgery, he could speak less and less. At first he had only lost a few words or left a few thoughts unfinished. But now, just three months after he'd fallen dizzy in Brooklyn, he was mostly unable to complete a sentence. So this speech after the bris was all the more remarkable for its eloquence. Bobby stood on the podium with Tamar and the baby. The family stood there together. Bobby told us that just a week ago Benjamin had been born at six o'clock in the morning. Then Bobby had gone down the hospital hallway for his own chemotherapy. "But that's not important," he said. His own health didn't matter anymore. "That's not my life."

Whatever can he mean? I thought.

We all held our breaths as Bobby struggled for his next set of words. Then suddenly he lifted his forefinger. "Benjamin and Tamar—" he said, pointing among the triangle of them standing together. "This is my life."

Bobby concluded in gratitude and thanks to God for giving him the gift of fatherhood. We all blinked back tears. At that moment I couldn't help but look over at Bobby's parents. There they were, Mr. and Mrs. Lichtman, identical in my mind to when I first met them coming home after school with Bobby. *What about their son?* I thought. *What's happened to their lives?*

After the buffet lunch, much of the crowd from the Orthodox community had left, though Bobby's family still milled around. I saw Mrs. Lichtman with Tamar and her mother, all three now admiring the baby. Bobby was again focusing intently on the rabbi, reviewing some last-minute ritual questions. It was late enough in the afternoon that I knew I needed to beat rush hour traffic on the interstate back to Los Angeles. So I put my hand on Bobby's shoulder and turned him away from the rabbi for a brief moment, just to say goodbye and to tell him that I'd get back to see him in Irvine as soon as I could. I quickly shook his hand and smiled, I thanked the rabbi, and then I left to allow the two to complete their important discussion. We could catch up later. I didn't know when, but from now on I'd make time.

I'd already grabbed my sport coat, descended the stairs, and was pushing through the front door of the synagogue when I heard Bobby shout my name.

"Mick!" he called.

He had chased me all the way through the building. I guess he'd been unable to get any words out to call my attention. When I turned, I saw he held up his forefinger, kind of pointing it in the air. He wanted a minute with me. He wasn't wearing his fedora now. I could see a flat spot on the side of his head where his skull used to be.

"Yeah, Bob. What's up?"

His face screwed up, and he stuttered.

"Is there a . . . a . . ."

What was he saying? I didn't understand.

"a *problem?*" he spat out.

He couldn't get out any more words. Instead, he flicked his forefinger between us. He pointed to me and then back to him. Then he repeated the motion. His finger traversed and noted the short distance between us.

He was communicating perfectly. *Is there a problem between us.* That's what he was trying to say with the flick of his fingers. *Is there a problem between us?*

I died right there. I fell straight into his arms, utterly penetrated by shame. "Oh no, Bobby, never." I said. "Not now, not ever!"

With all these things on his mind, still in the full glow and pallor of the ceremony marking the full spectrum of his profound life changes, amidst all this he'd run after *me*. His *friend. I'd* been on his mind. So he'd decided to break away from his other troubles and joys for a minute to make this extraordinary effort to repair our friendship. With everything else going on, *this* had been on his mind. Our friendship mattered that much to him.

How can it be that only in that moment did I realize our friendship mattered as much to me, too?

"Not ever," I whispered.

Bobby went back inside to join his family, and I went outside to crawl up behind the steering wheel of my gray Toyota. I sat there looking out over the parking lot of the Irvine strip mall. Then I fell apart.

ROCK STAR

The next time I see Bobby, he has his red Stratocaster slung across his back and he's just stepped up to the microphone. I've been thrown back a quarter-century to this moment in the archive of my memory, the Oceanside High School talent show of 1987. Bobby will graduate in just another month. His band is vamping a rock rhythm, very tight and slightly funky, like the early Bruce Springsteen records he adores. But the room of shouting and laughing kids hasn't settled down yet from waiting for the band to set up. Suddenly Bobby barks into the mic.

"Parents got you down?"

Only six months older than me, but in the next grade, I look up to Bobby. Seeing him there onstage, I'm completely in awe. But that's just me. Only half the audience has bothered to turn around at all. Some kids are high on cans of Budweiser or reek of different kinds of cigarettes, mostly Marlboro Lights and Virginia Slims. Other kids are waiting for their friends to take the stage and are talking through every other act. Bobby looks out over this impossible audience, surveying the terrain before him like a crusty general.

"I said something, people," he snarls. *"PARENTS GOT YOU DOWN?!"*

More kids turn around. "Yeah!" they cheer. The rest drop their conversations and turn toward the stage. They're getting into it! In this moment I realize something about my friend Robert Lichtman, honors class of Oceanside High School of 1987, that nobody heretofore has suspected except maybe Bobby himself. He is going to be a rock star.

"Tests got you down?"

"Yeah!"

"DLTs got you down?" (Deficient Learning Time—Oceanside High School Orwellian for detention).

"Yeah! *Yeah! YEAH!*"

"Are you an outlaw? A desperado? Are you a loner like *me*?"

The sound of uncontrollable teenage wrath thunders through the room.

"Well there's something you can do about it!" He swings his red Stratocaster around and hits the first blister of chords. The noise in the room is soon beyond my capacity to actually hear Bobby, despite the best attempts of the auditorium's sound tiles to silence our teenage rage. It's his squirming on his back during the solo that I see most clearly. His red T-shirt bunches up as he executes the rock 'n' roll maneuver, his body sliding across the polished wooden stage. His guitar squeals out his own adolescent fury, but it also proclaims something more. This solo is beyond a mere expression of hormones; it's already something adult, something existential. To me his guitar seems to scream: *I'm here, goddamn it. Goddamn it, I'm here.*

"Al Jolson?" Bobby says. "You're really going to write a book about Jolie?"

"I'm thinking about it," I say. "First it would be a Ph.D. dissertation, but later maybe if it's any good it could be a book."

"Like a popular book?" he asks.

"I don't think I could do that."

"Why not?" he says.

We're passing through West Virginia. Bobby drives my car. I'm looking out the passenger window, gazing over a scene of raw beauty like I've never seen before, and by this time I've been through a lot of Europe and the Middle East for my studies, so I have some capacity to compare beautiful places. Yet here we both are, two Americans, Long Island born, well into our adulthoods, and in our own country we haven't spent any time outside the borders of exurbia. Forested mountains, rollicking rivers, eagles—who knew America still possessed any of these?

"You see any wild reefers growing out there?," Bobby asks.

I'd forgotten to line up the marijuana before we left. Then I'd discovered as we crossed the George Washington Bridge that Bobby didn't have any either.

"I'll let you know when I see some," I say.

This is Bobby's trip. Nineteen-ninety-five is going to be a slow summer in the rhythm of my academic career, so I'm able to join him. I've just finished my coursework. We're taking my car and splitting the gas. We've only planned to go out for a week or so. I want to get started with my qualifying exams, but Bobby has convinced me otherwise. What can taking the week off possibly matter in the grand scheme of my life?

"Al Jolson started everything," Bobby says. "He had so many hits. 'April Showers,' 'You Made Me Love You,' 'Sonny Boy.'"

"'Toot, Toot, Tootsie,'" I contribute.

"Of course, he introduced Gershwin's 'Swannee,'" Bobby says.

Our ludicrous archive of nostalgia is exactly what Bobby and I hold in common. We're talking about a mediocre baritone whose last hit landed during the Great Depression. When Bobby and I get together, either we're talking about girls or Jews or popular music, ideally all three together. These themes comprise the entire Venn diagram of our conversations. What began as teenage idiosyncrasies are now developing into our careers, his in music, mine in the academic study of Jewry. Bob dropped out of Columbia University, but he's still an autodidact, a voracious reader, especially of anything vaguely pertaining to Jewish history. He seems to know more about the content of my graduate classes than I do.

Then in New York, through talent, charisma, and much pounding of the pavement, Bobby managed to get himself signed with Columbia Records, also the label of Bob Dylan, Bruce Springsteen, and Leonard Cohen—all of them Bobby's idols. Bobby released his own record for Columbia in May of 1994, *From a Sympathetical Hurricane*. I still don't know what the title means. I never really understand his esoteric lyrical style, but I feel the same way about the lyrics of Dylan, Springsteen, and Cohen, so I figure I must be wrong. Bobby's got a hermetic mind tending toward conspiracy, especially linking the political with the metaphysical. Bobby sees secret connections below the surface of everything, and, when I do ask about lyrics, it's usually these secret theories that animate them. Often Bobby's ideas come out of the Kabbalah, for which I have little feeling. So I don't try to understand. It's just Bob O'Bedlam, I usually think.

Bobby supported his record the previous summer with a European tour that he thought had gone exceedingly well. Crowds in Germany and Prague knew his lyrics. He even had groupies. But that all was last summer. For Columbia Records, that's ancient history, and Bobby hasn't yet produced another album.

The label isn't supporting him, he says. Of the pool of singer-songwriters Columbia had picked up in 1994, they'd put their resources behind Jeff Buckley and Dave Matthews, not Bobby. Those two exploded in summer and fall of 1994, after Bobby's own album had been released, and back then Bobby had taken me to scout out their shows. As we'd stood at the back of packed Manhattan auditoriums, I saw him watching, baffled. What did those guys have? Why had the label supported them and not him? Now, a year later, he and Matthews and Buckley are all still with Columbia, but the label has left Bobby out on his own. He has no money for a second album. Creatively, he's struggling. I think he doesn't know what to do.

Still he's always writing, always producing songs, and some of these happen to be Christmas songs. He admires the Christmas genre. ("Listen to the *anticipation* in 'The Little Drummer Boy,'" he says, "the drum announcing the coming of the newborn King!"). So he's gotten the idea to visit Columbia offices in Nashville to pitch his Christmas songs down there. Maybe a country artist will pick one up and put it on a holiday record. It could mean royalties to float Bobby until he gets his own act together.

Bobby and I planned our itinerary together. It is the stupidest, goofiest, most ill-informed tour of Americana that two New

York Jews could possibly piece together from the information on the records we adore. Bobby has a couple of cassette mix tapes for the trip. He's got Lefty Frizzell on one tape, a crooner from the 1950s who captured Bobby's interest because Bob Dylan had mentioned him in an interview as being a forgotten American master. We also have our requisite Neil Diamond tape. That's my contribution, but Bobby loves him too. As we roll through Kentucky, Bobby turns up the stereo to full capacity, lets down the windows, and blasts "Kentucky Woman."

We're so dumb.

In Kentucky a big stop for Bobby is Lincoln's birthplace. We spend a lot of time at the largely unvisited monument. Bobby comments that the log house compares to the trailer park where our sitting President Clinton was born. We then hightail it to Memphis and go directly to Sun Records before it closes for the day. This place, like the Lincoln homestead, also feels sacred in a quintessentially American way—pulsing with the emotion of the improbable come true. The next day in Memphis we tour Graceland. On a bookstand in the Jungle Room some mischievous curator has placed Elvis's own heavily marked copy of *Gods from Outer Space* (1972). The book is turned open to a paragraph discussing feminism. In the column the King himself had cryptically noted his own hermetic thoughts, writing there the word *karate*.

"Look," I say to Bobby, pointing out the royal gloss. "The King was as crazy as you."

"He may also have been a Jew," says Bobby.

"Elvis?" I say.

"From his great-great-grandmother," he says.

Bobby nods knowingly, and I ask no more questions about it.

Before we leave Memphis, we tour Beale Street. Then we head out toward Jackson, Tennessee, where we intended to breakfast, believing incorrectly that the Johnny Cash song takes place there and not in Jackson, Mississippi. Finally we head to Nashville to kick around Music Row for a day before Bobby's meeting at the Columbia offices.

By the time we've gotten to the campsite outside of Nashville it's really late. The air is thick with mosquitoes, and I'm beat anyway, so I crawl into the tent and try to get some sleep. Bobby doesn't bother lighting a fire. He's just out there sitting on a rock, strumming softly, singing just below his breath, practicing his same set over and over to get each chord change and vocal nuance just right. I watch the vague shadow of him and his acoustic guitar from inside the tent and I listen as if this was a lullaby until I fall asleep. I don't think Bob put the guitar down all night.

The next morning I walk around the parking lot of the record label while Bobby goes and sings his songs. He had a nine o'clock appointment, and it's already an hour later, so he's been in there a long time. When he comes out, we both get in the car, this time to head back to New York. I ask him how it went.

"OK," he says. "The suit liked the Christmas song. He told me to open with the chorus and repeat it a couple more times, but that was it. Otherwise he liked it."

"Great," I say. "Do you think he'll buy it?"

"He didn't say. But he wanted to hear the rest of my set, that's what took so long."

"Sounds like it went all right," I offer.

Bobby kind of grimaces while he looks off somewhere out beyond his window.

"We'll see," he says. "This ain't my first rodeo."

Even so, at this point in our lives each episode still glistens with the tinsel of naive courage and hope. Having had virtually no life experiences, I fully expect myself to think up something profound to say to the world. That's my dream. But Bobby at this point isn't only a dreamer. He's had achievements. He's become a Columbia recording artist just like his heroes Dylan and

Springsteen and he's put out a Columbia record; he's gone on a European tour and has the groupie stories to prove it; and here he is in Music City pitching Christmas songs like a latter-day Irving Berlin, Phil Spector, or Neil Diamond. At twenty-five, he's made his adolescent dreams actually manifest in the world. *Who does that?* Bob O'Bedlam, that's who.

I take the first stretch at the wheel as we drive back through Knoxville on the way to Appalachia and then toward home. Bobby wants to make it back to New York before sunset on the next night, Friday. He's begun to keep the Sabbath and attend synagogue and now has standing dinner invitations from all sorts of ultra-Orthodox families back in New York. I don't understand his new religious impulse, although I admire his commitment, and so we are headed home kind of quickly to make the Sabbath in time.

"I think you should write the book," he says. "Jolie was the biggest Jew that ever was. He started everything." He winks at me and nods as though I understand, but this is exactly the hermeticism that I never understand.

"I don't understand," I say. "What did he start?"

Bobby sighs. "He was the first guy to strip it down and say, 'Forget all the schmaltz. American music is just black music. That's it.'"

I consider this.

"So he painted his face in burnt cork so he could sing like he was black?" I say.

"Exactly," says Bobby. "And maybe he schmeered it on his tuchas, too. We don't know."

My eyebrows go up. I have to think about that one.

"That's messed up," I say.

"That's entertainment," says Bobby. "It's the same today."

He sighs. As we reach the Virginia line, I can see Bobby looking out the window, surveying. I think maybe he's trying not to miss any of the journey we have left before us. Too soon we'll be back, him to New York and me to Connecticut, both of us with careers and money issues and romantic disasters and all the anxieties that take up a young man's life. In just another day, the clarity of our daydreams will mist over and we'll be back to the realities that those eastern places mean to us. That's something like how I'm feeling.

"Look, over there!" Bobby says suddenly.

"What?"

"Why Mickey Bones, just look over there. Can't you see them?"

Nothing but Tennessee shrubs stretch out in every direction.

"Bobby, I don't see anything. What is it?"

"Reefers!" he shouts. "Reefers yea high! Reefers growing like weeds right there along the side of the road!"

So of course I pull over. If there's a chance to locate some Tennessee Wild, we have to look. I realize that no such plant exists—Bobby knows it too—but I don't care. In this moment I'm happy to play sidekick in Bob's buddy flick. We step out along some strip of ancient asphalt and walk among the weeds for a while, smiling, breathing in, letting go, best of friends, crazy in our youth, crazy in our hopes, and thick in our shared hallucination that God's own bounty might spring up anywhere, waiting to be picked, even here among the Tennessee shrubs.

NOT FADE AWAY

"What do you mean you can't have the baby?"

That's me a decade later in 2006 on the phone with Cathy. I'm in the lobby of a movie theater in West Philadelphia waiting for *Borat* to start, while she's back in Los Angeles at home with our toddler, Nick. I've just called in before the movie to find out about the IVF results, and Cathy has told me she's pregnant and this time it seems to be holding. Pregnant! *Finally.* This was her third round of IVF, our last try. As I had heard the news, the change in my life immediately registered, and I couldn't even process my happiness. We're finally successful. *We're having another baby.* It's been nearly three years of trying. Nick is going to have a *sister.* Or maybe it will be a brother—it doesn't matter to me. *I'd been right! Trying was worth it! Facing failure has paid off.*

But I had only had seconds to enjoy this feeling of triumph. Just then Cathy had burst into tears and wailed at me through my phone in nearly indecipherable sobs: *"I can't have this baby. How am I going to have this baby?"*

Now she's hysterical, totally hysterical. She's in the middle of a panic attack. I can hear the waves of anxiety pulse through her voice. I can hear her heightened breathing over my flip phone. And now I realize what she's thinking. She's thinking about the half-dozen miscarriages she's already endured. All that hope for birth and motherhood built up and up—and then instantly vanished. Six times. *Go back to work, people, nothing to see here.* All that time spent imagining the future life of a baby and how it will change our lives—gone. *Six times.*

I've been so wrapped up in finding a sibling for Nick. *Have I even been thinking of Cathy at all?* I can't possibly understand what she's going through emotionally, let alone hormonally. I can't imagine the PTSD scenes that she's replaying in her head from six episodes of hope and grief. And now I'm frozen. Because I understand that I actually *don't* know what she's thinking. Naturally my imagination takes me to the most horrible possible thought: How rash could she be? Could she just *snap?* Could she just go and get rid of the pregnancy?

How quickly could that happen? My mind is crazy. Maybe Cathy could be done with it *tonight* while I'm three thousand miles away.

"Cathy," I say. "Promise me that you'll chill out until I get back in a couple of days. In two days I'll be back. Can you sit tight?"

"Yeah," she says. But she doesn't say it with conviction. I'm not convinced. But what can I do?

"Sit tight then," I say. "And try to be happy. I'm so happy! Everything is going to be OK."

"OK," she says.

We say a few awkward I-love-yous and the phone goes silent. I'm alone again. And I'm helpless. What should I do? Who can I talk to about this? Nobody. None of my friends will understand this position. What advice or moral support can anyone possibly give me anyway? This beyond sucks. This is the excremental character of the universe, choosing to reveal itself with perfectly symmetrical irony in the announcement of my beloved second child. This is how life goes: no triumph without pain and confusion. No joy without bitter irony. I have to suck it up and deal. I can only hope that Cathy will not freak out. That's all I can do. So I snap the phone shut and go into the theater to see *Borat*.

Columbia dropped Bobby a few weeks after we'd come back from Nashville. He'd only just turned twenty-six, but that was already too old for the label. They'd given him two years to become a star. Dave Matthews and Jeff Buckley had done that; Bobby hadn't. So Bobby was on his own again. The youthful life of potential then began its midlife retreat. He floundered for the next decade.

Those ten years had done a job on me too. In 2006 I'm now on airplanes twice a week between Los Angeles and Philadelphia. I've got a teaching job on one coast; Cathy has one on the other. I don't want to give up my career, Cathy doesn't want to give up hers, and we don't want each other to make the sacrifice either. Cathy seems happy when she's busy at work. Work seems good for her. Besides, I like what Cathy does. Like me, she also writes history, and besides this she does museum shows and other public work. Unlike me, she goes out into different communities and actually talks to people. She especially favors the stories of disenfranchised people. People on Skid Row. People living along the Los Angeles River. People getting shuffled in and out of the penal system on account of poverty and the insane failure of public education. She tries to hear these people. Then she tries to create some space for them to represent themselves. Most times I see one of her finished shows or programs, or when I read her publications, I think to myself: *That's good work.*

As for my own work, I'd never think to talk to a living person. My purview is the dead. Dead souls, that's who I like being around. I'm scared of living people. An immobilizing, almost cryogenic panic comes with the thought that I might have to talk to one. It's difficult enough trying to keep my own vital issues clamped down tight below my own hood, thank you very much. No reason to enter vital human spaces that are actually warm; no reason to engage with life. That's too messy. I prefer dead.

Despite my dedication to persons already gone and moments already past, I still hope to contribute something significant to my own world. Why I believe this, I have no idea. How can my compulsion over dead souls amount to something in the present? I don't know. At the same time, I also feel I have no choice. The dust of the library and chalkboard seem to me to be the only possible arena of my contribution, so I push forward.

The solution to our career paradoxes (I mean Cathy's and mine) had been obvious to me. We'd take both jobs, hers in Southern California and mine in Philadelphia. I'd make weekly flights. We'd watch the job market for two years, maybe three. Nobody knows the future, that's the only lesson history teaches, so we would have to see what came up. I had thought this was a solid three-year plan. Even Stalin and Mao couldn't do much better than that.

Cathy had nodded. She'd agreed. But I can tell she hasn't had my confidence in the plan. I guess looking back I can see she didn't exactly agree. She'd consented. Either I hadn't noticed this distinction at the time or I hadn't cared. In any event, I still can't see another option. So I'd taken the Philadelphia job and avoided thinking through the emotional implications, and we all went forward with my rational Three-Year Plan.

The air miles have earned me much needed drink coupons. Among the only benefits of the arrangement is that I get to see Bobby occasionally when I can make it up to New York after teaching in Philadelphia. That had been my plan for this week. The night after *Borat*, I'd planned to take a train to Manhattan to visit Bobby and check out a guitarist. So I headed up.

I meet Bobby over at the Living Room on Stanton Street to catch Jim Campilongo's guitar trio. We're both fans. I'm the bigger fan, having introduced Bobby to the music, but he loved it immediately. A virtuoso is a virtuoso, there's just no further argument. Campilongo plays a Telecaster straight into a Princeton Reverb, couldn't be simpler. Hearing him in a hundred-person venue is something like it must have been to hear Wes Montgomery play the Village Vanguard a few generations earlier or Charlie Christian bop it up at Minton's Playhouse a generation even before that. And here in SoHo we're not five blocks from where Irving Berlin once worked as a singing waiter at the turn of the previous century. Music runs through every cobblestone of these Manhattan streets, and Bobby knows each bump and turn in that noble history.

"How's your fornicating going?" Bobby asks while we wait for Campilongo's set to start.

"Pretty good," I say. "Cathy's pregnant."

"Really?"

"She's had a bunch of false starts, but this one seems good. The doctor said so. She told me on the phone."

I omit telling Bobby the critical details about the IVF, or about Cathy's panic and my frozen immobility in the face of terror. Am I here having dinner and drinks in SoHo while Cathy scours the phone book looking for a twenty-four-hour women's clinic? That's the insanity going through my mind.

"That's pretty good fornicating," Bobby says.

"I get by," I lie.

Campilongo's trio begins its first blistering set. While the music plays, my troubles churn. Campilongo's ethereal squeals and detuning antics seem to match the exact state of my own panic. Forty-five minutes go by quickly. When the band takes its break, half the place clears out onto the sidewalk to smoke cigarettes, but Bobby and I linger at the bar. When Bobby throws his coat from one arm to the other, I see in his inside pocket he has a compact disc stuffed into a CD envelope. Bobby has scribbled some words with a black marker which I can't quite make out. I guess it's some tunes he's working on.

"I envy you," Bobby says. "And my friend Morty, too. You married guys get action any night you want. It's like Gan Eden."

"Bobby, it's not Eden by a long shot," I say. I can feel myself getting annoyed. This is exactly the kind of Bobby conversation that I can't stand. He understands nothing about this. I can't even remember him ever having a serious girlfriend. Still he'll bring up things about my relationship that belong firmly shoved in the closet. I feel myself getting sucked into a bad conversation. I don't want to discuss this stuff with anyone, let alone with Dr. O'Bedlam.

"What's going on?" he insists.

"Nothing's going on," I snap. "Cathy's full of it, that's all. It's the same domestic inferno as everybody. Lack of communication, misunderstanding, all followed by resentment."

He considers for a minute.

"I don't think everybody suffers from lack of communication," he says pointedly. "What if you just tell her she's full of crap?"

Tell Cathy she's full of crap? *Are you crazy?* Tell her she's full of crap and send her running off to the twenty-four-hour clinic? *Bobby.—Just. Shut. Up.*

"I'll try that," I mutter.

"What are you doing with yourself?" I ask him, deflecting matters to a safer zone. "How's your music?"

"Now I don't want to talk about it," he says. "I'm doing eyesight now. Natural eyesight, that's what I do."

"Why don't you want to talk about music?" I push, now suddenly feeling communicative.

He doesn't say anything. To me it looks as though he's both trying to formulate a response and to manage his emotions for having to say it.

"Mick," he says finally. "It's been years since I've made any money in the music industry. I failed. Asking me about my music just hurts. Don't you see that? You always do this. It's like the last thing I want to talk about."

I guess it's true. I'd thought he was still sort of in the game, but maybe he's finally slipped out. We stand there at the bar in silence for a while, not knowing what to say. Campilongo is back on stage, and I know the band will start up in a minute, so I take this closed moment to reveal one among my own fears, during the safety of the few seconds before guitars and drums drown us out.

"I feel that way about my work," I say.

"Mick, that's ridiculous," he says. "You're a terrific writer."

"It doesn't feel that way," I say. "I don't say anything. I don't reach anybody. I don't know what I'm doing. Whatever."

The second set comes and goes. Campilongo is amazing, but somehow his virtuosity tonight doesn't inspire me as it usually does. It is affecting the opposite. I feel immobilized and generally awful about what my life has come to. Of course Cathy and the unborn baby are still hovering in the forefront of my mind. And I'm thinking about my gorgeous little toddler Nick, whom I now imagine being shuffled between lousy apartments like a piece of luggage, a result of the inevitable divorce that will come after the abortion. Because in my anxious fantasy Cathy is already aborting the baby, probably right now as I suck down cocktails in this SoHo nightclub. As the Campilongo trio finishes up, all my problems intertwine into a great Gordian knot so complicated and thick that even a sword stroke would just bounce off. In my domestic life, in my work life, in my core of meaning and self, I have no strength left to untangle or cut through. Yet I know the next day will inevitably come. I'll be on yet another airplane and once again I'll be back in Los Angeles, forced to face reality.

After the show, Bobby and I take a long route walking to the subway. I can feel autumn in New York, the air already has that great leafy smell, nothing at all like Los Angeles. Bobby is headed out to some shared apartment in Brooklyn and I'm going to Penn Station to catch the last train back to Philadelphia to my own pathetic rented room.

"You've got to keep writing," Bobby says. "Your stuff is *torah lishma*—learning for its own sake. That's why I love your book. It's about a kook like Al Jolson, but still I feel like I'm learning Torah."

That registers. "Thanks," I say.

"You're welcome," he says. "It happens to be true."

We are actually crossing though Union Square, 14th Street, the original site of the Tin Pan Alley music publishing industry. So many of the great lyricists and composers of the American Songbook first worked in steam-heated offices all along this very street. One hundred years ago, Harry von Tilzer named the place for the sound of the cheap piano notes tinkling from each second-floor window. Bob knows this history better than anyone.

"OK, my turn." I say to Bob. "How much would it cost you to produce all those songs that I know you have running around in your head? What would it cost for you just to say, screw it, I'm putting it into the world, I don't care what happens?"

I don't expect Bobby to answer me.

"Five thousand dollars," he blurts out. "I could do it for five grand."

There in Union Square I take out a check and write it for that amount. I don't actually have the money in the bank, but I'll figure it out.

"Take this as an investment," I say. "Take this as a permanent loan. Pay it back. Don't pay it back. I don't care. But go ahead and make that record. It belongs in the world. Torah lishma, for its own sake."

I'm surprised that he takes the check—typically he's so proud. But he does take it. We walk silently for a while. I can only imagine the content of his thoughts, but if it's anything like what I'm feeling, in these moments Bobby and I have never been closer.

We get to his subway entrance and embrace, as we usually do. Then I turn away to catch my own train.

"I should have joined the army," Bobby says suddenly. I've already turned away in my thoughts and am back among my own troubles, but I face him again.

"Now I'm too old," he says.

"You're crazy," I say. "But it so happens Bush just raised the enlistment age to forty. I heard it on the news. We're having another surge in Iraq."

"No joke?" Bobby says.

"You could sign up tomorrow," I say.

JAH GUIDE (AND ME I'LL
JUST FOLLOW)

The next six years saw me generally fading out of the lives of the people I loved. I faded out of Bobby's life. I faded out of my wife Cathy's life. We started counseling and then ended it. In my work I sometimes had epiphanies, insights, rushes in the joy of learning, so I turned to the ancient places I found edifying and began writing this book. I did this every day in silent libraries, never talking to anyone, and then I'd come home, close a door, and continue my fantasies into the night. I dedicated all my emotional energy into trying to empathize with the thoughts and feelings of dead people—Socrates, Mary Lou Williams, Abu Hamid al-Ghazali, Chinggis Khan, and many other dead souls too. Typically I did this while Cathy clicked away on her computer and my kids watched Netflix. And so in a sense I had also faded out of my own life.

Meanwhile Bobby the bachelor—the desperado, outlaw, and loner—was locking in. He was making the requisite human commitments. Bobby had gone ahead and signed up for the U.S. National Guard, indeed the day after I told him he could. So Lieutenant Lichtman began patrolling and securing the tunnels and bridges of New York City. When we talked on the phone, I could tell he was enormously proud of his work and totally engaged with the lives of the soldiers in his unit.

At the same time, somehow he'd firmly entered the world of Orthodox Jewry. He didn't wear a skullcap while in uniform, but other than that he'd begun to keep the fundamental laws. He settled in among a Hasidic group in Brooklyn, and most evenings and holidays he'd spend at their synagogue, and then the next morning he'd suit up in uniform to oversee the patrol of the Queensboro Bridge or the Queens-Midtown Tunnel.

In those years he also made that album he'd been carrying around in his head, calling it *Peddler in Babylon*. It enacts a Western landscape, with a Jewish peddler crossing that frontier. That's the most I can figure out regarding the album's concept. Since the time of his first album, Bobby had now moved from the guitar over to the harmonica as the instrument of his inner voice. He blew it gently, in a wail, as though over a plain, like the plains he and I had imagined as kids from the movies, and like those which we'd then both had the fortune to see in real life. This sound is the album's motivic timbre. Tumbleweed blows through the music.

It's motivic spirit, if that can be articulated at all, I think is found in several of the album's great songs, including "Song of the Open Road," and the title song "Peddler in Babylon." But I think Bobby best conveyed the spirit of the album with a Rasta prayer, "Jah Guide (And Me I'll Just Follow):"

Jah Guide! And me, I'll just follow
Through joy, pain, or rain,
Heartbreak, love, and sorrow . . .

Through this world I was born to wander
Though aloneness made me strong
It nearly drove me under

Jah Guide! And me, I'll just follow
Don't know where I'll be tomorrow
I have gotten nothing
Outside its time
He's given me no mountain
That I can't climb

Jah Guide!

I don't think he sold any copies of the CD at all. I think he gave most away. I don't know how he felt about that; it couldn't have felt very good. But as I've listened to it over the years, it's held up as the minor spiritual masterpiece I think it actually is. Back then, I kept the disc in my car and listened to it constantly. This became my driving music, my own songs of the open road. These days, even well after his passing, I'm only just beginning to be able to listen to it again, but I'm starting to. This amazing album was his gift. Maybe he'd even made this masterpiece just for me. I don't know.

Bobby paid back every penny of the five thousand dollars. He didn't have to, but he did.

Sometime in these later years he met Tamar. I don't know how, actually. Probably it had happened through Jewish circles. When I first learned of Tamar, I think she was doing computer programming jobs in New York, but she was also on the job market for a professorship in computer science. She and Bobby came to Los Angeles for Thanksgiving at my house one year, and I met her. It was telling because Bobby had never brought anyone "home" before. The next thing I knew, they were married. In the meantime, by total serendipity she got a job on my own campus in Riverside, California, and Bobby began his Ph.D. program down at Irvine in psychology. He was pursuing a dissertation regarding ocular perception. He had it in his head to start a practice in teaching natural eyesight. I didn't know what to think of all this except what I'd already known since high school: Bobby was crazy. But he also made his dreams happen in the world, so who was I to say?

When he reached out to me (and when I bothered to pick up the phone), I could tell that he seemed really happy. Did I feel jealous? I think I did. I resented his seemingly effortless ability to connect with different groups of people. I didn't realize how hard he had actually worked to overcome the shyness that had propelled him to become a desperado rock star in the first place. Rather, I understood these new obligations he'd taken on as being rash. Join the army at age thirty-seven? Enter a Hasidic cult of Jews? Become a homeopath? Make brash plunges into marriage and fatherhood? What was a reasonable person to think? And then when I finally dedicated some time to think about Bobby, when I finally got around to making an effort to understand him by simply picking up the phone, Bobby went and got brain cancer.

Just days after Benjamin's circumcision, Bobby began acting erratically again, especially losing speech. Tamar took him back to the hospital, and the doctors diagnosed a regrowth of the tumor, this time to the size of a lemon. They checked him in on the spot, and in this, his third open brain surgery, they removed the tumor. He never recovered significant language control from that point on. Strictly speaking, I suppose we never spoke again, but that's not really true. There was one more point my friend managed to coax out of his rebelling neurological system to get through to me, one final piece of advice, friend to friend.

In May of 2014, Bobby had been deteriorating for over a year. The circumstances of that decline I will not recount as I did not know them nearly as well as Tamar did. Tamar, for her part, managed his care with attention that I thought superhuman. The conditions of any body ailment are complicated, but that of neurological shutdown affects every single cell in the body. Nevertheless, Bobby and Tamar had decided to have him spend his last months and days in their home. They did not want him spending his nights alone in hospice. They wanted Bobby to hear the sounds of their son Benjamin's increasing youthful tumult and to enjoy the click of Tamar's computer keyboard as she wrote lectures. So Tamar brought Bobby home.

Most days Tamar schlepped him to hospitals and doctor's offices down in Orange County. But in May of 2014 Tamar had found one last experimental treatment being offered up at UCLA. Because of her own intense professional and parental schedule, she couldn't be with Bobby to oversee this visit. When I rang their bell, Bobby came up to the door right away. He was wearing his Orthodox fedora, ready to go, so we headed straight up to UCLA.

The plan was to get there about an hour before his appointment and have some lunch. It was perfect spring weather, so I took our cafeteria plate outside and we began our simple meal. I did a lot of babbling. Bobby sometimes would try to say something. He'd sort of squirm up his face as though to ask me for the word he meant to say, the word stuck still inchoate in his mind . . . and then he'd just give up. But he could nod and shake his head, so I filled the awkward moments with my own chatter.

"I'll be on this retreat for the whole month of June," I told him. "These are Burmese monks, called *sayadaws*. They invented this technique of 'noting' that I was telling you about. It helps you focus. Meditation is all about focus."

He nodded and chewed on his food, interested and engaged.

"Thirty days of silence," I said. "No having to talk to anyone. It will be heaven!"

Bobby looked back at me. Immediately I regretted my words.

"I thought I might have to go to Burma to learn this stuff," I added quickly. "But a community of Vietnamese immigrants in San Jose has set up a meditation center there, and they ship the sayadaws over from Burma for retreats a few times a year. It's four hundred bucks for the month including lodging and vegetarian meals, so I'm going."

He nodded. We sat quietly for a while. I didn't know what else to say. Should I try to penetrate his feelings about his situation? Or did he want to take this time with me to relax and take his mind off of things? I chose a middle route.

"Do you think fatherhood has changed you?" I asked.

He thought about it for a second and shrugged.

"Same time . . ." he managed to say as he pointed to his head.

"You haven't had time to untangle them," I said.

He nodded yes. Then Bobby took off his fedora.

"Look," he said. He was pointing directly at the back quarter of his skull which by now had been totally removed. Skin lay flat across it.

"I know, Bob," I said. "But you know, some women go for that."

He smiled.

We had about fifteen minutes before his appointment at UCLA Medical Center began, so we walked north, away from the hospital and up toward campus. Summer school must have been starting. There were all kinds of banners and young people with matching T-shirts for the summer programs they were attending, and I thought about the vitality and youth of my own campus. Bobby wouldn't see his son Benjamin through to his days of glory. Why was Bob being robbed of this? Why was he being robbed of his gift of fatherhood and family? I became angry and sad and inarticulate. A great weight sunk my chest inward as I thought about how I couldn't find any meaningful words to say to my friend. And so I decided to change the subject of my heart. I turned back to talking about my coming month of silence on the meditation bench.

"I think the focus techniques the Burmese use are a lot like what Rabbi Abulafia was doing a thousand years ago. You know, all his memorizing of long names of God and stuff. You still interested in the Kabbalah?"

Bobby shook his head. His expression managed to say: "Not really."

"Why not?" I asked.

Bobby stopped walking, and so I stopped also and turned toward him. His face screwed up a little, like he was going to lose the word, as he typically did. But he made a colossal effort and pushed the thought through.

"Distraction," he managed to say.

It was the most complicated thought I'd heard him say in months.

"Distraction?" I repeated. "Can you tell me what you mean?"

He grimaced and went through a moment of frustration. I thought for sure he was about to lose the thought and give up. But he didn't. Instead he took his index finger and swiped it across the space between us. He pointed to me and then back to him. Then he repeated the motion. His finger traversed the short distance between friends.

This is what matters, he was saying. *What matters are the relationships between people.*

THE EVIDENCE OF THINGS UNSEEN

Bobby died nine months later after twenty-two months of illness. In that final period I'd been largely unable to communicate with him. But I think we were both OK with that. He'd indicated everything he needed to tell me silently in our last conversation. That wordless sentence, pointing to the space between us, had instantly summarized my lifelong study of spirituality, and it had done a lot more. It had healed our friendship. I realized with Bobby's finger swipe that it's the space between us where the divine presence resides. That's what Bobby taught me.

Still, I wondered whether I had done enough. "I should have been a better friend to Bobby" I confessed to Cathy when I got home that day and relayed the terrible news of his death.

"You did your best," Cathy said.

"I feel bad about the last few years. I let things go, always expecting there would be time to make things right, to become closer again, and then suddenly there wasn't."

I looked at Cathy. Another lost friend.

"We should get a babysitter when I get back from the funeral," I said suddenly. The words just burst out. I knew the moment was wrong, but if not now, when? "It wasn't just with Bobby. I've been distant. But I could really use some Cathy time."

Cathy pulled our best bottle from the liquor cabinet. "You've had a lot on your mind," she said. "I have too. I can never seem to catch up."

"It goes so fast."

Then as I looked at my wife across the kitchen, I finally understood what I'd wanted and needed to say to her for so long.

"Bobby turned out to be a pretty good marriage counselor," I said.

"Really? How's that?"

"I learned something from him and from Tamar" I said. "Marriage is just being there for one another. That's it. That's all it is. Me being there for you. You being there for me."

"In sickness and in health," Cathy said, leaving the rest of the vow unspoken.

"I'm here for you," I said.

"Me too," she said.

She poured two shots of whiskey and shook a drop of bitters into mine. Just how I like it.

"The first round is to Bobby," she said.

With the fiery gulp, the entire complex of warmth and sadness of mortal friendship somehow coursed through me.

"To Bobby," I said.

"And to those who loved him," Cathy said.

My red-eye landed at Kennedy at six o'clock in the morning, giving me enough time to rent a car and beat some of Long Island rush hour. I was headed out against traffic anyway, back to a funeral parlor in my own hometown where I'd been raised. I hadn't been back in twenty years, ever since my folks had moved out. It was freezing and snowy and dreary, just like I remembered it, the sky swaddled in the thick gray fog of winter. I parked behind the plain funeral parlor, which could easily have been confused for a warehouse. In a tight stall in the bathroom I changed into a suit I now wore once a year on Yom Kippur. I threw my tie over my shoulder and brushed my teeth. Then I looked at myself in the mirror for what seemed to be a very a long time. I was asking myself whether I was able to do this and telling myself that I was not.

Bobby's brothers Steve and Dave were already there. Mr. and Mrs. Lichtman greeted incoming guests.

"I'm so sorry, Mrs. Lichtman," I said when I met her.

"Michael," she said, even managing to smile. "After all this time I think you can call me Phyllis!"

"Same goes for me," said Bobby's father, Irving. "Robbie didn't have a better friend."

A lot of my old friends from high school trickled in, but I didn't get a chance to see them. I spent most time consoling Bobby's old girlfriends and puppy loves from different periods in his life. Some had shown up. He'd connected with his girlfriends back then much more than he had let on to me. Some had even remained on as friends.

None of these trial relationships compared to what I'd seen he'd found with Tamar. Here she was, surrounded by all her brothers and sisters and family, still holding fast to her baby Benjamin. She'd cared for Bobby over these past twenty-two unfathomable months fueled by the force of sheer love. When I saw her we didn't really speak. I said only that she knew how sorry I was. She said only that indeed she knew, and she thanked me. There wasn't much else to say.

As we were called into the pews, the officers of Bobby's U.S. National Guard unit lined the way for us. His Hasidic rabbi from Brooklyn sat in the front row with some of his disciples. I think Bobby's younger brother Dave took the podium first. He was having a hard time controlling his emotions, but he managed to hold it together. He listed each of Bobby's impossible dreams and their ensuing impossible achievements: Columbia recording artist; filmmaker; United States military officer; scientist; husband, and father. Who does that? Who thinks he can do the impossible and then goes and does it? His big brother Bobby. Dave held the rail tightly as he descended the dais steps.

Steve ascended next. He seemed more confident in his composure, but then again he had been in California and had borne visceral witness to an awful lot of Bobby's physical deterioration. Knowing an end had come to that suffering I think tempered Steve's grief. I felt that too. But whereas I had allowed Bobby's sickness to impede my better memories of him, Steve hadn't. He spoke with the composed grief of an older brother, someone who had witnessed his first sibling come into the world and then be taken out of it. He'd thought an awful lot about Bobby over those decades of fraternity, and it all came out with a few words.

"My brother Bobby was an unlikely mix of passions and influences in his life and in his music," Steve said. "But they were never unlikely to him. It always made perfect sense to him to love Al Jolson and Robert Johnson, Sly Stone and *SCTV*, Howlin' Wolf and *The Honeymooners*, Bob Dylan, Chris Elliott, Bruce Springsteen, Public Enemy, William Shatner, Rick Rubin, and the Lubavitcher Rebbe. And you know what? He was right. And if he contradicted himself, well, he contained multitudes. Bobby saw and (especially) heard things and made connections that were obvious to him, if invisible and inaudible to the rest of us— at least until he noticed and made art out of it. He believed with all his soul and all his might in the evidence of things unseen. But he resisted with just as much stubborn determination the possibility that there were ideas or feelings he couldn't eventually find a way to express."

Then Steve took out an MP3 player and seemed to be cuing up a song. I started to shake. I'd been avoiding listening to Bobby's music all the time he had been sick. I can't handle it, I thought. I'm going to lose it right here in the pews. I'm going to lose it in this dreary funeral home on this dreary Long Island road in the dreary town where I grew up, on this dreary freezing day where the snowpack is already grayed over with soot. I'm going to lose it. This is the excremental character of the universe coming to prove itself.

"Here's one of my favorite songs of his to remember him by," Steve said as he clicked on the MP3 player in front of the microphone. "Rest in peace, my brother."

And then Bobby's voice rang out. Coherently. Without succumbing to the frustration of losing a thought. Without stammer or stutter. It was so *musical*. It was his voice! It was the voice I'd carried with me only in my mind now for nearly two years of having a voiceless Bobby. What that moment of hearing meant to me I can't begin to capture, though maybe its spirit is in fact best relayed by the very song Bobby was singing to me from the next life. Its words were adapted from Whitman's own "Song of the Open Road." These are from Bobby's version:

Aloof and lighthearted I go
Healthy and free, don't you know
The world before me
The long brown path that leads
Wherever else I choose to go

I won't ask for fortune no more
'Cause I am my fortune, you know.
I won't cry or whimper no more
Or postpone;
I'm through with complaining.
Strong and content I'm on the open road

The earth is sufficient for me
I don't need the stars necessarily
I carry the names of the people
That I'd like to see.
And have more faith in things unseen

From this moment on I am free
Awe seems so beautiful to me
I never realized that I held
So much Godliness, I
I'm larger, better than at first it seemed

On the airplane back to Los Angeles I kept thinking about how freezing it had been at graveside and about how much Bobby had always detested the cold. It had been unbearable to watch shovel after shovel of frozen dirt being thrown on the pine coffin. As I'd thrown my own shovelful I couldn't stop thinking, *Bobby, what the hell are you doing in the ground?*

Now as my airplane chased twilight across the west, in my mind I had a kind of strange conversation with Bobby. Actually it was more like a movie scene. Even these days the scene still sometimes comes out to play in my imagination. It's about finally sitting down to do that script Bobby always wanted to write with me. One diner booth. One old ninety-minute cassette tape, forty-five minutes per side, just like in the old days. Two friends. This is how I imagine it kicking off.

FADE IN

INT. DINER — NIGHT

A diner booth. A bottle of whiskey and a cassette recorder sit on the table between two friends.

                    MICKEY
    Do you think God laughs?

                    BOBBY
    Most definitely. He's a big kibitzer, bigger
    than Jerry Seinfeld or Mel Brooks.

                    MICKEY
    Really?

                    BOBBY
    For sure. Even bigger than Jolie.

                    MICKEY
    Bigger than Jolie? Wow. That's some-
    kibitzer.

Bobby pours a stevia packet on his tongue.

                    BOBBY
    He's the Biggest.

THE DIVINE PRESENCE

Three months later, Beau Biden was dead of the same ailment, tugging the heartstrings of the nation. Bobby and Beau had suffered through the very same weeks and months. In those same months *Time* magazine had put yet another young glioblastoma patient on the front page, Brittany Maynard, and continued to cover her when she chose to end her own life legally in Oregon. My god the bravery! From every walk of life, and supported by every conceivable human therapeutic tradition—religious, secular, medical, whatever, the dignity with which people face death is *awe*-inspiring in the deepest sense of that word. It is inspiring of divine fear and wonder. It invokes the awe of having oneself set before the entire horror and strange beauty of existence. It is realizing that this horror and beauty is all *me*—and then it's over.

Tamar later told me something that might initially seem callous to some, but which made sense to me.

"I'm glad for having gone through it," she said. But she immediately corrected herself. "'Glad' isn't the right word. There *is* no word. Of course I wish none of it had happened. I feel absolutely awful about Bobby's suffering. And I wish he was still here with me. But somehow I'm *more* for all of this. And that's not exactly what I mean, either."

I thought I understood Tamar because independently, though by severely less strenuous circumstances, I had come to a similar place. There is no other path than the one we are given. Our only choice is how we view it. We can make of life a path of friendship and joy and let love build us up, or we can allow life to overcome us. That's all there is to it.

I don't distinguish between joy and pain anymore, or between happiness and sorrow. I don't distinguish between sacred and profane either. One's stance before the universe, whatever it may throw at us, must be either/or. Either all moments deserve awe or none do. And this means, I think, that I ought to be grateful not only for the mountains I think I can climb but also for those that seem to topple me. Because I've withstood each landslide so far. I'm here. Right now. Another moment thinking and feeling. Another moment breathing. Another moment longing. Another moment in triumph and then in tragedy. Another moment in grief for the memory of my friend in his hospice gurney and yet a strange joy regarding the very same memory. These moments are all gifts, even the worst ones.

Unless, of course, they aren't, which I also take to be a valid point of view. I sometimes live with that dark perspective of ingratitude and nihilism. I don't think it's coincidence that these are also my moments of worst suffering. I've started to recognize this mood. And it's exactly that, a *mood*. It comes when it will and, typically, it disappears by the same mysterious means. But sometimes, when I am aware of the impending suffering and dark interpretation of the world, I can muster up the will to hold up my own hand against it and say: *I am grateful for all this. I know the alternative.* My circumstances so far have permitted me to utter that prayer in truth. I realize I have been privileged. Circumstances for many people may not have made life a privilege. Believe me, I understand that point of view. In many moments I hold it myself. But for me, and perhaps for Tamar, so far it has come down to a matter of faith.

This wasn't Bobby's faith. His was less abstract. He filled his faith with people. He had faith in his wife and son and in his brothers and parents. He adored his friends and expected the world from us. He believed in the soldiers of his military unit and bonded with them more profoundly than even he had expected to happen. He had faith in the people and the God of Israel. Each and every one of these folks came through for Bobby, except for maybe God himself. I don't know. But Bobby knew. Bobby's faith consisted of these specific personal relations, the invisible webs that tether us to one another. I wish I shared Bobby's faith in connection with people. I'm working on it, starting with my own family. Bob charted a life of these human connections through his music as much as through his friendship and love, even when the universe sent an insurmountable landslide to crush the instrument of his body. I think he climbed that mountain too.

He's given me no mountain that I can't climb.

BOBBY SICHRAN

I miss Bobby. I still wonder whether God let him down or whether, in fact, God saved him. That question encapsulates the mood swings of my grief. But I know the question has no answer, and so these days I just try to do my best. I try to submit myself in assent to the circumstances of whatever reality I face: whether during the ecstasy of reaching mountaintop, as I did one lost summer somewhere along the road to Nashville (where the reefers sprout up just like weeds), or amidst the mortal hollow of losing my best friend. I've now had this faith work miracles in my own life. When I submit, it gives death meaning. It affords life purpose. It tinges suffering with joy. It eliminates all barriers to God.

But let me conclude by remembering the most important moment I shared in Bobby's brief life. I had come to see him down in

Irvine in his new home with Tamar and Benjamin. Tamar had set up his hospital gurney in a lovely alcove of the house, attached to the family room, where Bobby could hear each little family activity. I pulled a chair up to one side of the gurney, Bobby's father Irving sat on the other side. His mother Phyllis fiddled with some of the medical equipment that buzzed and beeped around us. Tamar played with Benjamin just across the threshold in the family room. Occasionally Benjamin, now eighteen months old, would stumble into the alcove hoisted up on his own two feet. "Daddy!" he'd shout and then toddle out again.

"Look who's here," Irving said to Bobby's unresponsive body as I sat down beside the gurney. By this time his skin had shriveled up to his very bones, a victim of the worst human hunger. No longer able to swallow or otherwise process food, the body was well beyond eating whatever fat he had stored. He had little muscle left and his breathing was more shallow than I thought possible. I took Bobby's hand gently, not knowing what to say.

"It's Mike," I said.

And then Bobby did something extraordinary. From the very depth of his depleting life energy he squeezed back against my hand. When I felt this, his life pulse shot right through my body. Our last word together was this touch, this closure of human boundary. It meant so many things. I'm here. I love you. Eternal thanks for being my friend. The squeeze meant these and an infinite array of ineffable communications that we once passed back between one another with the arch of an eyebrow or a wink, or that Bobby told with the grin which I already missed so much. But in that moment, in that pulse of friendship and love, I swear I also actually heard his voice.

"Mickey Bones!" he seemed to shout out.

And I thought I could see God's divine presence, the Shechinah, light up Bobby's face for me one more time.

CONCLUSION

Giving Into Gravity

To return to the words and spirit of William James, which have been such a resource for me, I hope this journey has revealed something like "a true record of the inner experiences of great-souled persons wrestling with the crises of their fate."[1] These are the agonizing human backstories to some spiritual masterpieces. Normal, suffering people, when facing the doubt and panic common to times of illness, midlife, patterns of addiction, and other reminders of the human condition, tried only to figure out their own few next steps forward. By taking some time to locate their personal feelings of gravity and significance, and accordingly reorienting their lives, they came through the terror. The affect achieved was a kind of spiritual mood, a peace with the universe and with their places in it. Perhaps stated less grandly, they achieved an integrative psychological health. Almost incidentally, in so reorienting themselves they also managed to pull entire spiritual traditions forward through the gift of having recorded their insights.

As I mentioned in the introduction to this book, the oldest continuing human experiments regarding affect, or how things feel, have been recorded for us in the annals of religion. Religions cultivate particular affects, which themselves are organized to bring the feelings of healing, orientation, and fulfillment. These original experiments in positive psychology and happiness studies may still be available to us, should we wish to seek them.

Also in the introduction I promised to return to discuss my difference with William James. I mentioned there that in *The Varieties of Religious Experience* James suggested how to characterize the saving spiritual point of view. "One might say," he finally offered, "that it consists of the belief that there is an unseen order, and that our supreme good lies in harmoniously adjusting ourselves thereto." He considered the qualitative psychological affects associated with belief in this unseen order to comprise "the reality of the unseen."[2] My own understanding of spirituality is, of course, deeply indebted to James's formulation, including his focus on the integrative therapeutic efficacy of spirituality. More significant still is his insight regarding the means of spiritual therapy, which is assent and adjustment to that which is beyond our capacity to control. So understood, religions are ultimately the world's classic *therapies of commitment* to higher orienting powers. James himself must be counted among the classical theorists of therapy, sided as he was with proponents of self-limitation through higher commitment, from Augustine among the ancients to Tolstoy in James's own day, and indeed also among all of the theorists and practitioners that we have met in these cases.

In contradistinction, Sigmund Freud in James's time began advocating for therapies of release—typically from higher powers and gravities that had grown oppressive in our neglect of them. But the limbic system (which Freud called the id) faces a cold universe. Our instinctual needs confront almost infinite frustrations when set before the scarce resources of the environment. Therapeutic exercises in release after release from these frustrations, tempered by stoic consent to the interminable process of making all things meaningless just as soon as they become too painful, are the most Freud ever promised. In favoring Freud's pathological view and medical approach, modern therapy came mostly to follow tactics of release, even after so much else of Freudian theory became disfavored. Current practices of cognitive behavior therapy, for instance, in their pathological rather than integrative focuses, also offer very specific redirection and recommitment and have not put forward a therapeutic strategy for overall integrative homeostasis. This is not peace with the universe but a series of untrustworthy and temporary cease-fires.[3]

Still the question remains as to whether one can do any better.

As much as I owe to James, here at the end of my study I find myself quibbling with his formulation. Although James claimed to be "bent on rehabilitating the element of feeling in religion and subordinating its intellectual part," nevertheless his definition—"belief that there is an unseen order"—supports the opposite.[4] With this formula, James came to emphasize the primacy of cognition and thought ("belief"), even to the point of contradicting his case for the precognizant, even autonomic, power of affects. Of course, beliefs may sometimes play a role in spiritual experiences, but not always. One may have experiences without coming to some cognitive conclusion about them, as one may believe in unseen orders and yet not feel affects. As an example highlighting the discrepancy in James's final formula, Nietzsche famously also believed in an unseen order, one of totalizing and meaningless chaos, and he also advocated self-adjustment to that order. Strictly speaking, I think James's definition of spirituality, relying as it does on belief and cognition, would have to accept Nietzsche's scheme as being a spiritual one, which in fact James explicitly did not believe.

So in the introduction I suggested that gravitas, the affect of spiritual weight, perhaps better characterizes the set of myriad spiritual experiences. Gravitas in particular is precisely what distinguishes James's spiritual mood from Nietzsche's advocacy of a carefree science in which the fundamental *weightlessness* of the world is the unseen order to which one assents. I come to the gravitational distinction actually by following Nietzsche's most famous passage. "Whither is God?" Nietzsche's madman cried; "I will tell you. We have killed him—you and I. All of us are his murderers." But then follows Nietzsche's remarkable report of his own feelings for having abandoned all higher orientation.

> What were we doing when we unchained this earth from its sun? Whither is it moving now? Whither are we moving? Away from all suns? Are we not plunging continually? Backward, sideward, forward, in all directions? Is there still any up or down? Are we not straying as through an infinite nothing? Do we not feel the breath of empty space? Has it not become colder? Is not night continually closing in on us?[5]

Nietzsche's own visceral response to the notion of no higher order—his free fall into infinite cold—indicates, to me at least, the premature declaration of God's death. Spiritual orientations are only "unseen" in the sense that they are rationally unavailable. But they are known and verifiable empirically by human faculties other than cognition, namely by affect and feeling. Nietzsche's own panicked feelings of ultimate disorder, having thought through the coldest implications of reason, flew out almost uncontrollably from his pen.

Nietzsche himself, brilliantly but I think fancifully, also proposed the primacy of cognition and belief, recommending that we might somehow grow capable of reinterpreting feelings of disorientation and weightlessness not as pains or guilts but as the sensations of carefree frolic. In this ultimate therapy of release, he anticipated much of what therapy has become. It may work for *Übermenschen* and other sociopaths, but it does not work for me. When the dark night of the soul chimes me awake, I know a carefree revaluation is not under my control to employ. I may stand stoic against the panic. Or I may give in to the many limbic temptations of weightless release that are instantly available to me now online and everywhere else. But in the end, my many experiments with weightlessness just end up with me feeling badly about myself. On the other hand, when I finally come to abide by my feelings of gravitas my recovery comes quickly, even instantly.

Which is all to say, spiritual affects don't necessarily require "belief," "over-belief," "faith," or a "faith-state" (to use James's final intellect-privileging nomenclature) to do their work.[6] In the arenas of human affect and feeling beyond cognition and reason—which James himself lauded and psychologists now know to constitute so much of human knowledge—qualitative evidence piles up for the existence of higher orders of feeling, quite beyond belief.[7] The observation is as old as Ghazali. For instance, real therapeutic orientation sometimes *is* seen, as when Ghazali saw the Lake of Fire. It can be heard, as Socrates heard from his daemon and Mary Lou Williams heard during private prayer. And it is felt, as Chinggis Khan came to feel in the pulse of the life force, and even as Nietzsche felt while falling into all directions of cold void and night. By these suprarational means, we feel joys, we feel temptations, we feel guilts, we feel pains. We are oriented or disoriented typically by every single thing that we do, whether or not we believe. Too often it is in *not* believing them that affects grow to become our torments. These pushes and pulls take no leap of faith to feel. Rather, these affects constitute *therapeutic reality*.

We are now totally surrounded by interminable promises of weightless release. A billboard assures us we can "Open Happiness" in a can of carbonated sugar water. "Social" and "news" media feeds hack our dopamine cycles, doing nothing for communal

feeling except to package us together as markets. Even our story-
tellers no longer leave us with guidance for life, but rouse us
merely to binge on sexual, violent, and laughable titillations.
These limbic activities, detached from higher orientations such as
learning, laboring, and loving, typically leave us empty and without edification. Who among us hasn't spent hours clicking away
at a browser and then ended the vapid search only to think: *What
kind of black hole was that?* When in the middle of the last century
my own teacher, the sociologist Philip Rieff, noted the increasing
legitimacy of these therapies of release, in the marketplace no less
than on the psychiatric couch, he thought we had already become
"permanently engaged in the task of achieving a gorgeous variety
of satisfactions." "That a sense of well-being has become the end,
rather than a by-product of striving after some superior communal end," he predicted "announces a fundamental change of focus
in the entire cast of our culture."[8]

As difficult as we now have it in the twenty-first century, we
are not the first generations to face helium temptations. I hope
I have shown here that the classic therapies of commitment are
still available to us. Of course, we must each locate our own personal orientations and edifying attachments by noticing how
our own behaviors make us feel. No saved soul ever did otherwise. But we are not entirely without compass in this adventure.
I think we each do have a therapeutic reality, subjective to each
of us and yet still very much beyond our control, especially when
dread tells us we're on the wrong path. This therapeutic reality
is not ours to choose; it's only ours to receive as though by revelation. It orients like the unseen pull of gravity. It's one and the
same with the daemonion voice that spoke to Socrates, telling
him No. It's what insisted to Mary Lou Williams that her music
could achieve something more. It's what whispered to Ghazali
that his time was short and his road still long. It's what beck-
oned the mighty Chinggis Khan when he suspected something

more worth knowing about the treasure of life. And it's what strengthened my friends Bobby and Tamar even in the final moments of human frailty.

It's also what I hear in my conscience when I face the mirror. For me, realizing the Reality of therapeutic reality—that my own best way exists, that I can come to discover it, and that it is beyond my control to define—this Reality of my own inwardly felt gravitas has been my most significant finding along this journey. These days, for every questionable action that I am aware enough to consider, I ask myself: *Is this a tug toward helium weightlessness, or is it an orienting gravity?* Typically my inner voice answers this question with staggering clarity. I hope further review of the world's diverse array of spiritual insights may prompt us to heed our own interior reckonings. Perhaps thereby we may finally make peace with the universe and also with ourselves.

ACKNOWLEDGMENTS

In the writing of this book I leaned heavily on the help of very good friends. Thanks to those who read, commented honestly, and pushed me forward, in roughly the order I appealed to them for help: Thomas LeBien, Thomas Crofts, John Jones, Jonathan Walton, Sanjay Sharma, Yuli Masinovsky, Mark Oppenheimer, Noah Feldman, Bruce Haynes, Syma Solovitch, Bryant Simon, Joel Friedlander, Shawn Callahan, Brian Kopell, Phil Dow, Amanda Lucia, Matthew King, Paul Chang, Jack Miles, Norman Watkins, John Malpede, Jenny Price, Bonnie Nadell, Aaron Sachs, Dana Calvo, Casey Affleck, Mike Pesca, Shmully Hecht, Peter Sellars, Julia Carnahan, Steven Zipperstein, David Stern, Molly Callender, Peter Curtis, Norman Stillman, Tudor Parfitt, Sandra Seligman, and Ellen Sweeney. Also thanks to the family of Robert Lichtman: Phyllis, Irving, Steven, and David Lichtman; Tamar Shinar, Shai, Benjamin and Daniel, and their whole family.

Special thanks go to my editor Wendy Lochner, who has graciously included my work among so many classics she has produced, and to the team at Columbia University Press, including Lowell Frye, Susan Pensak, and Meredith Howard. Thanks to Kelly Hughes of Dechant Hughes for helping me navigate the marketplace of ideas. Thanks also to the faculties and staffs of the Huntington Library, the University of California at Riverside Library, the Institute of Jazz Studies of Rutgers University Libraries, the Dunhuang Academy, the Boethius Initiative of UCLA, and the UCLA Confucius Institute.

Sincere thanks to John Malpede and Henriëtte Brouwers of the Los Angeles Poverty Department for inviting me to present portions of this work at the Skid Row History Museum and Archive. Thanks also to my rabbi, Shmully Hecht, for inviting me to discuss the project with Shabtai Los Angeles.

I am grateful to my brother Alan Alexander and my parents Ellen and Paul Alexander for their continuous love and support, while I am indebted to my children, Nick for locating a crucial article in *Sepia* magazine, and Thea for putting up with way too much jazz during carpool. Finally, thanks and love to Catherine Gudis for building us all up, especially me.

NOTES

1. THE PATH OF JOY

1. Katha Upanishad 1:20–29, 2:1–9. Translation adapted from Juan Mascaro, ed. and trans., *The Upanishads* (London: Penguin, 1965), 57–58. I translate the Sanskrit *s'reya* as joy, and *preya* as pleasure. Thanks to Justin McDaniel for his Sanskrit lessons.

2. MAKING PEACE WITH THE UNIVERSE

1. Martin E. P. Seligman and Mihaly Csikszentmihalyi, "Positive Psychology: An Introduction," *American Psychologist* 55, no. 1 (2000): 5–14, https://doi.org/10.1037/0003-066X.55.1.5.
2. Dante Alighieri, *The Divine Comedy*, trans. Henry Wadsworth Longfellow (Boston: Houghton, Mifflin, 1867), 1.
3. Letter to Benjamin Paul Blood, in William James, *The Letters of William James*, ed. Henry James (Boston: Atlantic Monthly, 1920), 39, cited in John J. McDermott, ed. *The Writings of William James* (New York: Random House, 1967), xiv. McDermott comments: "James spent a good part of life rationalizing his decision not to commit suicide." For the James biography, see Robert D. Richardson, *William James: In the Maelstrom of American Modernism* (New York: Houghton Mifflin, 2006).
4. Here and throughout the book, I mean *affect* as it is utilized in psychology, as a noun indicating the experience of feeling and emotion.

Affect, emotion, and mood are distinguished from cognition and thought, even by their corresponding neuroanatomy. As an introduction to the scientific field, I prefer Antonio R. Damasio, *Descartes' Error: Emotion, Reason, and the Human Brain* (New York: Penguin, 2005). Humanities scholarship has also developed significant affect theory, although they tend to emphasize social and political aspects of affect, which are not my interests here; for an overview, see Melissa Gregg and Gregory J. Seigworth, eds., *The Affect Theory Reader* (Durham: Duke University Press, 2010). For some recent work on religious affects, see Donovan O. Shaefer, *Religious Affects: Animality, Evolution, and Power* (Durham: Duke University Press, 2015); and Karen Bray and Stephen D. Moore, eds., *Religion, Emotion, Sensation: Affect Theories and Theologies* (New York: Fordham University Press, 2019).

5. William James, *The Varieties of Religious Experience* (New York: Modern Library, 2002), 48.

6. See James, 31–60. I agree with James's understanding of stoicism—and specifically of the equanimity and peace of mind (*ataraxia*) of Epictetus—as something less than "enthusiastic assent" and "passionate happiness." But I understand that others do not; see, for instance, William B. Irvine, *A Guide to the Good Life: The Ancient Art of Stoic Joy* (New York: Oxford University Press, 2008). For more a general interpretation of philosophy as exercises in spirituality, see Pierre Hadot, *Philosophy as a Way of Life: Spiritual Exercises from Socrates to Foucault,* ed. Arnold I. Davidson, trans. Michael Chase (Oxford: Blackwell, 1995).

7. Some will notice my use of the words *religion* and *spirituality* nearly interchangeably. In this, I follow William James's spirit, if not his nomenclature, as laid out in *The Varieties of Religious Experiences.* For James's purpose of determining the therapeutic value of religious affect (also my purpose here), he felt it "very important to insist on the distinction between religion as a personal function, and religion as an institutional, corporate, or tribal product." In his day, he could still say "the word 'religion,' as it is ordinarily used, is equivocal" (James, 366). In our day it is less equivocal. Many people now distinguish themselves as being "spiritual but not religious," and are probably right to feel institutionalism, corporatism, and tribalism in the latter. James, though obviously aware of the social perspective, for his purpose was interested in the "personal function" of religion—the therapeutic one. In these

pages, when I use either word, *spiritual* or *religious,* I too mean the personal psychological function. I am aware of the social and political blinders set up by so circumscribing the topic. For recent discussions of the importance of individual experiences, see Ann Taves, *Religious Experience Reconsidered: A Building-Block Approach to the Study of Religion and Other Special Things* (Princeton: Princeton University Press, 2011); Howard Wettstein, *The Significance of Religious Experience* (New York: Oxford University Press, 2014). For recent work regarding "the spiritual but not religious," see Linda A. Mercadante, *Belief Without Borders: Inside the Minds of the Spiritual but not Religious* (New York: Oxford University Press, 2014). On the emerging field of the history of spirituality itself, see especially the foundational work of Philip Sheldrake, *Spirituality: A Brief History* (Oxford: Wiley-Blackwell, 2013).

8. The science and medicine of spiritual experience is a highly technical and rapidly changing field. A recent overview is Andrew Newberg, *Neurotheology: How Science Can Enlighten Us About Spirituality* (New York: Columbia University Press, 2018). Accessible introductions to the science can also be found through the work of Andrew Newberg and Mark Robert Waldman, *How God Changes Your Brain: Breakthrough Findings from a Leading Neuroscientist* (New York: Ballantine, 2010); Malcolm Jeeves and Warren S. Brown, *Neuroscience, Psychology, and Religion: Illusions, Delusions, and Realities About Human Nature* (West Conshohocken, PA: Templeton Foundation, 2009); Patrick McNamara, *The Neuroscience of Religious Experience* (New York: Cambridge University Press, 2014). See also Mark Cobb, Christina M Puchlaski, and Bruce Rumbold, *Oxford Textbook of Spirituality in Healthcare* (New York: Oxford University Press, 2012). For the view of a leading cognitive neuroscientist working in the field, see Justin L. Barrett, *Cognitive Science, Religion, and Theology: From Human Minds to Divine Minds* (West Conshohocken, PA: Templeton Foundation, 2011). Historical work linking general medicine and religion has also been achieved recently; for an overview, see especially Gary B. Ferngren, *Medicine and Religion: A Historical Introduction* (Baltimore: Johns Hopkins University Press, 2014).

9. Sigmund Freud, "Analysis Terminable and Interminable," in *The Standard Edition of the Complete Psychological Works of Sigmund Freud,* trans. James Strachey, 24 vols. (London: Hogarth, 1974), 24:209–12;

Philip Rieff, *Freud: The Mind of the Moralist* (Chicago: University of Chicago Press, 1979), 28–64.

10. James, *The Varieties of Religious Experience*, 195. See especially the chapters "The Religion of Healthy-Mindedness" and "The Sick Soul" in *The Varieties of Religious Experience*, 90–184.

11. James, 61.

12. See the work of John Corrigan, particularly *Business of the Heart: Religion and Emotion in the Nineteenth Century* (Berkeley: University of California Press, 2002), and Corrigan's edited volume *The Oxford Handbook of Religion and Emotion* (New York: Oxford University Press, 2008). See also Shaefer, *Religious Affects*; Bray and Moore, *Religion, Emotion, Sensation*.

13. James himself toyed with the analogy of magnetism to describe unseen and unnamable foundations of spiritual beliefs: "The sentiment of reality can indeed attach itself so strongly to our object of belief that our whole life is polarized through and through, so to speak, by its sense of the existence of the thing believed in, and yet that thing, for purpose of definite description, can hardly be said to be present to our mind at all. It is as if a bar of iron, without touch or sight, with no representative faculty whatever, might nevertheless be strongly endowed with an inner capacity for magnetic feeling; and as if, through the various arousals of its magnetism by magnets coming and going in its neighborhood, it might be consciously determined to different attitudes and tendencies. Such a bar of iron could never give you an outward description of the agencies that had the power of stirring it so strongly; yet of their presence, and of their significance for its life, it would be intensely aware through every fibre of its being." James, *The Varieties of Religious Experience*, 63–64.

14. As it happens, an extraordinary amount of the neural activity occurring during spiritual experiences is, in fact, the tempering of limbic system activities (that typically accompany primary, innate, preorganized emotions and instincts) by activities of the prefrontal cortex (the seat of abstraction, executive function, planning, and especially prediction of consequence). Looking at these neurological functions cognitively, spiritual practices appear to provoke a consort of mind activity where private appetites and emotions are tempered by higher-order

contextualization. See Newberg and Waldman, *How God Changes Your Brain*, 41–66, as well as their more recent work on mysticism, *How Enlightenment Changes Your Brain* (New York: Avery, 2016). See also R. Joseph, "The Limbic System and the Soul: Evolution and the Neuroanatomy of Religious Experience," *Zygon* 36 (2001): 105–36, https://doi.org/10.1111/0591-2385.00343; Amy D. Owen et al., "Religious Factors and Hippocampal Atrophy in Late Life, *PLOS ONE* 6 (2011): e17006, https://doi.org/10.1371/journal.pone.0017006.

15. The distinction between therapies of commitment and those of release I borrow from my late teacher Philip Rieff, although I deploy them in a manner he would have have considered far too divorced from the social order. See Philip Rieff, *The Triumph of the Therapeutic: Uses of Faith After Freud* (Chicago: University of Chicago Press, 1987), 241, 261. I return to Rieff's contribution in the conclusion.

16. The principles are similar to contemporary acceptance and commitment therapy, although the generalized scope of traditional spiritual commitments—acceptance of one's place in the universe itself—goes well beyond the scope of contemporary clinical commitments, which focus on specific acceptances and goals. Which is to say, ACT remains pathology based and does not offer an integrative, homeostatic state of health, even as ACT theorists have recently adapted certain Buddhist languages of mindfulness. See especially Steven C. Hayes, Kirk D. Strosahl, and Kelly G. Wilson, *Acceptance and Commitment Therapy: The Process and Practice of Mindful Change* (New York: Guilford, 2016).

17. See for instance the organization of Tal Ben-Shahar, *Happier: Learn the Secrets to Daily Joy and Lasting Fulfillment* (New York: McGraw-Hill, 2007), 82–122.

18. With the recent advent of narrative psychology, even scientific psychology has enjoyed a revival of interest in narrative, self-reporting, and the qualitative analytic case history. So perhaps there is some room to view the great spiritual confessions as classic examples of such self-reporting, narrative sense making, and sometimes even competent qualitative analysis. For the foundations of the new narrative psychology, see especially Theodore R. Sarbin, ed., *Narrative Psychology: The Storied Nature of Human Conduct* (New York: Praeger, 1986); Jerome S. Bruner, *Actual Minds, Possible Worlds* (Cambridge: Harvard University

Press, 1986). A précis and manifesto of the twenty-first-century field of narrative psychology can be found in Brian Schiff, *A New Narrative for Psychology* (New York: Oxford University Press, 2017).

19. For a recent précis and review of sympathetic introspection, see Ryan Gunderson, "Sympathetic Introspection as Method and Practice: Cooley's Contributions to Critical Qualitative Inquiry and the Theory of Mind Debate," *Journal for the Theory of Social Behavior* 47, no. 4 (2017): 463–80, https://doi.org/10.1111/jtsb.12142.

3. SOCRATES

1. *Meno* 80a–b. All translations are adapted from Plato, *Five Dialogues: Euthyphro, Apology, Crito, Meno, Phaedo,* ed. John M. Cooper, trans. G. M. A. Grube (Indianapolis: Hackett, 2002). *Arete* is used differently throughout the Hellenic corpus. In fact, the word was most commonly utilized to judge athletic achievement, a use that Socrates thought dubious. See Debra Hawhee, "Agonism and Arete," *Philosophy and Rhetoric* 35, no. 3 (2002): 185–207.

2. *Apology* 21d.

3. *Apology* 19b–c.

4. W. K. C. Gutherie, *The Greek Philosophers: From Thales to Aristotle* (New York: Harper and Row, 1960), 183–204.

5. *Apology* 21d.

6. *Apology* 22d; see also *Euthyphro* 14a.

7. *Meno* 80c–d. Stupefied is my translation, Grube says "perplexed." But the torpedo fish sting is not merely perplexing, it is discombobulating.

8. Sean D. Kirkland, *The Ontology of Socratic Questioning in Plato's Early Dialogues* (Albany: State University of New York, 2012), 103–105.

9. Plato through Socrates explores these qualities respectively in *Laches, Republic,* book 1, *Meno, Charmides, Euthyphro,* and *Lysis.* On the Socratic paradox, see Alexander Nehamas, *The Art of Living* (Berkeley: University of California Press, 2000), 85.

10. *Euthyphro* 3a–b. When referring to *daemon* or *daemonion,* I've replaced some instances of Grube's "divine" with "spirit" or "spiritual."

11. *Republic* 496c2; *Euthydemus* 272e4.

12. See *Symposium,* especially Socrates's discussion of eros as the desire for happiness, literally *daemon eudaemonia.*

13. Heraclitus Fragment 54. *Daemon* differs from the idea of a "self," or a personal animating spirit, which in Greek would be *psyche*, best translated as "soul," and not what Socrates is talking about here. Socrates does speak extensively of *psyche* in the *Phaedo* when discussing the possibility of an afterlife.

14. *Apology* 31c–d.

15. *Republic* 6 496c.

16. *Apology* 36d.

17. *Apology* 36d–7a.

18. *Apology* 40a–c.

19. *Euthydemus* 279c–280a. There's a word in Greek for good fortune, *eutuchia*, which is the subject of another Socratic dialogue in which Socrates considers whether good fortune leads to eudaemonia—and concludes that it doesn't.

4. ABU HAMID AL-GHAZALI

1. Omid Safi, *The Politics of Knowledge in Premodern Islam: Negotiating Ideology and Religious Inquiry* (Chapel Hill: University of North Carolina Press, 2006), 18.

2. Massimo Campanini, "In Defense of Sunnism: Ghazali and the Seljuqs," in *The Seljuqs: Politics, Society, and Culture*, ed. Christian Lange and Songül Mecit (Edinburgh: Edinburgh University Press, 2011), 228–39.

3. Safi, *The Politics of Knowledge*, 78.

4. See Frank Griffel, *Ghazālī's Philosophical Theology* (Oxford: Oxford University Press, 2009), 37–40.

5. Eric J. Hanne, *Putting the Caliph in His Place: Power, Authority, and the Late Abbasid Caliphate* (Cranbury, NJ: Associated University Presses, 2007), 118–41.

6. ʿAṭā-Malik Juvaynī, cited in Griffel, *Ghazālī's Philosophical Theology*, 37.

7. Cited in Griffel, *Ghazālī's Philosophical Theology*, 39.

8. See Abu Hamid al-Ghazali, *Al-Ghazali's Path to Sufism: His Deliverance from Error*, trans. R. J. McCarthy (Louisville, KY: Fons Vitae, 2000), 53–54. All translations of this source have been adapted from McCarthy.

9. The anonymous reviewer of this book's manuscript noted that Griffel is more agnostic regarding Ghazali's motives in leaving Baghdad; see

Griffel, *Ghazālī's Philosophical Theology*, 39–45. See also the interpretations documented in Safi, *Politics of Knowledge*, 107–10. I would also like to thank the same reviewer for suggesting that the theme of conversion (*tawba*), the turning of one's life toward concern for the afterlife, shapes the entirety of Ghazali's interpretation and presentation of his narrative. See Griffel, *Ghazālī's Philosophical Theology*, 43; see also Eric L. Ormsby, "The Taste of Truth: The Structure of Experience in al-Ghazali's *al-Munqidh min al-dalāl*," in Wael B. Hallaq and Donald P. Little, eds., *Islamic Studies Presented to Charles J. Adams* (Leiden: Brill, 1991), 147.

10. Ghazali, *Deliverance from Error*, 53–54.

11. Ghazali, *Deliverance from Error*, 24–28.

12. Ghazali, *Deliverance from Error*, 20. Those who wish to follow Ghazali's remarkable experiment in skepticism might keep in mind that it preceded Descartes's "hyperbolic doubt" by five hundred years and, at least to my mind, came to more sustainable conclusions. See Tamara Albertini, "Crisis and Certainty of Knowledge in al-Ghazālī (1058–1111) and Descartes (1596–1650)," *Philosophy East and West: A Quarterly of Comparative Philosophy* 55 no. 1 (January 2005): 1–14.

13. "The connection between what is habitually believed to be a cause and what is habitually believed to be an effect is not necessary, according to us," in Abu Hamid al-Ghazali, *The Incoherence of the Philosophers*, trans. Michael E. Marmura (Provo, UT: Brigham Young University Press, 2002), 17:1. Although there is no indication that David Hume read Ghazali, this is exactly Hume's argument against causal necessity in *A Treatise on Human Nature* (1738). Hume there considers the perception of causal necessity to be a kind of human habit, not a fundamental rule of the universe. Kant's reading of Hume, precisely on the troubling issue of causality, led him to compose the *Critique of Pure Reason* (1781).

14. Ghazali, *Deliverance from Error*, 23.

15. ʿAbd al-Ghafir al-Farisi, a biographer of Ghazali, said that Ghazali actually started studying with this influential Sufi teacher back in Tus, Abu ʿAli al-Faramadhi (d. in 1084 when Ghazali was twenty-eight). See Griffel, *Ghazālī's Philosophical Theology*, 52.

16. Ghazali, *Deliverance from Error*, 51.

17. Adapted from Ghazali, *The Incoherence of the Philosophers*, trans. Marmura, 20:6. Marmura translates *dhawq* as "direct experience" where I prefer the literal "taste."

18. John Renard, ed. and trans., *Knowledge of God in Classical Sufism: Foundations of Islamic Mystical Theology* (Mahwah, NJ: Paulist Press, 2004), 196.

19. See Antonio R. Damasio, *Descartes' Error: Emotion, Reason, and the Human Brain* (New York: Penguin, 2005).

20. Ghazali, *Deliverance from Error*, 23. Compare to another formulation in the *Revival of the Religious Sciences:* "A hidden subtlety is understood only by those who have received so much grace from God as to grasp things by a divine light, rather than by the traditional authority." Cited in Kojiro Nakamura, *Ghazali and Prayer* (Kuala Lumpur: Islamic Book Trust, 2001), 29. In the same paragraph, Ghazali calls this the "light of spiritual certainty (*nūr al-yaqīn*)." Summary of idea of light in the works of Ghazali: "Chapter IV: Symbolism of Light in Al-Ghazzālī's Writings," in Hava Lazarus-Yafeh, *Studies in al-Ghazzālī* (Jerusalem: Magnes, 1975), 264–348.

21. Neurologists have since named this the Eureka Effect, consisting of a sudden information exchange between the two brain hemispheres, particularly activating the hippocampus and anterior superior temporal gyrus of the right hemisphere. There are, of course, also evolutionary theories explaining why this response developed in humans over time. WangBing Shen, Jing Luo, Chang Liu, and Yuan Yuan, "New Advances in the Neural Correlates of Insight: A Decade in Review of the Insightful Brain," *Chinese Science Bulletin* 58, no. 13 (2013): 1497–511.

22. Cited in Renard, *Knowledge of God in Classical Sufism*, 115.

23. Ghazali, *Deliverance from Error*, 51.

24. Cited in William C. Chittick, "Dhikr," in *Encyclopedia of Religion* (New York: Macmillan, 1987), 4:343.

25. Adapted from *Ghazali, Deliverance from Error*, 52, substituting "taste" for "fruitional experience."

26. Ghazali, *Deliverance from Error*, 53.

27. Ghazali, *Deliverance from Error*, 54.

28. Ghazali, *Deliverance from Error*, 53–54.

29. Abu Hamid al-Ghazali, *Letter to a Disciple,* ed. and trans. Tobias Mayer (Cambridge: Islamic Texts Society, 2010), 24.

30. From book 21 of the *Revival of the Religious Sciences*, translated in Nakamura, *Ghazali and Prayer*, 71f. A less poetic translation appears in Abu Hamid al-Ghazali, *The Marvels of the Heart: Science of the Spirit*, trans. Walter James Skellie (Louisville, KY: Fons Vitae, 2010), 54–56.

31. Ghazali is always exceedingly careful to maintain an orthodox differentiation between God and people, maintaining, for instance, in *The Niche of Lights* (1:45–46) that the gnosis experience "[is] not the reality of unification but [is] similar to unification." Ghazali, *The Niche of Lights*, trans. and annotated by David Buchman (Promo, UT: Brigham Young University Press, 1998), 18. See further book 35 of *The Revival of the Religious Sciences*, in Abu Hamid al-Ghazali, *Faith in Divine Unity and Trust in Divine Providence*, trans. David B. Burrell (Louisville, KY: Fons Vitae, 2001).

32. From book 21 of the *Revival*, translated in Nakamura, *Ghazali and Prayer*, 71–72.

33. Ghazali, *Deliverance from Error*, 56f. Also consider the following from *Deliverance* 64–65: "For nearly ten years, I assiduously cultivated seclusion and solitude. During that time several points became clear to me." No Sufi would have described mere intellectual study as the cultivation of "seclusion and solitude." In this sentence, Ghazali referred to his own mystical experiences.

34. Ghazali, *Deliverance from Error*, 57. In one place Ghazali goes rather far in his description of these states, in his *The Niche of Lights* 1:48: "When this state gets the upper hand, it is called 'extinction' in relation to the one who possesses it. Or, rather, it is called 'extinction from extinction,' since the possessor of the state is extinct from himself and from his own extinction. For he is conscious neither of himself in that state, nor of his own unconsciousness of himself." Ghazali, *Niche of Lights*, 18.

35. Cited in Renard, *Knowledge of God in Classical Sufism*, 115. "The knowledge of certitude cannot be found except among those who have certitude. It is among the deeds of those who possess certitude and is found uniquely in the hearts of those endowed with experiential knowledge."

36. Ghazali, *Niche of Lights*, 38 (2:53).

37. Griffel, *Ghazālī's Philosophical Theology*, 34.

38. Ghazali, *Deliverance from Error*, 64–65.

39. See especially books 21–23 of Ghazali's *The Revival of the Religious Sciences*, available in Ghazali, *Marvels*; and Abu Hamid al-Ghazali, *On Disciplining the Soul and Breaking the Two Desires*, trans. T. J. Winter (Louisville, KY: Fons Vitae, 2017).

40. Abu Hamid al-Ghazali, *On the Remembrance of Death and the Afterlife*, trans. T. J. Winter (Louisville, KY: Fons Vitae, 2016). See an excellent treatment of Ghazali's "psycho-cosmology" in Timothy J. Gianotti, *Al-Ghazālī's Unspeakable Doctrine of the Soul: Unveiling the Esoteric Psychology and Eschatology of the Iḥyāʾ* (Boston: Brill, 2001).

41. Ghazali, *Marvels*, 41.

42. *Saʿada* is the "happiness" in *The Alchemy of Happiness*, meaning something akin to "joy." See H. Daiber, "Saʿāda," in *Encyclopaedia of Islam*, vol. 8, ed. P. Bearman, Th. Bianquis, C. E. Bosworth, E. van Donzel, and W. P. Heinrichs, 2d ed., 12 vols. (Leiden: Brill, 1995 [1960–2005]). I thank William C. Chittick for indulging my emailed questions.

43. Adapted from Abu Hamid al-Ghazali, *The Alchemy of Happiness*, trans. Jay R. Crook (Chicago: Kazi, 2008), 860–62. I have only substituted the archaic second-person familiar ("thee") with the current form ("you").

44. The "hard problem" was named by D. J. Chalmers, "Facing Up to the Problem of Consciousness," *Journal of Consciousness Studies* (1995): 2:200–19. See also Rodolfo R. Llinas, *I of the Vortex: From Neurons to Self* (Cambridge: MIT Press, 2002).

45. Ghazali seems to have come to phenomenology seven hundred years before Kant clarified the idea of the synthetic a priori for the West: "The aim of this account is to emphasize that one should be most diligent in seeking the truth until he finally comes to seeking the unseekable. For primary truths are unseekable, because they are present in the mind; and when what is present is sought, it is lost and hides itself." Ghazali, *Deliverance from Error*, 24.

46. Ghazali, *Niche of Lights*, 23 (1:62).

47. Griffel, *Ghazālī's Philosophical Theology*, 55.

5. QIU CHUJI

1. Timothy May, *The Mongol Art of War: Chinggis Khan and the Mongol Military System* (Yardley, PA: Westholme, 2007), 46.

2. "The Travels of Friar Oderic," in Henry Yule, *Cathay and the Way Thither* (Millwood, NY: Kraus, 1967), 2:235, cited in George Lane, *Daily Life in the Mongol Empire* (Indianapolis: Hackett, 2009), 108.

3. Passages adopted from 'Ata Malik Juvaini, *Genghis Khan: The History of the World-Conqueror*, trans. John Andrew Boyle (Seattle: University of Washington Press, 1997), 27–28.

4. Juvaini, 28.

5. Li Zhichang, *Changchun zhenren xiyou ji*, translated as Li Chih-Ch'ang, *The Travels of an Alchemist: The Journey of the Taoist Ch'ang-ch'un from China to the Hindukush at the Summons of Chingiz Khan*, trans. Arthur Waley (London: Routledge, 1931), 48. All translations of this source have been adapted from Waley.

6. Li Chih-Ch'ang, 48.

7. Ruth W. Dunnell says *Yeke Mongol Ulus, Great Mongol Nation,* and claims the title came around 1210. Ruth W. Dunnell, *Chinggis Khan: World Conqueror* (Boston: Longman, 2010), 52. Timothy May says Chinggis Khan wiped out ethnic divisions between Mongol, Tatar, Kereit, Naiman, and eventually other ethnicities and created *Qamuq Monggol Ulus*, the whole Mongol nation. May, *The Mongol Art of War*, 32.

8. According to Chinggis Khan's Chinese secretary: "Formerly someone whose surname was Liu and given name Wen was introduced at court on account of his medical skill. He said that His Excellency Ch'iu was three hundred years old and that he possessed a secret technique of preserving health and prolonging life, and addressed a memorial to the Emperor recommending him." Igor de Rachewiltz, trans., "The Hsi-Yu Lu by Yeh-lu Ch'u-Ts'ai," *Monumenta Serica* 21 (1962): 25.

   In my depiction of these events, some readers will notice that I do not follow Jack Weatherford's account, or accept his view that "Qiu Chuji and his sect specialized in spiritual quackery, mainly selling longevity through magic." See Jack Weatherford, *Genghis Khan and the Quest for God: How the World's Greatest Conqueror Gave Us Religious Freedom* (New York: Penguin, 2016), 231, 223–40.

9. Igor de Rachewiltz thinks that it is highly probable that Yelu Chucai (1189–1243), Chinggis Khan's "scribe-secretary" and "astrologer-astronomer" after 1218, drafted this letter. See de Rachewiltz, "The Hsi-yu lu by Yeh-li Ch'u-ts'ai," 3.

10. Adapted from Emilii Bretschneider, *Mediaeval Researches from Eastern Asiatic Sources* (London: Trubner, 1888), 1:37–38.

11. Li Chih-Ch'ang, *The Travels of an Alchemist*, 54.

12. Bretschneider, *Mediaeval Researches*, 40–41.

13. Li Chih-Ch'ang, *The Travels of an Alchemist*, 55. The painting itself had been done by Yan Liben (d. 673) of the early Tang dynasty, whose works seem remarkably contemporary. A facsimile of his *Thirteen Emperor's Scroll* is available at https://en.wikipedia.org/wiki/Yan_Liben, retrieved January 8, 2020.

14. Daodejing 16; translation from D. C. Lao, *Chinese Classics: Tao Te Ching* (Hong Kong: Chinese University Press, 1982), 23.

15. Dunnell, *Chinggis Khan*, 51: "Although the Mongols kept their troop strength secret, estimates for 1206 . . . range from a high of ninety-five thousand to a more likely fifty thousand to seventy-five thousand soldiers. By the end of Chinggis's reign, troop strength had grown to about 129,000, largely as a result of the absorption of sedentary and other nomadic elements."

16. W. Barthold, *Turkestan Down to the Mongol Invasion* (London: Messrs Luzac, 1968), 406. Barthold thinks five months is an exaggeration. Juvaini, *Genghis Khan*, 81–86.

17. May, *The Mongol Art of War*, 2f.

18. Adapted from Juvaini, *Genghis Khan*, 103–5.

19. Komjathy says "Tomb for Reviving the Dead." See Louis Komjathy, *Cultivating Perfection: Mysticism and Self-transformation in Early Quanzhen Daoism* (Boston: Brill, 2007), 40.

20. Stephen Eskildsen, *The Teachings and Practices of the Early Quanzhen Taoist Masters*, (Albany: State University of New York Press, 2004), 4–5.

21. Yin Zhiping (1169–1251), *Qinqhe zhenren beiyou yulu*, 2/9a–10b. Translation adapted from Eskildsen, 47–49.

22. Adapted from Lao Tzu, *Tao Te Ching*, trans. Arthur Waley (London: Wordsworth Classics, 1997), 1, 56.

23. Zhuangzi, *Basic Writings,* trans. Burton Watson (New York: Columbia University Press, 2003), 36.

24. Yin Zhiping (1169–1251), *Qinqhe zhenren beiyou yulu* (1237), 2/9a–10b; translation adapted from Eskildsen, *The Teachings and Practices*, 47–49.

25. Zhuangzi, *Basic Writings*, 86.

26. Li Chih-Ch'ang, *The Travels of an Alchemist*, 94.

27. Adapted from Florian C. Reiter, "'A Praise of Buddha' by the Taoist Patriarch Qiu Chuji and Its Source," *Zeitschrift des deutschen morgenländischen Gesellschaft* 143 (1993): 179–91.

28. Tao-Chung Yao, "Ch'iu Ch'u-chi and Chinggis Khan," *Harvard Journal of Asiatic Studies* 46, no. 1 (1986): 201–19, 211n34.

29. Li Chih-Ch'ang, *The Travels of an Alchemist*, 99.

30. Li Chih-Ch'ang, 99.

31. Li Chih-Ch'ang, 100–2.

32. Ma Yu (1123–1184), *Dongxuan jinyu ji*, translation adapted from Eskildsen, *The Teachings and Practices*, 166.

33. "One-hundred years is the greatest limit from the womb until death." Wang Zhe (1113–1170), *Chongyang quanzhen ji*, adapted from Eskildsen, *The Teachings and Practices*, 57.

34. Wang Zhe, *Chongyang lijiao shiwu lun*, adapted from Eskildsen, *The Teachings and Practices*, 58.

35. Cited in Paulino T. Belamide, "Self-Cultivation and Quanzhen Daoism with Special Reference to the Legacy of Qiu Chuji" (PhD diss., University of Toronto, 2002), 129.

36. Following Waley's interpretation of the Mongolian, see Li Chih-Ch'ang, *The Travels of an Alchemist*, 101n1.

37. Li Chih-Ch'ang, 100–2.

38. Li Chih-Ch'ang, 111.

39. Li Chih-Ch'ang, 111–12.

40. Tradition holds that it was the khan's Chinese secretary Yelu Chucai who published a summary of the lectures as *Xuanfeng qinghui lu* (Record of celebrated meetings of mysterious winds), though after the khan's death he wrote a nasty rebuttal of them; see Rachewiltz, "Hsi-Yu Lu" 1–128. Key portions of the summary have been translated into English, though remarkably not the entirety of it. Waley provides a loose translation and précis of *Xuanfeng qinghui lu* in the introduction to *The Travels of an Alchemist*. Belamide has translated portions (125–27 and 133–35). Eskildsen has translated some short fragments: Eskildsen, *The Teachings and Practices*, 117. See also Louis Komjathy, "Technical Glossary of Early Quanzhen Daoism," in *Cultivating Perfection:*

Mysticism and Self-Transformation in Early Quanzhen Daoism (Leiden: Brill, 2007), 434–89. What follows must therefore be my imaginative recreation of the meetings between Chinggis Khan and Qiu Chuji, although, to my knowledge, my account is consistent with both the historical record and with Quanzhen Daoist theory, insofar as I understand it. I should like to say that I regret not being able to read contemporary Chinese and cannot evaluate W. Guo's biography of Qiu Chuji: W. Guo, *Qiu Chuji xue'an* (Jinan: Qilu Shushe, 2011). I have no doubt that my own thought would have been greatly enhanced with access to it.

41. Contemporary readers are quite correct to think forward to *différance* and to imagine that Derrida's neologism is an awfully good translation of Dao. Komjathy defines yang as celestial, ethereal/transcendent and yin as terrestrial/substantial/prone to decay; see Komjathy, *Cultivating Perfection,* 70; see also Komjathy 117: "Etymologically speaking, yin depicts a hill covered by shadows, while yang depicts a hill covered by sunlight. . . . As the characters suggest, yin and yang are used to represent different dimensions of the same phenomenon or situation. There are various association: yin/female/earth/dark/heavy/turbidity/rest and yang/male/heavens/light/light/clarity/activity."

42. Wang Zhe, *Chongyang quanzhen ji,* adapted from Eskildsen, *The Teachings and Practices,* 57.

43. See the medical work attributed Qiu Chuji, *Dadan zhizhi* (compiled late thirteenth century), translated as "Direct Pointers to the Great Elixir" in Louis Komjathy, trans., *The Way of Complete Perfection: A Quanzhen Daoist Anthology* (Albany: State University of New York Press, 2013), chapter 4. Portions are also translated throughout Belamide, "Self-Cultivation and Quanzhen Daoism."

44. Dunnell, *Chinggis Khan,* 33: "The Mongols shared a taboo against shedding blood, which they believed to house the human soul. If possible, one should kill without splattering a lot of gore about, thus redirecting the potency of the deceased spirit to serve oneself. Custom decreed that honorable adversaries be executed by suffocation through one means or another, although custom did not always hold sway."

45. Yelu Chucai (1190–1244), ed. *Xuanfeng qinghui lu,* adapted from Eskildsen, *The Teachings and Practices,* 69.

46. Dunnell, *Chinggis Khan*, 41: "According to Rashid ad-Din, Chinggis had nearly five hundred wives and concubines (perhaps an exaggeration) of which five ranked as grand ladies with an ordo, including the Tatar sisters. Lady Börte, number one wife, presided over her own ordo at the tip of the hierarchy."

47. Li Chih-Ch'ang, *The Travels of an Alchemist*, 23.

48. Arthur Waley concludes his own discussion of these lectures with a necessary historical comment. This interview between Qiu Chuji and the Jin emperor, Waley says, "took place in 1188 and by 1189 the monarch was dead. The improvement to his health was evidently of a very temporary nature." Li Chih-Ch'ang, *The Travels of an Alchemist*, 25.

49. Li Chih-Ch'ang, *The Travels of an Alchemist*, 24. Daoism indeed had a regimen of utilizing sexual asceticism and the withholding of orgasm called *huanjing bunao*, or "returning the sperm to fortify the brain." See Farzeen Baldrian-Hussein, "Inner Alchemy: Notes on the Origin and the Use of the Term Neidan," *Cahiers d'Extrême-Asie* 5 (1989): 163–90. See also Eskildsen, *The Teachings and Practices*, 78–83.

50. Since notes of this lecture were intentionally omitted from the original record, I have pieced it together from other Quanzhen sources available in Belamide, "Self-Cultivation and Quanzhen Daoism"; Eskildsen, *The Teachings and Practices;* and Komjathy, *The Way of Complete Perfection.*

51. Xuanquanzi (ca. 1300), ed. *Zhenian zhizhi yulu*, adapted from Eskildsen, *The Teachings and Practices*, 27–28.

52. Li Chih-Ch'ang, *The Travels of an Alchemist*, 113.

53. Translation of the conclusion of the lecture document by Rachelwitz, "Hsi-yu lu," 69–7n168.

54. Li Chih-Ch'ang, *The Travels of an Alchemist*, 113. Dunnell, *Chinggis Khan: World Conqueror*, 84: "By the autumn of 1222 the armies under Chinggis Khan moved out of Afghanistan (the Hindu Kush) and, reuniting with the other Mongol forces in central Asia, returned to their staging camp on the Irtysh River in the summer of 1224. Chinggis Khan was back at his *ordo* in Mongolia the following spring, planning the Tangut campaign, his last."

55. Li Chih-Ch'ang, *The Travels of an Alchemist*, 116–18.

56. Li Chih- Ch'ang, 117.

57. Qin Zhi'an (1188–1244), *Jinlian zhengzong ji* (1241), cited in Eskildsen, *The Teachings and Practices*, 157–58. See also Jinping Wang, *In the Wake of the Mongols: The Making of a New Social Order in North China, 1200–1600* (Cambridge: Harvard University Press, 2018).

58. The research is growing daily. I thank Dr. Brian Harris Kopell of the departments of neurosurgery, neurology, neuroscience, and psychiatry at the Icahn School of Medicine at Mount Sinai for answering so many of my questions. For a good introduction to the field of the neuropsychology of spiritual experience, see Newberg and Waldman, *How God Changes Your Brain*, 41–66. Regarding specific changes to the limbic system, see Newberg and Waldman, *How Enlightenment Changes Your Brain*; R. Joseph, "The Limbic System and the Soul: Evolution and the Neuroanatomy of Religious Experience," *Zygon* 36 (2001): 105–36, https://doi.org/10.1111/0591-2385.00343; Amy D. Owen et al., "Religious Factors and Hippocampal Atrophy in Late Life, *PLOS ONE* 6 (2011): e17006, https://doi.org/10.1371/journal.pone.0017006.

59. See the neiyeh chapters in Guanzi in Harold D. Roth, *Original Tao: Inward Training (Nei-yeh) and the Foundations of Taoist Mysticism* (New York: Columbia University Press, 2004).

60. Li Chih-Ch'ang, *The Travels of an Alchemist*, 158–59.

61. May, *The Mongol Art of War*, 17.

62. May, 143.

63. Tatiana Zerjal et al., "The Genetic Legacy of the Mongols," *American Journal of Human Genetics* 72, no. 3 (2003): 717–21.

64. Li Chih- Ch'ang, *The Travels of an Alchemist*, 129.

6. MARY LOU WILLIAMS

1. Mary Lou Williams Archive at the Institute of Jazz Studies, Rutgers University, Newark, Series 5, Box 1, Notebook 1. Citations of this collection herein are abbreviated as such: IJS 5.1 Notebook 1. The archive is massive, and papers are not yet entirely labeled. Specific locations cannot always be indicated. Sincere thanks to the librarians and archivists of the institute.

2. Linda Dahl, *Morning Glory: A Biography of Mary Lou Williams* (New York: Pantheon, 2000), 185.

3. Music critic John S. Wilson conducted an oral history interview with Mary Lou Williams on June 26, 1973, for the Smithsonian. A tape and paginated transcription of that interview is kept at the Institute of Jazz Studies, Rutgers University, Newark, as part of the Jazz Oral History Project and is referred to herein as IJS Oral History, 96.

4. IJS Oral History, 70; IJS 5.1 Autobiographical Notebook 3, 298–300.

5. Mary Lou Williams and Peter O'Brien, interview by Martha Oneppo, Yale Oral History American Music Series, 1981, 21. Herein cited as Yale Oral History. See also IJS 5.2 "Don't Destroy the Roots," 7: "Today musicians should all kneel to Monk—he suggested the modern era; he sent everyone on a return to school and the library. I was there when it all began at Minton's."

6. Scott Hubbard, "Mary Lou Started at 3 and Stays in Key," *Wilmington Evening Journal*, November 3, 1975.

7. Dahl, *Morning Glory*, 187.

8. Eric C. Schneider, *Smack: Heroin and the American City* (Philadelphia: University of Pennsylvania Press, 2008).

9. Ross Russell, *Bird Lives!: The High Life and Hard Times of Charlie (Yardbird) Parker* (New York: Da Capo, 1996), 199–243. IJS 5.1 Autobiographical Notebook 3, 401–402.

10. Johann Hari, *The First and Last Days of the War on Drugs* (London: Bloomsbury, 2015), 19–32.

11. Yale Oral History, 20.

12. IJS 5.1 Autobiographical Notebook 3, 328f. IJS 5.1 Autobiographical Notebook 2, 280–83 recounts an episode with two benzedrine tablets and coffee, which motivated the club's owner Barney Josephson to call upon a doctor in the audience, who sent Williams home for 10 days.

13. IJS 5.2 Williams, "All Musicians are in Need of God," unpublished manuscript.

14. IJS Oral History, 143–44.

15. IJS 5.1 1/10, 39–43.

16. IJS 5.1 1/10, 45, 48.

17. IJS 5.1 1/10, 39–56.

18. IJS 5.1 1/10, 67 (emphasis in the original).

19. Mary Lou Williams, "What I Learned from God About Jazz," *Sepia*, April 1958, 57–60. Thanks to Nick Gudis for tracking down a copy of this crucial article.

20. Yale Oral History, 8.

21. Thomas Albright, "Mary Lou—a Heritage That's Strictly American," *World Sunday*, May 1, 1977.

22. IJS 5.1 1/10, 67.

23. Mary Lou Williams, "What I Learned from God About Jazz," 59.

24. IJHS 5.1 1/10, 69–71 (emphasis in the original).

25. Williams, "What I Learned from God About Jazz," 57–58.

26. IJS 5.2 "Has the Black American Lost His Creativeness and Heritage in Jazz?" unpublished manuscript.

27. "We stopped in at the cathedral for a few minutes," Edith Stein remembered in her autobiography, "and, while we looked around in respectful silence, a woman carrying a market basket came in and knelt down in one of the pews to pray briefly. This was something entirely new to me. To the synagogues or to the Protestant churches which I had visited, one went only for services. But here was someone interrupting her everyday shopping errands to come into this church, although no other person was in it, as though she were here for an intimate conversation. I could never forget that." Edith Stein, *Life in a Jewish Family: Her Unfinished Autobiographical Account*, ed. L. Gelber and Romaeus Leuven, trans. Josephine Koeppel (Washington, DC: ICS, 1986), 401.

28. IJS Oral History, 136.

29. John S. Wilson, "Mary Lou Williams, A Jazz Great, Dies," *New York Times*, May 30, 1981. In IJS Oral History, 145, with Wilson she in fact indicated a sound to be the sign: "I got a sound that everybody should pray in the church every day."

30. IJS Oral History, 155.

31. IJS Oral History, 151.

32. IJS 5.3 Williams's Private Liturgy.

33. IJS 5.1 folder 2, Prayer List.

34. IJS 8.13 Publicity Document.

35. "The Catholic Church and the Negro," *Ebony*, December 1957, 19–21.

36. Yale Oral History, 9.

37. Williams, "What I Learned from God About Jazz," 59.

38. IJS Oral History, 156.

39. IJS 5.2 "Has the Black American Lost His Creativeness and Heritage in Jazz?" unpublished manuscript.

40. Williams, "What I Learned from God About Jazz," 59.

41. Yale Oral History, 9.

42. Williams, "What I Learned from God About Jazz," 59.

43. IJS 5.3 Publicity Interview.

44. Cited and translated by John W. O'Malley, *What Happened at Vatican II* (Cambridge: Harvard University Press, 2008), 17.

45. Giuliana Cavallini, *St. Martin de Porres: Apostle of Charity*, trans. Caroline Holland (St. Louis: Herder, 1963).

46. Mary Lou Williams, *Mary Lou Williams Presents Black Christ of the Andes*, Smithsonian Folkways SFW CD 40816.

47. Fran Goulart, *Sounds and Fury*, December 1965, cited along with other similar reviews in Dahl, *Morning Glory*, 276f; also see reviews collected by Tammy L. Kernodle, *Soul on Soul: The Life and Music of Mary Lou Williams* (Boston: Northeastern University Press, 2004), 202–3.

48. My own favorite treatment of John Coltrane and of sixties jazz generally is Scott Saul, *Freedom Is, Freedom Ain't: Jazz and the Making of the Sixties* (Cambridge: Harvard University Press, 2003).

49. IJS 8.1 Syllabus for Music 074 and African-American Studies 074, "Introduction to Jazz," Fall Semester 1979, Duke University.

50. IJS 5.2 "Has the Black American Lost His Creativeness and Heritage in Jazz?" unpublished manuscript.

51. Dahl, *Morning Glory*, 292–93.

52. The best history of the musical questions discussed and decided at Vatican II, made by an observer of those proceedings, is Archbishop Piero Marini, *A Challenging Reform: Realizing the Vision of the Liturgical Renewal* (Collegeville, MN: Liturgical Press, 2007).

53. Especially helpful at this time was Brother Mario Hancock, an African-American Franciscan then stationed in Rome, with whom Mary Lou carried on a lifelong correspondence and deep relationship. At the Mary Lou Williams Archive at the Institute of Jazz Studies, the correspondence takes up many folders (series 3, boxes 19 and 20). Those interested in Williams's developed articulations of suffering, sacrifice, and the African American status as God's chosen people are directed to these remarkable communications. See also communications with Sister Martha Morris of the Cenacle Retreat House of Lancaster, Massachusetts, Williams's favorite hermitage (IJS 3.20–21).

54. IJS 8.2 AP Wire Report of February 2, 1969.

55. Mary Lou Williams, *Mary Lou's Mass*, Smithsonian Folkways SFW CD 40815.

56. Frances Herridge, "New Ailey 'Rites' at City Center," *New York Post*, May 18, 1973; Hubert Saal, "The Spirit of Mary Lou," *Newsweek*, December 20, 1971, 67.

57. Vernon D. Jarrett, "Mary Lou Williams Is Jazz," *Chicago Tribune*, July 2, 1971. She also made this related comment: "Whenever I play I throw myself away. It doesn't matter where I am. I close my eyes and leave this earth. The music comes through my mind, into my heart, and out my fingertips." Peter Keepnews, "Liturgy of Jazz at St. Patrick's," *New York Post*, February 19, 1975.

58. John S. Wilson, "Mary Lou Williams, at Piano, Leads Her Jazz Mass at St. Patrick's," *New York Times*, February 19, 1975.

CONCLUSION

1. William James, *The Varieties of Religious Experience* (New York: Modern Library, 2002), 7.

2. James, 61. James expanded this definition in the conclusion to *The Varieties of Religious Experience*, 528.

3. The distinction between therapies of commitment from those of release I borrow from my late teacher Philip Rieff, although I deploy these in a manner he would have have considered far too divorced from the social order. See Philip Rieff, *The Triumph of the Therapeutic: Uses of Faith After Freud* (Chicago: University of Chicago Press, 1987), 241, 261. See also Philip Rieff, *Freud: The Mind of the Moralist* (Chicago: University of Chicago Press, 1979).

  Recently there have been fascinating pushes toward an integrative cognitive behavioral therapy approach, even from the field's founder Aaron T. Beck. See especially Brad A. Alford and Aaron T. Beck, *The Integrative Power of Cognitive Therapy* (New York: Guilford, 1997). On the increasing use of traditional Buddhist theory and practices to achieve psychological integration, see James D. Herbert and Evan M. Forman, eds., *Acceptance and Mindfulness in Cognitive Behavior Therapy: Understanding and Applying the New Therapies* (Hoboken, NJ: Wiley, 2011).

4. James, *The Varieties of Religious Experience*, 545.

5. Friedrich Nietzsche, *The Gay Science*, trans. Walter Kaufman (New York: Random House, 1974), section 125. See also Nietzsche's magnificent attempt (in concluding section 383) to revalue the cold, sinking feeling (*The Gay Science*, 374–75).

6. James, *The Varieties of Religious Experience*, 528–64. Yet in places James indeed seems to have considered superseding the need for cognitive belief entirely, focusing rather on affect alone: "In the distinctively religious sphere of experience, many persons . . . possess the objects of their belief, not in the form of mere conceptions which their intellect accepts as true, but rather in the form of quasi-sensible realities directly apprehended. . . . The feeling of reality may be something more like a sensation than an intellectual operation properly so-called" (James, 73–74).

7. Especially important for this feeling intellect seems to be the orbitofrontal cortex. See the fascinating study in which patients with prefrontal damage could not quite get the feel of a card game (that is, they could not cultivate "nonconscious biases"), although they rationally understood its rules. Antoine Bechara, Hanna Damasio, Daniel Tranel, and Antonio R. Damasio, "Deciding Advantageously Before Knowing the Advantageous Strategy," *Science* 275, no. 5304 (1997): 1293–95. See also Antonio Damasio, *The Feeling of What Happens: Body and Emotion in the Making of Consciousness* (New York: Mariner, 2000). On the differences between cognition and affect, see especially Antonio Damasio, *Descartes' Error: Emotion, Reason, and the Human Brain* (New York: Penguin, 2005).

8. Rieff, *The Triumph of the Therapeutic*, 241, 261.

BIBLIOGRAPHY

Albertini, Tamara. "Crisis and Certainty of Knowledge in al-Ghazālī (1058–
  1111) and Descartes (1596–1650)." *Philosophy East and West: A Quarterly of
  Comparative Philosophy* 55, no. 1 (2005): 1–14.
Albright, Thomas. "Mary Lou—a Heritage That's Strictly American." *World
  Sunday*, May 1, 1977.
Alighieri, Dante. *The Divine Comedy.* Trans. Henry Wadsworth Longfel-
  low. Boston: Houghton Mifflin, 1867.
Baldrian-Hussein, Farzeen. "Inner Alchemy: Notes on the Origin and the
  Use of the Term Neidan." *Cahiers d'Extrême-Asie* 5 (1989): 163–90.
Barrett, Justin L. *Cognitive Science, Religion, and Theology: From Human
  Minds to Divine Minds.* West Conshohocken, PA: Templeton Founda-
  tion Press, 2011.
Barthold, W. *Turkestan Down to the Mongol Invasion* London: Messrs Luzac,
  1968.
Bechara, Antoine, Hanna Damasio, Daniel Tranel, and Antonio R. Dama-
  sio. "Deciding Advantageously Before Knowing the Advantageous Strat-
  egy." *Science* 275, no. 5304 (1997): 1293–95.
Beck, Aaron T. *The Integrative Power of Cognitive Therapy.* New York: Guilford, 1997.
Belamide, Paulino T. "Self-Cultivation and Quanzhen Daoism with Special Reference to the Legacy of Qiu Chuji." PhD diss., University of
  Toronto, 2002.
Ben-Shahar, Tal. *Happier: Learn the Secrets to Daily Joy and Lasting Fulfillment.* New York: McGraw-Hill, 2007.

Bray, Karen and Stephen D. Moore, eds. *Religion, Emotion, Sensation: Affect Theories and Theologies*. New York: Fordham University Press, 2019.

Bretschneider, Emilii. *Mediaeval Researches From Eastern Asiatic Sources*. London: Trubner, 1888.

Bruner, Jerome S. *Actual Minds, Possible Worlds*. Cambridge: Harvard University Press, 1986.

Campanini, Massimo. "In Defense of Sunnism: Ghazali and the Seljuqs." In *The Seljuqs: Politics, Society and Culture*. Ed. Christian Lange and Songül Mecit, 228–39. Edinburgh: Edinburgh University Press, 2011.

"The Catholic Church and the Negro." *Ebony*, December 1957, 19–21.

Cavallini, Giuliana. *St. Martin de Porres: Apostle of Charity*. Trans. Caroline Holland. St. Louis: B. Herder, 1963.

Chalmers, D. J. "Facing up to the problem of consciousness." *Journal of Consciousness Studies* 2, no. 3 (1995): 200–19.

Chittick, William C. "Dhikr." In *Encyclopedia of Religion*, 4:343. New York: Macmillan, 1987.

Cobb, Mark, Christina M. Puchlaski, and Bruce Rumbold. *Oxford Textbook of Spirituality in Healthcare*. New York: Oxford University Press, 2012.

Corrigan, John. *Business of the Heart: Religion and Emotion in the Nineteenth Century*. Berkeley: University of California Press, 2002.

——, ed. *The Oxford Handbook of Religion and Emotion*. New York: Oxford University Press, 2008.

Dahl, Linda. *Morning Glory: A Biography of Mary Lou Williams*. New York: Pantheon, 2000.

Daiber, H. "Saʿāda" In *Encyclopaedia of Islam*, vol. 8. 2d ed. Ed. P. Bearman, Th. Bianquis, C. E. Bosworth, E. van Donzel, and W. P. Heinrichs. 12 vols. Leiden: Brill, 1995.

Damasio, Antonio R. *Descartes' Error: Emotion, Reason, and the Human Brain*. New York: Penguin, 2005.

——. *The Feeling of What Happens: Body and Emotion in the Making of Consciousness*. New York: Mariner, 2000.

Dunnell, Ruth W. *Chinggis Khan: World Conqueror*. Boston: Longman, 2010.

Eskildsen, Stephen. *The Teachings and Practices of the Early Quanzhen Taoist Masters*. Albany: State University of New York Press, 2004.

Ferngren, Gary B. *Medicine and Religion: A Historical Introduction*. Baltimore: Johns Hopkins University Press, 2014.

Freud, Sigmund. "Analysis Terminable and Interminable." In *The Standard Edition of the Complete Psychological Works of Sigmund Freud*, 24:209–12. Trans. James Strachey. 24 vols. London: Hogarth, 1974.

al-Ghazali, Abu Hamid. *The Alchemy of Happiness*. Trans. Jay R. Crook. Chicago: Kazi, 2008.

——. *On Disciplining the Soul and Breaking the Two Desires*. Trans. T. J. Winter. Louisville, KY: Fons Vitae, 2017.

——. *Faith in Divine Unity and Trust in Divine Providence*. Trans. David B. Burrell. Louisville, KY: Fons Vitae, 2001.

——. *Al-Ghazali's Path to Sufism: His Deliverance from Error*. Trans. R. J. McCarthy. Louisville, KY: Fons Vitae, 2000.

——. *The Incoherence of the Philosophers*. Trans. Michael E. Marmura. Provo, UT: Brigham Young University Press, 2002.

——. *Letter to a Disciple*. Trans. Tobias Mayer. Cambridge: Islamic Texts Society, 2010.

——. *The Marvels of the Heart: Science of the Spirit*. Trans. Walter James Skellie. Louisville, KY: Fons Vitae, 2010.

——. *The Niche of Lights*. Trans. David Buchman. Provo, UT: Brigham Young University Press, 1998.

——. *On the Remembrance of Death and the Afterlife*. Trans. T. J. Winter. Louisville, KY: Fons Vitae, 2016.

Gianotti, Timothy J. *Al-Ghazālī's Unspeakable Doctrine of the Soul: Unveiling the Esoteric Psychology and Eschatology of the Iḥyāʾ*. Boston: Brill, 2001.

Gregg, Melissa and Gregory J. Seigworth, eds. *The Affect Theory Reader*. Durham: Duke University Press, 2010.

Griffel, Frank. *Ghazālī's Philosophical Theology*. Oxford: Oxford University Press, 2009.

Gunderson, Ryan. "Sympathetic Introspection as Method and Practice: Cooley's Contributions to Critical Qualitative Inquiry and the Theory of Mind Debate." *Journal for the Theory of Social Behavior* 47, no. 4 (2017): 463–80. https://doi.org/10.1111/jtsb.12142.

Guo, W. *Qiu Chuji xue'an*. Jinan: Qilu Shushe, 2011.

Gutherie, W. K. C. *The Greek Philosophers: From Thales to Aristotle*. New York: Harper and Row, 1960.

Hadot, Pierre. *Philosophy as a Way of Life: Spiritual Exercises from Socrates to Foucault*. Ed. Arnold I. Davidson. Trans. Michael Chase. Oxford: Blackwell, 1995.

Hanne, Eric J. *Putting the Caliph in His Place: Power, Authority, and the Late Abbasid Caliphate.* Cranbury, NJ: Associated University Presses, 2007.

Hari, Johann. *The First and Last Days of the War on Drugs.* London: Bloomsbury, 2015.

Hawhee, Debra. "Agonism and Arete." *Philosophy and Rhetoric* 35, no. 3 (2002): 185–207.

Hayes, Steven C., Kirk D. Strosahl, Kelly G. Wilson. *Acceptance and Commitment Therapy: The Process and Practice of Mindful Change.* New York: Guilford, 2016.

Herbert, James D., and Evan M. Forman, eds. *Acceptance and Mindfulness in Cognitive Behavior Therapy: Understanding and Applying the New Therapies.* Hoboken, NJ: Wiley, 2011.

Herridge, Frances. "New Ailey 'Rites' at City Center." *New York Post*, May 18, 1973.

Hubbard, Scott. "Mary Lou Started at 3 and Stays in Key." *Wilmington Evening Journal*, November 3, 1975.

Irvine, William B. *A Guide to the Good Life: The Ancient Art of Stoic Joy.* New York: Oxford University Press, 2008.

James, William. *The Letters of William James.* Ed. Henry James. Boston: Atlantic Monthly, 1920.

——. *The Varieties of Religious Experience.* New York: Modern Library, 2002.

——. *The Writings of William James.* Ed. John J. McDermott. New York: Random House, 1967.

Jarrett, Vernon D. "Mary Lou Williams is Jazz." *Chicago Tribune*, July 2, 1971.

Jeeves, Malcolm and Warren S. Brown. *Neuroscience, Psychology, and Religion: Illusions, Delusions, and Realities About Human Nature.* West Conshohocken, PA: Templeton Foundation, 2009.

Joseph, R. "The Limbic System and the Soul: Evolution and the Neuroanatomy of Religious Experience." *Zygon* 36 (2001): 105–36. https://doi.org/10.1111/0591-2385.00343.

Juvaini, ʿAta Malik. *Genghis Khan: The History of the World-Conqueror.* Trans. John Andrew Boyle. Seattle: University of Washington Press, 1997.

Keepnews, Peter. "Liturgy of Jazz at St. Patrick's." *New York Post*, February 19, 1975.

Kernodle, Tammy L. *Soul on Soul: The Life and Music of Mary Lou Williams.* Boston: Northeastern University Press, 2004.

Kirkland, Sean D. *The Ontology of Socratic Questioning in Plato's Early Dialogues.* Albany: State University of New York, 2012.

Komjathy, Louis. *Cultivating Perfection: Mysticism and Self-Transformation in Early Quanzhen Daoism.* Boston: Brill, 2007.

———, ed. and trans. *The Way of Complete Perfection: A Quanzhen Daoist Anthology.* Albany: State University of New York Press, 2013.

Lane, George. *Daily Life in the Mongol Empire.* Indianapolis: Hackett, 2009.

Lao, Tzu. *Chinese Classics: Tao Te Ching.* Trans. D. C. Lao. Hong Kong: Chinese University Press, 1982.

———. *Tao Te Ching.* Trans. Arthur Waley. London: Wordsworth Classics, 1997.

Lazarus-Yafeh, Hava. *Studies in al-Ghazzālī.* Jerusalem: Magnes, 1975.

Li, Chih-Ch'ang. *The Travels of an Alchemist: The Journey of the Taoist Ch'ang-ch'un from China to the Hindukush at the Summons of Chingiz Khan.* Trans. Arthur Waley. London: George Routledge, 1931.

Llinas, Rodolfo R. *I of the Vortex: From Neurons to Self.* Cambridge: MIT Press, 2002.

Marini, Piero. *A Challenging Reform: Realizing the Vision of the Liturgical Renewal.* Collegeville, MN: Liturgical Press, 2007.

May, Timothy. *The Mongol Art of War: Chinggis Khan and the Mongol Military System.* Yardley, PA: Westholme, 2007.

McNamara, Patrick. *The Neuroscience of Religious Experience.* New York: Cambridge University Press, 2014.

Mercadante, Linda A. *Belief Without Borders: Inside the Minds of the Spiritual but not Religious.* New York: Oxford University Press, 2014.

Nakamura, Kojiro. *Ghazali and Prayer.* Kuala Lumpur: Islamic Book Trust, 2001.

Nehamas, Alexander. *The Art of Living.* Berkeley: University of California Press, 2000.

Newberg, Andrew. *Neurotheology: How Science Can Enlighten Us About Spirituality.* New York: Columbia University Press, 2018.

Newberg, Andrew, and Mark Robert Waldman. *How Enlightenment Changes Your Brain.* New York: Avery, 2016.

———. *How God Changes Your Brain: Breakthrough Findings from a Leading Neuroscientist.* New York: Ballantine, 2010.

Nietzsche, Friedrich. *The Gay Science.* Trans. Walter Kaufman. New York: Random House, 1974.

O'Malley, John W. *What Happened at Vatican II*. Cambridge: Harvard University Press, 2008.

Ormsby, Eric L. "The Taste of Truth: The Structure of Experience in al-Ghazālī's *al-Munqidh min al-dalāl*." In *Islamic Studies Presented to Charles J. Adams*, ed. Wael B. Hallaq and Donald P. Little, 133–52. Leiden: Brill, 1991.

Owen, Amy D., R. David Hayward, Harold G. Koenig, David C. Steffens, and Martha E. Payne. "Religious Factors and Hippocampal Atrophy in Late Life." *PLOS ONE* 6 (2011): e17006. https://doi.org/10.1371/journal.pone.0017006.

Plato. *Five Dialogues: Euthyphro, Apology, Crito, Meno, Phaedo*. Ed. John M. Cooper. Trans. G. M. A. Grube. Indianapolis: Hackett, 2002.

Rachewiltz, Igor de, "The Hsi-Yu Lu by Yeh-lu Ch'u-Ts'ai." *Monumenta Serica* 21 (1962): 1–128.

Reiter, Florian C. "'A Praise of Buddha' by the Taoist Patriarch Qiu Chuji and its Source." *Zeitschrift des deutschen morgenländischen Gesellschaft* 143 (1993): 179–91.

Renard, John, ed. and trans. *Knowledge of God in Classical Sufism: Foundations of Islamic Mystical Theology*. Mahwah, NJ: Paulist Press, 2004.

Richardson, Robert D. *William James: In the Maelstrom of American Modernism*. New York: Houghton Mifflin, 2006.

Rieff, Philip. *Freud: The Mind of the Moralist*. Chicago: University of Chicago Press, 1979.

——. *The Triumph of the Therapeutic: Uses of Faith After Freud*. Chicago: University of Chicago Press, 1987.

Roth, Harold D. *Original Tao: Inward Training (Nei-yeh) and the Foundations of Taoist Mysticism*. New York: Columbia University Press, 2004.

Russell, Ross. *Bird Lives!: The High Life and Hard Times of Charlie (Yardbird) Parker*. New York: Da Capo, 1996.

Saal, Hubert. "The Spirit of Mary Lou." *Newsweek*, December 20, 1971.

Safi, Omid. *The Politics of Knowledge in Premodern Islam: Negotiating Ideology and Religious Inquiry*. Chapel Hill: University of North Carolina Press, 2006.

Sarbin, Theodore R. ed. *Narrative Psychology: The Storied Nature of Human Conduct*. New York: Praeger, 1986.

Saul, Scott. *Freedom Is, Freedom Ain't: Jazz and the Making of the Sixties*. Cambridge: Harvard University Press, 2003.

Schneider, Eric C. *Smack: Heroin and the American City.* Philadelphia: University of Pennsylvania Press, 2008.

Schiff, Brian. *A New Narrative for Psychology.* New York: Oxford University Press, 2017.

Seligman, Martin E. P., and Mihaly Csikszentmihalyi. "Positive Psychology: An Introduction." *American Psychologist* 55, no. 1 (2000): 5–14. https://doi.org/10.1037/0003-066X.55.1.5.

Shaefer, Donovan O. *Religious Affects: Animality, Evolution, and Power.* Durham: Duke University Press, 2015.

Sheldrake, Philip. *Spirituality: A Brief History.* Oxford: Wiley-Blackwell, 2013.

Shen, WangBing, Jing Luo, Chang Liu and Yuan Yuan. "New Advances in the Neural Correlates of Insight: A Decade in Review of the Insightful Brain." *Chinese Science Bulletin* 58, no. 13 (2013): 1497–511.

Sichran, Bobby. *From a Sympathetical Hurricane.* Columbia Records CD, 1994.

——. *Peddler in Babylon.* Bombi Beat CD BB722, 2006.

Stein, Edith. *Life in a Jewish Family: Her Unfinished Autobiographical Account.* Ed. L. Gelber and Romaeus Leuven. Trans. Josephine Koeppel. Washington, DC: ICS, 1986.

Taves, Ann. *Religious Experience Reconsidered: A Building-Block Approach to the Study of Religion and Other Special Things.* Princeton: Princeton University Press, 2011.

The Upanishads. Trans. Juan Mascaro. London: Penguin, 1965.

Wang, Jinping. *In the Wake of the Mongols: The Making of a New Social Order in North China, 1200–1600.* Cambridge: Harvard University Press, 2018.

Weatherford, Jack. *Genghis Khan and the Quest for God: How the World's Greatest Conqueror Gave Us Religious Freedom.* New York: Penguin, 2016.

Wettstein, Howard. *The Significance of Religious Experience.* New York: Oxford University Press, 2014.

Williams, Mary Lou. Interview by John S. Wilson. Jazz Oral History Project. Institute of Jazz Studies, Rutgers University, Newark. 1973.

——. *Mary Lou's Mass.* Smithsonian Folkways SFW CD 40815, 2005.

——. Mary Lou Williams Archive. Institute of Jazz Studies, Rutgers University, Newark.

——. *Mary Lou Williams Presents Black Christ of the Andes.* Smithsonian Folkways SFW CD 40816, 2004.

———. "What I Learned from God About Jazz." *Sepia*, April 1958, 57–60.

Williams, Mary Lou, and Peter O'Brien. Interview by Martha Oneppo. Yale Oral History American Music Series, 1981.

Wilson, John S. "Mary Lou Williams, a Jazz Great, Dies." *New York Times*, May 30, 1981.

———. "Mary Lou Williams, at Piano, Leads Her Jazz Mass at St. Patrick's." *New York Times*, February 19, 1975.

Yao, Tao-Chung. "Ch'iu Ch'u-chi and Chinggis Khan." *Harvard Journal of Asiatic Studies* 46, no. 1 (1986): 201–19.

Zerjal, Tatiana, Yali Xue, Giorgio Bertorelle, R. Spencer Wells, Weidong Bao, Suling Zhu, Raheel Qamar et al. "The Genetic Legacy of the Mongols." *American Journal of Human Genetics* 72, no. 3 (2003): 717–21.

Zhuangzi. *Basic Writings*. Trans. Burton Watson. New York: Columbia University Press, 2003.

INDEX